REGNUM STUDIES IN MISSION

World Christianity in Western Europe

Diasporic Identity, Narratives and Missiology

Series Preface

Regnum Studies in Mission are born from the lived experience of Christians and Christian communities in mission, especially but not solely in the fast growing churches among the poor of the world. These churches have more to tell than stories of growth. They are making significant impacts on their cultures in the cause of Christ. They are producing 'cultural products' which express the reality of Christian faith, hope and love in their societies.

Regnum Studies in Mission are the fruit often of rigorous research to the highest international standards and always of authentic Christian engagement in the transformation of people and societies. And these are for the world. The formation of Christian theology, missiology and practice in the twenty-first century will depend to a great extent on the active participation of growing churches contributing biblical and culturally appropriate expressions of Christian practice to inform World Christianity.

Series Editors

Paul Bendor-Samuel   Oxford Centre for Mission Studies, Oxford, UK
Tony Gray   Words by Design, UK

REGNUM STUDIES IN MISSION

World Christianity in Western Europe
Diasporic Identity, Narratives and Missiology

Edited by

Israel Oluwole Olofinjana

Typeset by Words by Design

Cover photograph shows Majority World missionaries who are members of the Centre
for Missionaries from the Majority World at a Lausanne consultation in Liverpool last
year. The picture represents the theme of the book – here are four people, one West
African, one Southern African, one Latin American and one South Asian – and in the
background are flags of different nations.

Printed and bound in Great Britain

Contents

(1) World Christianity in Western Europe: Foundational Perspectives
Israel Oluwole Olofinjana

Background and Purpose of the Book

That Christianity is a world religion is attested to by the fact that it is currently the world's largest religious group in the world with about 2.3 billion Christians. According to the Pew Research Centre, that is a third, that is, 31.2 per cent of the world's population of 7.3 billion.[1] While Christianity's past centre used to be Europe in terms of size, significance and influence, we are living through a paradigm shift that now has other major centres such as Africa, Asia and Latin America. The recent data released by the Center for the Study of Global Christianity states that 66 per cent of all Christians now live in the Global South, leaving only 34 per cent in the Global North.[2] This is a reversal as indicated by research which shows that in 1910, 66 per cent of Christians resided in the Global North. This significant growth of Christianity in the Majority World has led to missionaries being sent to Europe and North America. Research projects have been commissioned and books have been written about this shift; three examples of the latter are Andrew Walls' two magisterial seminal texts, *The Missionary Movement in Christian History* (1996) and *The Cross-Cultural Process in Christian History* (2002), and Philip Jenkins' *Next Christendom: The Coming of Global Christianity* (2002).[3] Universities in Europe and North America have also developed research centres focusing on studying and teaching World Christianity. An example in the North American context is the Center for the Study of Global Christianity, now based at Gordon-Conwell Theological Seminary. Another is the recently founded Global Diaspora Institute, a partnership between Lausanne's Global Diaspora Network and Billy Graham Centre at Wheaton College. In the European scene, Andrew Walls pioneered the

---

[1] Pew research Centre Religion and Public Life
http://www.pewforum.org/2011/12/19/global-christianity-exec/ (Accessed 18th September 2017) http://www.pewforum.org/2017/04/05/the-changing-global-religious-landscape/#fn-27661-3 (Accessed 18th September 2017).
[2] Global Christianity: A look at the status of Christianity in 2018,
https://www.gordonconwell.edu/ockenga/research/Resources-and-Downloads.cfm (Accessed 16th September 2018).
[3] Andrew Walls has now published a third of these books, making them a trilogy. See Andrew Walls, *Crossing Cultural Frontiers: Studies in the History of World Christianity* (Maryknoll, NY: Orbis Books, 2017).

Centre for the Study of Christianity in the Non-Western World in 1982 at the University of Aberdeen. The Centre relocated in 1986 to the University of Edinburgh School of Divinity with the name changed in 2009 to the Centre for the Study of World Christianity. Through the pioneering work of Walls and the Centre, scholars from around the globe had the opportunity to study and major in an area of World Christianity.[4] What is more impressive is that this has led to more scholars from Africa, Asia, Latin America and the Pacific focusing their studies and research on their region. This has permitted fresh and original perspectives to be shared, thus helping us to understand the breadth and depth of World Christianity.

While World Christianity, with its attention on the growth of Christianity in Africa, Asia, Latin America, the Pacific and Oceania, is definitely significant, it is also important to consider World Christianity as it is developing in Europe. This is already happening in certain research centres and edited books; therefore, this volume builds on previous scholarship by looking at emerging forms of non-western Christianity in Europe. It examines the significant influx of Christians from the Majority World in Europe through the prisms of Diasporic Identity, Missional Narratives (that is, how migrant stories illustrate mission) and Missiological Insights. In essence, it considers the complex Christian identity of people migrating to Europe, their unfolding stories, and their mission practice. While these three broad areas can be studied exclusively, they are also interrelated and complimentary, and together, they enrich our understanding of the nature of World Christianity in Europe. Therefore, this book project takes an interdisciplinary approach, encompassing the fields of Diaspora Missiology, World Christianity, Contextual Theology, Pentecostal Studies and Practical Theology. Themes addressed include migration, intercultural mission, diasporic identity, globalisation, transnationalism, reverse mission, Pentecostalism and ecumenism. Contributors have been sought from different parts of Western Europe, including Germany, Sweden, Italy, Wales and, of course, England. These include Europeans as well as non-Europeans living and doing ministry in Europe. The contributors are also ministry practitioners who are serving in diaspora and refugee ministries. The majority are academics who study Diaspora Missiology in the European context and have taken the time to reflect on these issues. The three objectives of this book can be summarised as follows:

1) To document untold stories of Christians from the Majority World in Europe.
2) To document new diaspora missionary activities in Europe.

---

4 For a detailed history of the Centre, see Brian Stanley, 'Founding the Centre for the Study of Christianity in the Non-Western World', in William R. Burrows, Mark R. Gornik, and Janice A. McLean, eds., *Understanding World Christianity: The Vision and Work of Andrew F. Walls* (Maryknoll, New York: Orbis Books, 2011). *Christianity: The Vision and Work of Andrew F. Walls* (Maryknoll, New York: Orbis Books, 2011). *World Christianity: The Vision and the Work of Andrew F. Walls* (Maryknoll, NY: Orbis Books, 2011), 51-59.

3) To examine the complex diaspora identity of migrants and second-generation migrants.

History of World Christianity:
Important Themes in the Study of World Christianity

The subject of World Christianity might appear to be a newcomer when it comes to the history of Christianity. However, the history of World Christianity is inextricably bound to the genesis of Christianity itself: the birth of the church on the day of Pentecost is also the origin of World Christianity. On this particular day people who heard the gospel and were converted were Jews from the diaspora who migrated to Jerusalem for the purpose of keeping the Jewish feast of Pentecost. In this beginning we see important themes that emerge again and again throughout the history of Christian expansion. These themes include diaspora, migration and Pentecost, just to cite three examples. I will return to these themes later, but for now note the significance of the day of Pentecost for the study of World Christianity as the day when the Jewish diaspora from North Africa, Asia and Europe were converted. Here was God in his wisdom telling us that Christianity was never meant to be monopolised by one culture, but rather to be shared by different cultures, therefore making Christianity a multi-ethnic, polycentric faith. Multi-ethnic, because God himself embodies unity in diversity. Our understanding of the Trinity is that the Godhead consists of three distinct persons in the Father, the Son and the Holy Spirit, yet each person is co-equal and co-eternal. To conclude that the Trinity is one person manifested first as the Father and the Son and later as the Holy Spirit is to adopt one of the earliest anti-Trinitarian doctrines, termed modalism.5 The distinctiveness of the Father from the Son and the Son from the Holy Spirit, alongside their oneness in essence, points to God's vision of unity in diversity: a vision God enacted at creation when he created the bio-diversity that we are now so desperately trying to preserve after having failed to care for creation. Within that bio-diversity, God created one human race, yet he set them in different geographical contexts, as Paul affirms:

> From one man he made every nation of men, that they should inhabit the whole earth; and he determined the times for them and the exact places where they should live (Acts 17:26 NIV).6

God's vision of nations seeking him and reaching out for him – for that diversity is anchored in his person, and it is only in him that we have redemption – was why God called Abram (a name meaning, 'exalted Father') and changed

---

5 This is also sometimes called Sabellianism or Patripassianism.
6 Unless otherwise stated, all scriptural quotations are taken from the New International Version (NIV).

his name to Abraham ('Father of many nations'). Therefore, just as God embodies that vision of unity in diversity, Abraham, through his new name, purpose and nomadic journey, shared in that vision and helped to move it forward. This is why his calling was to be the father of many nations; the vision that through him all the families of the earth would be blessed was a signal that God's family was never meant to be homogeneous or monopolised. Paul understood this vision very clearly, which is why he insisted that salvation was not only to the Jews, but also to the Gentiles (Rom. 1:16-17). It is also this vision that underpins Paul's understanding of the new ecclesiology of two becoming one (Eph. 2: 11-22). This is, in essence, unity in diversity.

It appears that, while God's redemptive revelation started with families first (Adam, Noah and then Abraham's family), and then with Israel as a tribal nation (because God is particular and contextual), he nevertheless scattered seeds of his vision of unity in diversity throughout his journey with Israel. We see this with the 12 distinctive tribes of Israel gathering together to worship Yahweh, for although these tribes were different, their identity was rooted in the worship of Yahweh. We also see this seed in the story of Zipporah the Midianite, Ruth the Moabite and Cyrus the Persian. Perhaps God used these stories to remind Israel that his redemptive history will be shared and not monopolised. The prophetic literature is also loaded with God's vision of unity in diversity; two examples are Isaiah's prophecy that God's house shall become a house of prayer for all nations (Isaiah 56:3-8) and Joel's vision of God's Spirit being poured out on all people (Joel 2: 28-32). It is the fulfilment of this vision that we see in the events of the Day of Pentecost, as Peter himself realised and explained in Acts 2:16-21.

The Christian faith is polycentric because the Jewish Christians who resided in Jerusalem soon learned that the new faith could not be confined to Jerusalem as the first centre of Christianity. The faith started to spread first to Samaritans and then to Greeks. Its spread among the Greeks was so successful that the next centre of Christianity was Antioch in Syria. Before the end of the first century Christianity spread to Rome, so that Rome also emerged as a Christian centre. But again, Rome had to learn, like the Christians in Jerusalem, that the faith had to expand into other regions and territory. Both Alexandria and Carthage in North Africa became increasingly important centres during the Patristic period, with well-established theological institutions, theologians, monks and martyrs. Other centres subsequently emerged such as Constantinople, and by the time of the Reformations in the Middle Ages, European cities such as Geneva, Bern, Zurich, Basel, Freiburg, Strasbourg, Tubingen, Heidelberg, Augsburg, Trent, Orleans, Paris, Erfurt, Leipzig, London, Zwickau, Oxford, Wittenberg and Cambridge all became important centres for theological and ecclesiastical activity in Europe. The Reformations were indeed another reminder that Christianity was not meant to be monopolised by one group of people – in this case Rome – for it was more important that the church move away from theology to theologies, which is why we can talk of multiple Reformations, as opposed to a single Reformation. The theologians with different ecclesiastical and theological views that emerged during this period attest to this fact.

The modern missionary movement that went from Europe and later North America to Africa, Asia, Latin America, the Caribbean, Oceania and the Pacific – a shift, indeed, from a Christendom faith based in Europe to a World religion – saw the return of Christianity to its original vision as demonstrated on the Day of Pentecost. That vision, rooted in God's DNA, is that Christianity was meant to be a multi-ethnic, polycentric faith, and thus, inherently, World Christianity.

If Christianity is designed to be multi-ethnic and polycentric, other themes that cluster around this idea are diaspora, migration and Pentecost. As noted above, these are factors that developed within the historical origins of the church, so let us now return to them.

Diaspora and Migration

As the technical term employed by scripture and inter-testamental writings regarding the forced migration or scattering of Jews beyond their land is 'diaspora'. I shall consider diaspora as one example of migration. The term 'diaspora' is a Greek word meaning 'dispersion'. While it was Greek in usage, it nevertheless developed as a technical term that was used in places such as Egypt, Asia Minor and Mesopotamia to describe the dispersion of Jews. The first dispersion of the Israelites followed the Assyrian conquest of the northern kingdom around 722 BCE; the deportees did not, however, form a diaspora community.[7] It was during the displacement and deportation of Judah by the Babylonians around 587 BCE and then later by the Persians that led to the creation of a permanent diaspora community. By the time the Graeco-Roman period dawned, the word 'diaspora' had already gained wider usage, for it was used in the Septuagint to describe the forced migration that the children of Israel would experience if they disobeyed God's command. For example, in the Septuagint, the word 'diaspora' is used in Deuteronomy 28:25 to explain Israel's scattering among the kingdoms of the earth. Therefore, it appears that the usage of the term 'diaspora' in scripture is attached to forced migration or involuntary migration, thus representing one aspect of migration. The current European scene has so many migratory themes that are reminiscent of the biblical period, which are also re-shaping our context of mission and demanding of us fresh biblical insight on the subject of migration.

Firstly, there is our exit/Brexit from the European Union (EU), and all the implications that it has for us as a nation, politically, economically and socially. The Brexit vote also revealed our attitude on how we see the other in relation to ourselves – in essence, our views on migration and migrants. Brexit somehow gave people permission to voice their opinions on the issue of race and ethnicity.

---

[7] Philip Stern, 'Dispersion, Diaspora' in Bruce M Metzger and Michael D Coogan (eds), *The Oxford Companion to the Bible*, Oxford, Oxford University, 1993, 169.

We are also seeing the rise of a new nationalism across Europe with far-right political parties redefining politics and identity in countries such as France, Germany and Italy. In addition to this, there is the ongoing Syrian crisis, which is seeing families dislocated and moving into European countries in order to survive. This has raised the question of European hospitality towards Germany for taking the lead in welcoming Syrian refugees, whilst at the same time raising questions about German nationalism. Added to this was the situation we had in Calais, France, before it was demolished. One of the questions that Brexit and the rise of this new nationalism in some European countries definitely raises concerns our view of migration and migrants. For us as Christians, the question should be: what does the Bible have to say about migration, and what do we as Christians think of migrants? Should our opinion on this important subject be shaped and dictated by public opinion and political discourses only, or does the Bible have something to teach us as well?

Migration in the Old Testament

Chris Wright's seminal work, *The Mission of God*, argued that there is a missional basis to the entire Bible. This means that the Bible in its revelation and content is a missionary document.[8] To this perspective I would like to add that the Bible is a book of migrations, therefore making it a book of mission and migration. This means that the principle of mission and migration should form the hermeneutical lens through which we read and understand the Bible. Below are some examples drawn from the Old Testament and the New Testament.

The God of the Old Testament was certainly interested in migrants, as a casual perusal of the Old Testament reveals that he does. Often times God uses migration to accomplish his mission and purposes; therefore, mission and migration somehow complement each other. Take the classic case mentioned before of Abraham's call in Genesis 12:1-3. God's calling of Abraham meant that he had to cease to be a settled city dweller from Ur of the Chaldeans in Mesopotamia (modern day Iraq), and had to adopt a nomadic lifestyle and relocate to the new land God was showing him in Canaan (modern day Israel and Palestine). The writer of Hebrews was convinced enough about Abraham's status as a missionary migrant that he used the word 'migrate' (*parokesen*) in Hebrews 11:9 to describe Abraham's journey:

> By faith Abraham, when called to go to a place he would later receive as his inheritance, obeyed and went, even though he did not know where he was going. By faith he made his home in the Promised Land like a stranger in a foreign country; he lived in tents, as did Isaac and Jacob, who were heirs with him of the same

---

8 Chris Wright, *The Mission of God: Unlocking the Bible's Grand Narrative* (Downers Grove, IL, IVP Academic, 2006), 48-51.

promise. For he was looking forward to the city with foundations, whose architect and builder is God. (Hebrews 11:8-10 NIV).

Another way of rendering verse 9 in the Greek is: 'By faith he migrated into a land of promise as in a foreign land …'

Abraham as an Aramean nomad passed on this penchant for temporary residence to Isaac and Jacob, as we see in the Patriarch's stories in Genesis. There are others today like Abraham who are missionary migrants. In Chapter Six of this book, the story of Flavio Gurattos and his wife – missionary migrants from Brazil to the UK – demonstrates that not all migrants to the West are economic migrants. Flavio and his wife Karen left lucrative jobs, families and a growing church ministry to answer God's call in the UK.

Andrew Walls highlights two broad categories of migration in the Old Testament: 'One is involuntary and punitive, the other voluntary and hope driven. Underlying both categories is divine authority acting in judgement and mercy. One might call the first category Adamic and second Abrahamic.'[9] In essence, God uses migration to accomplish his redemptive purposes even in cases of exile or forced migration, such as what Adam and Eve experienced. God still demonstrated his grace towards them, firstly by clothing them, and secondly by giving them hope through a prophetic glimpse of the Messiah as God announced that the seed of the woman will bruise the head of the serpent (see Gen. 3:15).

Through jealousy and unfortunate circumstances, Joseph, Abraham's great grandson ended up an economic migrant in Egypt. He was sold by his brothers to traders – indeed, essentially trafficked as a slave labourer. Joseph's experience reminds us of the horrific trade in slaves known as the trans-atlantic slave trade. While the trans-atlantic slave trade was confined to a geographic location, modern slavery and human trafficking is global in scope, touching all continents. Modern human trafficking includes slave labour, domestic servitude, sex trafficking, prostitution and child labour. Joseph found himself in a strange land and difficult situations, such as being wrongly accused by Potiphar's wife (see Gen. 39). In all the suffering Joseph faced as an economic migrant in Egypt, God somehow used his journey and experience to fulfil his mission. This was in Joseph preparing the way to preserve his family from the terrible famine that occurred in the world at that time so that Joseph could declare in Genesis 50:20, 'You intended to harm me, but God intended it for good to accomplish what is now being done, the saving of many lives.' Here is another clear example of how God uses migration to carry out his mission.

Joseph living and settling as the Prime Minister in Egypt initially led to the children of Israel being welcomed in Egypt, but when the government of the day changed and power changed hands, the new government in authority felt the

---

[9] Andrew Walls, *Crossing Cultural Frontiers: Studies in the History of World Christianity* (NY, Orbis Books, 2017), 56.

borders were too loose and therefore needed to tighten border controls. The new Pharaoh introduced and implemented immigration policies that would control the many new immigrants in Egypt.

The first immigration policy Pharaoh introduced was forced labour and exploitation so that the Israelites helped build and develop the cities in Egypt (see Ex. 1:11-14). When it appeared that this measure neither worked nor halted the growing number of migrants, Pharaoh introduced a crueller measure: he asked the midwives systematically to eliminate all the boys born to Israelite families (see Gen. 1:15-20). This would mean reducing a community of people to nothing as men were the backbone of society in those days. When this policy failed as well, Pharaoh implemented another sadistic measure to combat increased migration. This time he decided to wipe out an entire generation by committing infant genocide:

> Then Pharaoh gave this order to all his people: 'Every Hebrew boy that is born you must throw into the Nile, but let every girl live' (Ex. 1:22 NIV).

It was in response to this injustice and oppression that God decided to liberate the Israelites from slavery; and in order for them not to forget, but instead to learn from this experience, God instructed them on how to treat strangers and foreigners. Below are some of the passages that instruct the Israelites on how to care for the strangers and foreigners among them:

> Do not mistreat or oppress a foreigner, for you were foreigners in Egypt (Ex. 22:21 NIV).

> Do not oppress a foreigner; you yourselves know how it feels to be foreigners, because you were foreigners in Egypt (Ex. 23:9 NIV).

> When a foreigner resides among you in your land, do not mistreat them. The foreigner residing among you must be treated as your native-born. Love them as yourself, for you were foreigners in Egypt. I am the Lord your God (Lev. 19:33-34 NIV).

> Do not deprive the foreigner or the fatherless of justice, or take the cloak of the widow as a pledge. Remember that you were slaves in Egypt and the Lord your God redeemed you from there. That is why I command you to do this. When you are harvesting in your field and you overlook a sheaf, do not go back to get it. Leave it for the foreigner, the fatherless and the widow, so that the Lord your God may bless you in all the work of your hands. When you beat the olives from your trees, do not go over the branches a second time. Leave what remains for the foreigner, the fatherless and the widow. When you harvest the grapes in your vineyard, do not go over the vines again. Leave what remains for the foreigner, the fatherless and the widow. Remember that you were slaves in Egypt. That is why I command you to do this (Deut. 24:17-22 NIV).

The last passage is of significance because it not only states why the Israelite community were to care for foreigners and strangers, but added in detail how they were to care by making provisions available for migrants. It was in following this pattern of care that Ruth, another migrant, connected with Boaz in the book of Ruth (see Ruth 2:1-7). The story of Ruth is that of an asylum seeker whom God used for the purposes of his kingdom. The story of Ruth exemplifies mission and migration once again as Ruth decided to follow Naomi's God and to leave her own people and home. Ruth was actually seeking asylum in God, which made her a different kind of asylum seeker:

'Look', said Naomi, 'your sister-in-law is going back to her people and her gods. Go back with her.' But Ruth replied, 'Don't urge me to leave you or to turn back from you. Where you go I will go, and where you stay I will stay. Your people will be my people and your God my God' (Ruth 1:15-16 NIV).

Here was Ruth's confession of faith and her calling into God's mission, but it only happened as she decided to relocate. We see this pattern repeated again in the story of Esther, another migrant, whom God used to accomplish his redemptive purposes. As an economic migrant in Persia (modern day Iran), God used Esther and Mordecai to preserve future generations and the posterity of the Israelites.

But the reason why the whole nation of Israel was in exile in the first place was because of disobedience to the Mosaic Law and covenant. The Babylonian exile and the return from it, the enforced migration, and the divinely-led remigration, were climactic events for Israel; but they did not mark the end of migration.[10]

Daniel and the three Hebrew children were also economic migrants in Babylon, but God again decided to use them to be agents of transformation in a corrupt and ruthless empire. Daniel and the three Hebrew children went from being economic migrants to missionary migrants. Perhaps it is the connection between mission and migration that led the immigrants in Calais to start a church amidst all the struggles they faced before they were evicted. One thing to also note here is that Daniel and the three Hebrew boys were from the noble stock and were well educated; therefore, their being in Babylon was actually a brain drain for their place of origin, Judah. One of the sad scenarios about modern migration is the brain drain of the nations from which people emigrate. This happens as people migrate to study and seek better employment, so that the skilled, the gifted and talented professionals are now contributing fully to a different society.

Over subsequent centuries after the Assyrian and Babylonian exiles into the inter-testamental period or second temple Judaism, thousands of Jews migrated

---

[10] Walls, *Cross Cultural*, 56.

all over the world. By the time of Jesus, the Greek word for migration, 'diaspora', was used to describe Jewish migration in the Roman Empire.

Jesus Was a Migrant

The word 'incarnation' refers to a Christian doctrine describing the process of God becoming human in the second person of the Trinity. The clearest biblical text that articulates this process is John 1:14, which reads, 'The Word became flesh and made his dwelling among us. We have seen his glory, the glory of the one and only Son, who came from the Father, full of grace and truth' (NIV). In order for God to achieve our redemption, he had to become one of us and blend in. He did this in the person of Jesus Christ, his only Son.

Jesus' incarnation was therefore a process that can be described as a journey. The following is a summary of that process:

Jesus' incarnation starts with the pre-existent Son of God, through whom the world was created, leaving the divine glory behind and stepping into the human realm. This is described in John's introduction in John 1:1-14, and it is emphasised by Paul in Philippians 2:5-11.

The birth of Jesus is the next stage in the incarnational process. Although he was born of supernatural means (virgin birth), He still needed protection when He was born (Matt. 2:13-18).

Jesus grew up normally like any child (Luke 2:41-52).

He was tempted like any human being (Matt. 4:1-11, Luke 4:1-13).

He slept like any human being (Matt. 9:23-27).

He wept when his friend Lazarus died (John 11:35).

The first stage of Jesus' suffering was a mental battle in facing his death, and this happened at Gethsemane (Luke 22:39-46). Luke gave a vivid description, recording that Jesus had sweat like blood, which clearly portrays the stress and the struggle he went through. After intense prayer he sacrificed his will and finally submitted to God's will.

He was betrayed by one of his friends (Luke 22:1-5, 47-48).

He was arrested and tried like a criminal (Mark 14:43-50, John 18:30-38).

He was denied by one of his closest friends (Mark 14:66-72).

He was accused by false witnesses (Mark 14:53-65).

He was mocked and flogged by the soldiers (Mark 15:16-20).

He was crucified among sinners (Mark 15:21-31, John 19:17-18).

While on the cross he was mocked by the soldiers and the people (Mark 15:29-32, John 19:23-27).

He struggled to face death on the cross (Luke 22:39-46).

He suffered, bled and eventually died on the cross (John 19:17-37).

If in the process of Jesus becoming human he had to leave one reality of existence for another, then in one sense his incarnation can be described as migration. This means that Jesus' first advent can be considered as migration, therefore making Jesus a migrant. The process of Jesus becoming human describes to some extent the journey of some migrants today. Most of the time, migrants have to adapt to new situations and contexts just as Jesus did. Jesus was born into a poor family and grew up poor; migrants are usually poor people seeking survival, security and the necessities of life. Although Jesus was poor, he nevertheless contributed to his community and society by challenging and changing societal taboos, such as healing people and restoring to community those who had been excluded because of their diseases. He also contributed by changing some of the social and cultural dynamics of his day by relating with women, the poor and the social misfits such as prostitutes. Some migrants do contribute to British and European societies. One example in this book is the contribution of the Majority World Christians in Wales, which is explored in Chapter Seven of this book by Jim Stewart.

Jesus also became a refugee when he was a baby. His parents had to flee to Egypt in order to keep him safe from the political powers of the day and to ensure his survival:

> When they had gone, an angel of the Lord appeared to Joseph in a dream. 'Get up', he said, 'take the child and his mother and escape to Egypt. Stay there until I tell you, for Herod is going to search for the child to kill him.'
>
> So he got up, took the child and his mother during the night and left for Egypt, where he stayed until the death of Herod. And so was fulfilled what the Lord had said through the prophet: 'Out of Egypt I called my son'. (Matt. 2:13-15 NIV).

Jesus' birth upset the royal establishment and was viewed as a threat to national security; his parents therefore had to flee to Egypt as refugees to protect his life. This means that Jesus himself experienced diaspora, that is, forced migration. There are political migrants, refugees and asylum seekers who have left their countries not because they wanted to leave but because it was not safe for them to stay. Families have been torn apart and dislocated as people have had to flee to survive. Jesus' status as a migrant was not meant to be exclusive; it appears that he expected his followers to be missionary migrants. The implication of the Great Commission in Matthew 28:18-20 is that it has migratory implications for mission. The new community of God's people known as disciples have to migrate to other nations and people groups in order to share the gospel. Paul's three missionary journeys in the Acts of the Apostle are examples of this migratory implication of mission.

The New Testament writers also appear to describe Christians as having heavenly citizenship. That is, an identity that can be described as trans-national in the sense of belonging to something much bigger than a nation-state identity: 'But our citizenship is in heaven. And we eagerly await a Saviour from there, the Lord Jesus Christ.' (Phil. 3:20 NIV).

Peter describes Christians as 'strangers in this world' in 1 Peter 1:1 (NIV). The NKJV describes us as 'sojourners', the Good News Bible as 'refugees', the

NRSV as 'exiles', and the New Living Translation (NLT) as 'foreigners'. All of these terms imply that we are not from this world but from somewhere else, and one day we will return home. Paul most of the time uses language that describes himself as a temporary resident on earth:

> Therefore we are always confident and know that as long as we are at home in the body we are away from the Lord. For we live by faith, not by sight. We are confident, I say, and would prefer to be away from the body and at home with the Lord. So we make it our goal to please him, whether we are at home in the body or away from it. For we must all appear before the judgment seat of Christ, so that each of us may receive what is due us for the things done while in the body, whether good or bad (2 Cor. 5:6-10 NIV).

> I am torn between the two: I desire to depart and be with Christ, which is better by far; but it is more necessary for you that I remain in the body (Phil. 1:23-24 NIV).

If Jesus' incarnation and first advent describes a migratory process which makes him a migrant, and if Christians are understood as temporary residents by New Testament writers, then the implication is that all Christians, irrespective of nationality, church tradition and ethnic or cultural background are missionary migrants.

Diaspora Studies and Diaspora Missiology

While the term 'diaspora' came initially to be associated and used exclusively to refer to Jewish forced dispersion, the term came to be used from around the 1960s to describe the enslavement and forced relocation of Africans in the barbaric trans-atlantic slave trade. The term was later extended to explain forced migration of other people groups. Within secular institutions and universities, diaspora studies emerged as an academic field encompassing areas such as politics, economics and the social sciences. In some cases, this area of research is referred to as migration studies. In the field of mission studies, Diaspora Missiology has developed as one of the areas of study from around 2010, when the third Lausanne Movement in Cape Town recognised officially the importance of diaspora mission and missiology.[11] The Cape Town commitment followed the Seoul Declaration on Diaspora Missiology in 2009. Hun Kim's contribution in Chapter Ten of this book shed's more light on how both ecumenicals and evangelicals have sought to engage theologically and missiologically with the diaspora phenomenon since 2010. In 2012, Enoch Wan, with his magisterial book, *Diaspora Missiology*, also helped to create this area of enquiry by situating diaspora studies within the Christian evangelical context

---

[11] Diaspora, Lausanne Movement, https://www.lausanne.org/networks/issues/diasporas (Accessed on 15th March 2018).

of mission.12 Around the same period, I started reflecting on the phenomenon of reverse mission as carried out by African pastors and missionaries in Britain, which has led towards the emerging subject of reverse missiology as a significant aspect of Diaspora Missiology. This occurred with the publication of my first book in 2010.13 The Global Diaspora Network (GDN) of the Lausanne Movement, through their Global Diaspora Forum in 2015, produced a significant book, *Scattered and Gathered: A Global Compendium of Diaspora Missiology*.14 This book, with international contributors with specialist knowledge and expertise on the field of study, has broadened the conversation on diaspora mission. A recent book on the subject is Sam George's edited book, *Diaspora Christianities*, which looks at issues and themes affecting South Asian Christian diaspora communities across the continents.15 The Global Diaspora Network (GDN), in partnership with Liverpool Hope University, also held a significant diaspora consultation in 2019 on the theme of the Global South and Diaspora Missions in Europe. This consultation was significant in that it marked the first time that practitioners, thinkers and scholars on the subject in Europe had gathered together to reflect and share papers on diaspora missions in the European context.16

It is now becoming standard within universities' Religious Studies and Theology departments and within Bible colleges in Europe for students to take a module on Diaspora Missiology when studying for an MA or MTh in Theology or Missiology. Students can now also focus their doctoral studies on an aspect of diaspora mission. An example of a European university offering postgraduate courses in this area is Vrije Universiteit Amsterdam (VU) Centre for Theology of Migration. They recently started postgraduate courses for migrant pastors and church leaders.17 As universities and Bible colleges are adapting their curriculum to reflect the shift in global migration, so are European mission agencies. Recognising that God is using migration and diaspora people in his mission, European mission agencies are now beginning to employ diaspora co-ordinators to focus their organisation's attention on this new dynamic of mission. African Inland Mission (AIM), Serving in Mission (SIM) and London City Mission

12 Enoch Wan, *Diaspora Missiology: Theory, Methodology, and Practice*, 2nd ed (Portland, OR, Institute of Diaspora Study, 2014), 123.
13 Israel Olofinjana, *Reverse in Ministry and Mission: Africans in the Dark Continent of Europe* (Milton Keynes, Author House, 2010).
14 Sadiri Joy Tira and Tetsunao Yamamori (eds), *Scattered and Gathered: A Global Compendium of Diaspora Missiology* (Oxford, Regnum Books International, 2016).
15 Sam George (eds), *Diaspora Christianities: Global Scattering and Gathering of South Asian Christians* (Minneapolis, MN, Fortress Press, 2019).
16 Some of the contributors to this volume – Hun Kim, Usha Reifsnider and myself – participated in the consultation.
17 Postgraduate Programme for Migrant Pastors and Church Leaders, https://www.godgeleerdheid.vu.nl/en/programmes/postgraduate/index.aspx (Accessed on 15th March 2018).

(LCM) are three examples of European mission agencies which have either employed a diaspora worker or are currently in the process of doing so.

All the contributors in this volume have engaged with Diaspora Missiology in their various chapter contributions. Section One of this book deals with Diasporic Identities by looking at the missional and transcultural identity of diaspora Christians in the context of Germany. Chapter two looks specifically at multicultural missionary identities of migrants within the German context. Chapters Three and Five explore identities through the lens of second-generation African and African Caribbean people in Britain, respectively. Chapter Five pays particular attention to the African Caribbean Pentecostal identity of the Windrush generation. Chapter Four is contributed by Rosalee Velloso Ewel, who looks at the biblical theology of Christian mission in Europe and its implications for how we understand the work of the Holy Spirit in shaping identities and in challenging pre-conceived notions of who is 'in' and who is 'out'. Section Two of this book explores Missional Narratives through the stories of migrant Christians in Europe. In Chapter Six, we have the story of a Brazilian missionary in Britain and Italy. In Chapter Seven, we have the stories of Majority World Christians and their missionary contributions in Wales. Chapter Eight explores migrant Pentecostal churches in the context of Sweden, while Chapter Nine contains the story of British missionaries in Italy and their engagement with multi-ethnic churches in the Italian context. In it, Claire and Mark Ord reflect on their experiences of how the migrant church transformed the Italian church during their 16 years of service in Italy.

The last section of the book is devoted to missiological insights that have emerged from the mission practices carried by migrants in Europe. Hun Kim in Chapter Ten looks at the case study of mission of South Koreans in Europe. This chapter also sheds more light on the Global Diaspora Network and the Lausanne Movement. Chapter Eleven looks at the post Indian independence Hindu migrants to Britain who have chosen to leave their inherited religious beliefs and become followers of Jesus; while Chapter Thirteen explores the African diaspora and mission. This chapter considers the significance of African identity in formulating a theological enterprise that can engage post-secular multicultural Britain in mission.

Pentecostals and Pentecostalism

Having considered diaspora and migration as important themes in understanding World Christianity, let us now return to another important theme, Pentecost. From the Acts narrative we see that God in his wisdom decided to give birth to the church on the Jewish feast day of Pentecost, or Harvest, as it is sometimes known. Today there is an expression of Christianity that is called Pentecostalism, which is a major player when it comes to World Christianity, for this expression of Christianity can be found on every continent in the world. It is fair to say that any study or research on World Christianity and World mission that does not include global Pentecostalism cannot be comprehensive. It is worth observing, however, that for some reason European mission practitioners and agencies do not often include Pentecostalism in their conversation. This is an oversight that needs correction for one obvious reason: the accelerated growth of Pentecostalism since the dawn of the twentieth century has been outstanding. Pentecostal Christianity is currently one of the fastest growing expressions of Christianity in the world. David Barrett estimates that Pentecostalism is likely to rise to 1,140 million, or 44 per cent of the total number of Christians by 2025.[18] Allan Anderson, a Pentecostal historian and theologian, adds that Pentecostalism is fast becoming the dominant expression of Christianity and one of the most extraordinary religious phenomena in the world today.[19] Pentecostalism as a global movement has large numbers of adherents in the Majority World. It is the expression of Christianity that is growing fastest in Africa, Asia and Latin America. Pentecostal missionaries and pastors from the Majority World are the ones who are taking the lead in planting churches in Europe. The continent of Europe, which used to include primarily white Pentecostals and, later, the white people who constituted the Charismatic Movements of the 1960s as the major players within those groups, now include black Pentecostals. These groups have thus become more diverse, to the extent that the history of European Pentecostals will not be complete without paying attention to the emerging black Pentecostals.[20]

To take the UK as an example in Europe, there are estimated to be 4,191 Pentecostal churches in the UK. About 2,848 of them are African and Caribbean Pentecostal churches.[21] These numbers attest to the diversity of Pentecostalism. This diversity must be included within the history and definition of Pentecostalism. So who are Pentecostals, and what is Pentecostalism? Allan Anderson, observed that the term 'Pentecostal refers to a wide variety of movements scattered around the world'.[22] In essence, any definition of modern Pentecostalism has to recognise that Pentecostalism is not just a North American or European phenomenon, but a worldwide movement of people of the Spirit. It

---

[18] David Barrett, Annual Statistical Table on Global Mission, *International Bulletin of Missionary Research* 21.1, 1997, 24-25.

[19] Alan Anderson 'Introduction: World Pentecostalism at a Crossroads' in Anderson Allan and Hollenweger Walter (eds), *Pentecostals After a Century: Global Perspectives on a Movement in Transition* (Sheffield, Sheffield Academic Press, 1999), 19.

[20] Israel Olofinjana, 'Historical Development of Black Pentecostal Churches in Britain: A Case Study of Apostolic Pastoral Congress (APC)', *Missio Africanus Journal* (Volume 1, Issue 2, 2016) http://missioafricanus.org/missio-africanus-journal-of-african-missiology/ (Accessed 19th March 2018).

[21] Peter Brierley (ed), *UK Church Statistics No 3: 2018 Edition* (Tonbridge, Kent, ADBC publishers, 2018), 10-19. Note that the figure of 2,848 dates back to African and Caribbean churches between the years 1948 and 2017. This does not, however, include some of the earlier African and Caribbean Pentecostal churches that started before 1948, such as Sumner Road Chapel, founded by Kwame-Brem Wilson in Peckham.

[22] Anderson, *World Pentecostalism*, 1999, 19.

is a truly global phenomenon characterised by the work of God's Spirit in shaping local narratives and contexts. This is why Asamoah-Gyadu, in his seminal work on *African Charismatics*, adopted a Pentecostal history with an intercultural perspective.[23] From this approach, his history of modern Pentecostalism incorporated not only the Azusa event in 1906, but also the outpouring of the Spirit in other places such as India and Haiti. In similar Fashion, Roswith Gerloff has shown that long before the outpourings in Azusa, there were Charismatic renewals happening in Asia, Africa and Latin America.[24] She cited the Jamaican Revival of 1860-1861 as an example of a renewal with African and Christian elements combined in the Caribbean with large-scale religious, social and political implications.[25]

Walter Hollenweger, the doyen of Pentecostal Studies, was one of the first to opt for a more inclusive definition of Pentecostals, taking into account the global nature of the modern movement. In his ground breaking book, *The Pentecostals*, he included Independent African churches, regarding them as Pentecostals.[26] From these discussions, it appears that a narrow Western understanding of Pentecostalism that dates back to the ministry of Charles Parham (1873-1929) in Topeka, Kansas, with his formulation of the Pentecostal theology of speaking in tongues as the initial evidence of the Baptism of the Holy Spirit, is not sufficient. We must add to this William J Seymour's (1870-1922) understanding that the Spirit breaks down racial barriers within places of worship and within missionary endeavours. With this understanding in the background, perhaps it is best to define Pentecostalism based on its biblical roots in the Acts of the Apostles. Such an approach will allow for a broader and more flexible view. Therefore, I have defined Pentecostalism in this chapter as an expression of Christianity that has its origin in Acts 2:1-13, when the disciples of our Lord were filled with the Holy Spirit on the Day of Pentecost. It is a modern church movement that is characterised by *glossolalia* (speaking in tongues), the use of the gifts of the Spirit, Spirit-filled experiences, the belief in miracles, healing, and free and ecstatic worship.

---

[23] Asamoah-Gyadu, J. Kwabena, *African Charismatics: Current Developments within Independent Indigenous Pentecostalism in Ghana* (Boston, Brill, 2005), 11.
[24] Roswith Gerloff, 'Churches of the Spirit: The Pentecostal/Charismatic Movement and Africa's Contribution to the Renewal of Christianity' in Afe Adogame, Roswith Gerloff, Klaus Hock (eds), *Christianity in Africa and the African Diaspora: The Appropriation of a Scattered heritage* (London, Continuum International Publishing, 2008), 208-221.
[25] Ibid, 209.
[26] Walter Hollenweger, *The Pentecostals* (London, SCM Press, 1972), 149.

Pentecostal Studies

While Pentecostalism has been around for a while, serious academic work on Pentecostalism only began in the 1950s.[27] Through the expertise and scholarship of Walter J. Hollenweger, Pentecostalism emerged in the 1970s as an area of academic enquiry. His ecclesiastical positioning as the secretary of World Council of Churches (WCC) from 1965 to 1971, and his scholarship as Professor of Mission at the University of Birmingham, helped to develop what we now know today as Pentecostal Studies. The University of Birmingham has since continued that tradition of Pentecostal Studies through the Centre for Pentecostal and Charismatic Studies. The Centre flourishes through research projects, research degrees and publications covering a wide range of Pentecostal and Charismatic expressions in Latin America, Africa and Asia. The Centre, in collaboration with other partners such as the Hollenweger Centre at the Vrije Universiteit in Amsterdam and the Department of History of Religions and Mission Studies at the faculty of Theology, University of Heidelberg in Germany, founded GloPent in 2004. GloPent is the European Research Network on Global Pentecostalism, and its main objective is to connect researchers on Global Pentecostalism and Charismatic Christianity in order to promote international and interdisciplinary approaches to the study of Pentecostal/Charismatic movements.[28] The University of Roehampton in London, with other stake holders such as The Redeemed Christian Church of God (RCCG) and the New Testament Assembly, has also recently founded the Centre for Pentecostalism and Community Engagement. This was partly due to the influx of students from Pentecostal and Charismatic backgrounds studying theology at the University. The Centre functions through its newly-constituted Pentecostal network, which draws together Pentecostal theologians and pastors who reflect on Pentecostal theology by giving seminar papers. There are also Bible colleges across Europe which offer modules on Pentecostal and Charismatic studies as part of their mission and theological training. Pentecostal scholarship is now a robust area of academic enquiry, and a recent anthology edited by Joe Aldred captures both the diversity and serious academic engagement of Pentecostals in Britain.[29] Some of the contributors in this book have engaged in Pentecostal and Charismatic Studies. A significant example is Dulcie Dixon McKenzie (herself a Pentecostal), who, in Chapter Five, explores the legacy of the African Caribbean Pentecostal churches of the Windrush generation. Nils Malmström's contribution in Chapter Eight investigates the rise of immigrant Pentecostal churches in Sweden, while Flavio Gurattos' story in

---

[27] Allan Anderson, Michael Bergunder, Andre Droogers and Cornelis Van Der Laan (eds), *Studying Global Pentecostalism: Theories and Methods* (Los Angeles, University of California Press, 2010), 4-5.

[28] Ibid, 9.

[29] Joe Aldred (ed), *Pentecostals and Charismatics in Britain: An Anthology* (London, SCM Press, 2019).

Chapter Six highlights significant partnerships that developed between Brazilian churches and some of the Charismatic churches in the UK.

Multi-ethnic Congregations: A New Approach in Studying World Christianity

It is befitting to end this chapter on a new approach to studying World Christianity. As observed earlier, Christianity was multi-ethnic from its beginnings, therefore making it a World religion. If World Christianity is multi-ethnic and international, how does this apply to the local context; or, to put the question another way, what can the local context teach us about World Christianity? As conversations continue on World Christianity, corresponding with the growth of churches in Africa, Latin America, South Korea, China and South Asia, and as missionaries continue to be sent from these places to the Western world, it is also important to look at multi-ethnic churches and congregations in Britain and in other European countries. These investigations allow us to consider the significance of these developments and to draw lessons and implications for World Christianity.

This approach has been used by some of the contributors in this book, and one that I will draw attention to is Stephen Dye's contribution in Chapter Two, which investigates three multi-ethnic churches in Germany. To shed more light on this approach, take for example the church I pastor in Woolwich in the Royal Borough of Greenwich (RBG) in south-east London. Our church consists of about 18 different nationalities, with representation drawn from African countries, the Caribbean and Europe. We have people from Nigeria, Cameroun, USA, Jamaica, Ghana, Trinidad, Barbados, Zimbabwe, Zambia, Martinique, Congo, Uganda, Vietnam, Kenya, Sierra Leone, Austria, St Dominic, Italy, England and India. These nationalities include layers of different ethnicities, such as white British, Black British, Black German and Black Austrian. We also have different generations, such as first-generation Africans and Caribbean people who came here from around the 1960s to the 1980s, and second-generation Africans and Caribbean people who were born in the UK, Germany and Austria. While English is our main language of communication as a church, we have people who can speak different languages such as Yoruba, France-French, West African French, German, Lingala, Igbo, Pidgeon English, Shona, Twi, Swahili, Vietnamese, Hindi and Patio.

These diversities, congregated in one location, have allowed me to have a taste of World Christianity in Britain, an experience similar to that of some of the other contributors to this book who have studied or engaged with multi-ethnic churches. I experienced a flavour of World Christianity whilst presiding over a Ghanaian naming ceremony, where I learned the deep meaning of Ghanaian names. I have also presided over Nigerian naming ceremonies (trust me, they are not the same!). This has been done either at people's homes (the traditional Yoruba way of doing naming ceremonies) or as part of a church service. In 2017, we had in the same service a Ghanaian naming ceremony, and a couple from Congo dedicated their daughter. The name of the Congolese couple's daughter was a Zulu name which means, 'the smart one'. The names of people at our church reflect World Christianity, as they have deep spiritual meaning and significance from different parts of the world. I have had conversations on Christian spirituality while enjoying a homemade curry and Indian tea. I have spent time listening to the stories and testimonies of Christians from around the world, which often elucidate different spiritualities and theologies. This process of listening and praying with people has enriched my own faith and spirituality.

Our congregation is one of many multi-ethnic churches now developing across European cities. While scholarly attention is on currents and developments within African Christianity, South Korean Christianity or Latin American Christianity (important as these regions are in their own right), it seems to me that multi-ethnic congregations in Europe are themselves a valid context within which to study World Christianity. There is a need to look at multi-ethnic congregations not just as places that permit deeper understanding of multicultural churches, but also as places within which to study World Christianity. These congregations often have rich theological significance in terms of our learning about and understanding of World Christianity. This does not, of course, constitute an arm-chair approach to the study of World Christianity, as it is still imperative to travel to Africa, Asia, Latin America, the Caribbean, the Pacific and Oceania to understand these Christianities. However, studying multi-ethnic congregations in Europe gives us a window into, and a flavour of, World Christianity in specific localities. In essence, this is contextual World Christianity!

Limitations of the Research

Whilst the title of the book suggests that the research in this book covers all of Europe, I must clarify that in reality, the research focuses on Western Europe. All of the contributors and the research areas are from Western European countries such as England, Wales, Sweden, Germany and Italy. It is hoped that further research can be carried out to explore World Christianity in Eastern Europe. This will all depend on how scholarship positions Eastern European Christians, whether as migrant Christians in Western Europe or just simply as Europeans. Another important limitation to mention is that of the language with which this book communicates, English. It would be very wrong to assume that English is the major language of Europe, given the other major European languages such as French, Spanish and German. These languages are spoken both by Europeans and by migrants in Europe.

References

Aldred, Joe (ed), *Pentecostals and Charismatics in Britain: An Anthology*, London, SCM Press, 2019.

Anderson, Alan, 'Introduction: World Pentecostalism at a Crossroads' in Anderson Allan and Hollenweger Walter, eds., *Pentecostals After a Century: Global Perspectives on a Movement in Transition,* Sheffield, Sheffield Academic Press, 1999.

Anderson, Allan, Bergunder, Michael, Droogers, Andre and Van Der Laan, Cornelis (eds), *Studying Global Pentecostalism: Theories and Methods*, Los Angeles, University of California Press, 2010.

Asamoah-Gyadu, J.K., *African Charismatics: Current Developments within Independent Indigenous Pentecostalism in Ghana*, Leiden, Brill, 2005.

Barrett, David, Annual Statistical Table on Global Mission, *International Bulletin of Missionary Research* 21.1, 1997.

Brierley, Peter, ed, *UK Church statistics No 3: 2018 Edition*, Tonbridge, Kent, ADBC publishers, 2018.

Gerloff, Roswith, 'Churches of the Spirit: The Pentecostal/Charismatic Movement and Africa's Contribution to the Renewal of Christianity' in Afe Adogame, Roswith Gerloff, Klaus Hock (eds), *Christianity in Africa and the African Diaspora: The Appropriation of a Scattered heritage,* London, Continuum International Publishing, 2008.

Jenkins, Philip,' *Next Christendom: The Coming of Global Christianity* Oxford, Oxford University Press, 2002.

Olofinjana, Israel, *Reverse in Ministry and Mission: Africans in the Dark Continent of Europe,* Milton Keynes, Author house, 2010.

Stanley, Brian, 'Founding the Centre for the Study of Christianity in the Non-Western World', in William R. Burrows, Mark R. Gornik, and Janice A. McLean, eds., *Understanding World Christianity: The Vision and Work of Andrew F. Walls* Maryknoll, New York: Orbis Books, 2011.

Stern, Philip, "Dispersion, Diaspora" in Bruce M Metzger and Michael D Coogan (eds), *The Oxford Companion to the Bible,* Oxford, Oxford University, 1993.

Walls, Andrew, *The Missionary Movement in Christian History*, New York, Orbis Books, 1996.

Walls, Andrew, *The Cross-Cultural Process in Christian History*, New York, Orbis Books, 2002.

Walls, Andrew, *Crossing Cultural Frontiers: Studies in the History of World Christianity* Maryknoll, NY: Orbis Books, 2017.

Walter Hollenweger, *The Pentecostals*, London, SCM Press, 1972.

Wan, Enoch, *Diaspora Missiology: Theory, Methodology, and Practice*, 2nd ed., Portland, OR, Institute of Diaspora Study, 2014.

Wright, Chris, *The Mission of God: Unlocking the Bible's Grand Narrative*, Downers Grove, IL, IVP Academic, 2006.

Internet Sources

Diaspora, Lausanne Movement, https://www.lausanne.org/networks/issues/diasporas (Accessed on 15th March 2018).

Global Christianity: A look at the status of Christianity in 2018, Center for the Study of Global Christianity, https://www.gordonconwell.edu/ockenga/research/Resources-and-Downloads.cfm (Accessed 16th September 2018).

Olofinjana, Israel, "Historical Development of Black Pentecostal Churches in Britain: A Case Study of Apostolic Pastoral Congress (APC)", *Missio Africanus Journal* (Volume 1, Issue 2, 2016) http://missioafricanus.org/missio-africanus-journal-of-african-missiology/ (Accessed 19th March 2018).

Pew research Centre Religion and Public Life http://www.pewforum.org/2011/12/19/global-christianity-exec/ (Accessed 18th September 2017) http://www.pewforum.org/2017/04/05/the-changing-global-religious-landscape/#fn-27661-3 (Accessed 18th September 2017).

Postgraduate Programme for Migrant Pastors and Church Leaders, https://www.godgeleerdheid.vu.nl/en/programmes/postgraduate/index.aspx (Accessed on 15th March 2018).

Section One

Diasporic Identity

(2) The Multicultural Missionary Identity of Diaspora Christians in Germany
Stephen Dye

One could argue that there is nothing unique about the movement of peoples today. After all, human migration has occurred since the beginning of the human race. In recent years, however, the migration of people has become more widespread and more pronounced. In the past 50 years, the number of international migrants has grown from around 79 million in 1960 to almost 250 million in 2015 – a 200 per cent increase.[1] Stephen Castles and Mark Miller even titled their book, *The Age of Migration*.[2] Unlike previous human migrations, today's migration, according to the authors, involves 'all regions of the world'.[3] They described some of the factors contributing to global diaspora:

> Mobilization has become much easier as a result of recent political and cultural changes, as well as the development of new transport and communication technologies. International migration is, in turn, a central dynamic within globalization.[4]

Castles and Miller further argued that human migration is a trend that will endure in coming years.[5]

Diaspora in Germany

The movement of peoples that is happening worldwide has been occurring in Europe, and in Germany in particular. As of the end of 2016, over 10 million foreigners were living in Germany – a 23 per cent increase since 2014.[6] The

---

[1] Phillip Connor, 'International Migration: Key Findings from the U.S., Europe and the World', *Pew Research Center* (blog), December 15, 2016, http://www.pewresearch.org/fact-tank/2016/12/15/international-migration-key-findings-from-the-u-s-europe-and-the-world/.

[2] Stephen Castles and Mark J. Miller, *The Age of Migration*, 4th ed. (Basingstoke, UK: Palgrave Macmillan, 2009).

[3] Castles and Miller, 2.

[4] Castles and Miller, 3.

[5] Castles and Miller, 3.

[6] 'Mehr Als 10 Millionen Ausländer in Deutschland' [More than 10 Million Foreigners in Germany], Statistisches Bundesamt [Federal Statistical Office], June 30, 2017,

increase was in large part due to the European migrant crisis, which reached its peak in 2015. The year 2015 saw more than 1.5 million immigrants coming into Germany, more than any previous year in the country's history.[7]

Berlin, the city where I presently reside, gives a glimpse of the shift that is taking place in the country at large. Berlin is one of Germany's most multicultural cities, its inhabitants representing 186 countries. More than 494,000 people of non-German citizenship live in Berlin.[8] The number of foreigners in Berlin is considerably higher when one includes individuals who migrated to Germany but now hold a German passport. Nearly one third of Berlin's population comes from an immigrant background.[9] What is especially noteworthy is how the city's immigrant population continues to increase. In 2016, the city's population grew by 60,500 people. Of this number of newcomers to Berlin, 55,700 (92 per cent) were immigrants from foreign countries.[10]

This demographic shift presents challenges to Germany. In a highly publicized speech given in the fall of 2010, Germany's chancellor, Angela Merkel, argued that the approach to building a multicultural society in which Germans and immigrants live happily side by side has 'failed, utterly failed'.[11] German politician Thilo Sarrazin went even further, asserting in his book *Deutschland schafft sich ab* (*Germany is Destroying Itself*) that immigrants who fail to integrate are contributing to such social ills as increasing crime, welfare dependency, and educational underachievement.[12] According to Sarrazin, if immigration in Germany continues unchecked, it will potentially bring about the ruin of the nation. Such opinions are not isolated to politicians. A survey conducted in the fall of 2010 showed that 'more than 30 per cent of Germans believed the country was "overrun by foreigners"'.[13] Arguably, the main reason for the stunning growth of Germany's new political party, the Alternative for

https://www.destatis.de/DE/PresseService/Presse/Pressemitteilungen/2017/06/PD17_22 7_12521.html.

[7] ,Mehr Als 10 Millionen Ausländer in Deutschland' [More than 10 Million Foreigners in Germany].

[8] 'Vielfalt' [Diversity], Berlin.de. March 16, 2016. http://www.berlin.de/berlin-im-ueberblick/hauptstadtleben/vielfalt/index.php.

[9] 'Berlin Wächst Im Ersten Halbjahr 2016 Weiter, Vor Allem Durch Zuzug Aus Dem Ausland' [Berlin Grows in First Half of 2016 through Influx of Foreigners], Amt Für Statistik Berlin-Brandenburg [Office for Statistics Berlin-Brandenburg], September 27, 2016, https://www.statistik-berlin-brandenburg.de/pms/2016/16-09-27.pdf.

[10] Andrew Bulkeley, 'Berlin's Population Growth Continues; Germans, Refugees', *Newsfeed.BERLIN* (blog), February 26, 2017, http://newsfeed.berlin/berlin-population-growth-continues.

[11] 'Merkel: "Multiculture Has Failed"', *BBC*, October 17, 2010, http://www.bbc.co.uk/news/world-europe-11559451, para. 1.

[12] Thilo Sarrazin, *Deutschland Schafft Sich Ab* [Germany Is Destroying Itself], (München, Germany: DVA Dt.Verlags-Anstalt, 2010).

[13] 'Merkel'," para. 4.

Germany (the AfD) has been its opposition to the government's allowance of the large influx of refugees to Germany, particularly in the fall of 2015.

A *Kairos* Moment

While there is no doubt that this period of increasing migration to Germany presents real challenges to the nation, it can also be seen as a *kairos* moment: a point in time ripe with opportunity for God to draw people from different cultures to himself. According to scripture, God sovereignly oversees the movement of peoples. In his sermon on Mars Hill, recorded in Acts 17:26-27, the Apostle Paul proclaimed:

> From one man he made all the nations, that they should inhabit the whole earth; and he marked out their appointed times in history and the boundaries of their lands. God did this so that they would seek him and perhaps reach out for him and find him, though he is not far from any one of us.[14]

This passage not only shows that God is involved in the movement and placement of peoples but also that he gives the reason why: 'so that people will perhaps reach out for him and find him'. One of God's purposes for diaspora, then, is to draw people to himself, and one of the ways in which he is accomplishing this purpose is through using diaspora Christians to give witness to Christ. Included in the wave of immigrants to Germany are Christians – many of whom believe that it is their missionary duty to spread the gospel in the land in which they now sojourn.

Although no one seems to know with certainty the number of immigrant Christians in Germany, one can get an idea by considering the number of immigrant churches in Germany. Benjamin Simon estimated that there were some 500 African-initiated immigrant congregations in Germany as of 2010.[15] This number is likely to be conservative given that, in the same year, the authors of the newsletter, 'Prayer for Berlin' reported that, in Berlin alone, between 80 and 100 African-initiated immigrant churches existed.[16] In one state of Germany, North Rhine-Westphalia, Claudia Währisch-Oblau identified more than 600 immigrant congregations.[17]

---

[14] Unless otherwise stated, all scripture references are from the New International Version (2011).

[15] Benjamin Simon, *From Migrants to Missionaries: Christians of African Origin in Germany* (Frankfurt am Main, Germany: Peter Lang, 2010).

[16] 'Immigrant Churches in Berlin', *Prayer for Berlin*, December 2010, http://gebetfuerberlin.files.wordpress.com/2010/11/gfb89e.pdf.

[17] Claudia Währisch-Oblau, 'Getting Ready to Receive? German Churches and the "New Mission" from the South', *Lausanne World Pulse Archives*, no. 7 (2008), http://www.lausanneworldpulse.com/themedarticles-php/971/07-2008.

Dual Identity of Diaspora Christians in Germany

Drawing upon qualitative case study research done for my PhD dissertation,[18] this chapter probes the dual identity of diaspora Christians in Germany. As part of my research, I examined three immigrant multicultural churches in three different urban contexts in Germany, each one initiated by a church planter (or church planters) coming from one of the three major regions of the Global South: Africa, Asia, and Latin America (see Figure 1 below). I interviewed a total of 35 participants[19] in the three churches (including the church planters). One of the findings of the research was that many of the immigrant participants exhibited a dual identity – a multicultural missionary identity.

Figure 1.1 Characteristics of the Immigrant Multicultural Churches in My Study

Name of church	Church planters and region of the Global South from which they come	Location of church in Germany	Denomination	Year planted
Akebulan Church	Peter Arthur-Africa (Ghana)	Berlin	Pentecostal	2006
Jesus for All People	Tony and Sarah Ibarra-Asia (Philippines)	Frankfurt and Giessen	Pentecostal	2002
New Life Church	Richard Aidoo-Africa (Ghana) Sigrid Aidoo-Latin America (Chile)	Düsseldorf	Baptist	1991

Multicultural Identity

I define a multicultural person as one who welcomes and engages racial, ethnic and cultural diversity. Several of the immigrant believers in my study were 'multicultural people' who could relate to a variety of immigrant cultures and, at the same time, had adapted to the dominant culture of their host country.

During my field visits to the three churches, I observed this characteristic of multiculturality in each of the first-generation immigrant church planters in my study. All three of the churches drew people from a variety of nations, and the church planting pastors welcomed and engaged the various cultures represented in their churches. Valencia, a Kenyan attendee of Jesus For All People, made an observation about Tony and Sarah Ibarra that is representative of the other immigrant church planters who were a part of my research:

---

[18] Stephen Dye, 'Mission in the Diaspora: Multicultural Churches in Urban Germany Initiated by Church Planters from the Global South' (Biola University, 2017).
[19] The actual name of each church planter is used. However, a pseudonym has been assigned for each of the other participants.

The pastor and his wife, they don't only go to Filipinos. They say, 'Greet everybody who is in the church'. They will walk up to everybody who is

in the church and say, 'Hi', and give them a hug. You feel yourself that this is a church for everybody. And that is the thing that makes you realize that it's not only for one race – because we are mixed. And, then, you can see when people sit in the church that here is not a corner where people say, 'This is only for Filipinos; this is only for Africans'. There are mixed people everywhere.

The immigrant church planters in my study demonstrated that they not only related to various immigrant cultures, but also adapted well to German culture. Each of the immigrant church planters had become sufficiently fluent in the German language. As Tony Ibarra of Jesus For All People put it, 'The Germans expect you to learn the language. I had it in my heart from the very beginning that I will learn German because it is important.' Paulus, a German attendee of Jesus For All People, made the following observation about Pastors Tony and Sarah: 'It seems like they are really willing to accept the Germans, to love this culture. They can speak fluent German, and they have really integrated themselves. They have an openness to our culture.' Andre, a German attendee of Akebulan Church in Berlin, observed something similar in Pastor Peter Arthur:

Peter married a German woman. For years, he attended a German church, and so he developed his language. I know other good African pastors in different churches in Berlin. They are doing good things for the Lord, but they are not so cross-cultural. The Lord led Peter to learn the German language. [And Peter has] encouraged other African sisters and brothers to learn the language of the country.

Each of the church planters also demonstrated a love and appreciation for the country and people of Germany. Martin, a German attendee of New Life Church, made the following comment about Pastor Richard Aidoo: '[He] really tries to connect to German society and mentality. I see the willingness of the pastor to reach Germans.' Both Tony and Sarah Ibarra manifested a love for and identification with Germany and the German people. Evidence of this is seen in the fact that they both renounced their Filipino citizenship and became German citizens. In my interview with Tony, he revealed his strong sense of identification with Germany. At one point in our conversation, he expressed his belief that racial prejudice is a problem in Germany. However, what was particularly striking was that he referred to racial prejudice in Germany as, '*our* sin as a nation' (as opposed to, '*their* sin as a nation'). Pastor Tony included himself as sharing this sin with the people of the country of which he has chosen to become a citizen.

This multicultural identity was even more accentuated in the 1.5 and 2.0 generation immigrants[20] who were a part of my study. In the three churches I visited, I interviewed nine teenagers and young adults who were either 1.5 or 2.0 generation immigrants.

One-point-five and 2.0 generation immigrants in Germany inhabit both their parents' culture and their host country's culture. While these individuals feel a connection to the culture of their country of origin, they also identify with German culture. As Michael Kisskalt put it, they 'have grown up in German kindergartens, in German schools with German friends'.[21] They are 'third-culture kids'[22] who fit David Pollock and Ruth Van Reken's description as someone 'who is living or has lived – or meaningfully interacted with – two or more cultural environments for a significant period of time during childhood'.[23] In addition to connecting with their parents' home culture and their host country's culture, they find themselves in between cultures, in a hybrid, third culture. They identify with both their home culture and their host culture but seem to feel most comfortable in a multicultural context.

In each of the churches, there were examples of 1.5/2.0 generation attendees who displayed a simultaneous affinity to immigrant cultures and to German culture, yet appeared to feel most at home in a multicultural setting. Ellen from Jesus For All People shared: 'I am a Filipino, born in the Philippines. I grew up in Germany, was raised here. I know a lot of people from different countries and nations, but also, I love the Germans.' Olamide, a second-generation immigrant from Togo attending New Life Church, expressed something similar in saying: 'I was born here, so I have a lot of German friends, of course – and a lot of friends from Ghana, from Spain, and other places. I'm not like, "So you're from Togo. I have to be with you because you're from Togo."' Darweshi, a young Tanzanian immigrant, expressed how Akebulan Church connected him to his home culture, while at the same time linking him to German culture:

> When I come to this church, I see black people, and ... it gives me a connection to where I was born. At the same time, the pastor has set up the service in a way that Germans can understand it. That way it is also kind of a little bit German – so I get both sides.

---

20 Individuals who were born in a different country but immigrated to the country of destination as a child or teenager are known as 1.5 generation immigrants. Second (2.0) generation immigrants are individuals
who were born in the new host country.
21 Michael Kisskalt, 'Cross-Cultural Learning: Issues of the Second Generation of Immigrant Churches', in Peter Penner (ed), *Ethnic Churches in Europe: A Baptist Response* (Schwarzenfeld, Germany: Neufeld Verlag, 2006), 134.
22 David C. Pollock and Ruth E. Van Reken, *Third Culture Kids: Growing Up Among Worlds*, 2nd edition (Boston, MA: Nicholas Brealey, 2009), 31.
23 Pollock and Van Reken.

Likewise, Jerod the son of Pastors Tony and Sarah Ibarra, stated:

> Because I grew up in Germany, German churches would not be a very big difference for me. But I love having people from different kinds of nations ... I'm used to it, that's why I couldn't imagine a place where there's only one culture. Like, for example, I hate going to a Filipino church.

The comments above reveal that the 1.5/2.0 generation immigrants I interviewed displayed a multicultural identity. On one hand, they felt a connection to the culture of their country of origin. On the other hand, they had become acculturated to Germany. They spent their formative years in Germany. Some of them – those who had a German parent – were half German themselves, and most of them had German citizenship. Yet, even more than in German culture or in their parents' culture, they felt most comfortable in a complex, multicultural setting.

Missionary Identity

In addition to a multicultural identity, many diaspora Christians in Germany also manifest a missionary identity. Immigrant believers with a missionary commitment and passion are part of the reverse mission[24] phenomenon happening in Germany, and throughout Europe. European missionaries in past centuries took the gospel to the Americas, Africa, and Asia. Now Christians from these regions of the world are returning the favour by bringing back the gospel to a continent where Christianity is in decline. These immigrants from the Global South are Europe's 'new Christians',[25] now living in a foreign land and carrying out what they believe to be their commission from Christ.

Each of the immigrant church planters in my study exhibited a missionary identity. They believed that the Lord sent them to Germany as missionaries and they identified themselves as part of the reverse mission movement.

This missionary commitment and passion was most clearly seen in Tony and Sarah Ibarra and Richard and Sigrid Aidoo. The Ibarras are part of the worldwide diaspora of over 8 million Filipinos living in some 130 countries around the world.[26] Although one could argue that most Filipinos leave their country of origin out of a desire for a better life elsewhere, the Ibarras had another

---

[24] J A B. Jongeneel, 'The Mission of Migrant Churches in Europe', *Missiology* 31, no. 1 (January 2003): 29-33; J. D. Payne, 'Missions in Reverse?', *Missiologically Thinking* (blog), December 8, 2010, http://www.jdpayne.org/2010/12/08/missions-in-reverse/; Claudia Währisch-Oblau, 'Missions in Reverse: Whose Image in the Mirror?', *Anvil* 18, no. 4 (2001): 261-67.

[25] Philip Jenkins, *God's Continent: Christianity, Islam, and Europe's Religious Crisis* (New York, NY: Oxford University Press, USA, 2007).

[26] Jr Luis L. Pantoja, Sadiri Joy B. Tira, and Enoch Wan (eds), *Scattered: The Filipino Global Presence* (Manila, Philippines: LifeChange Publishing, 2004).

motivation. Tony stated: 'We came here to Germany in obedience to God's word that he wanted us to be part of the labour force.' Likewise, Sigrid Aidoo of New Life Church stated:

> I was called as a missionary. A missionary looks for mission – and mission is everywhere – everywhere where needy people are – where the name of Jesus is not known. Where there is one unbeliever, there is mission. I came as a missionary. My husband came as a missionary as well. He was sent by God here. We came as missionaries. If you go to India, you want to reach Indians. If you go to Germany, you want to reach Germans too.

Each of the church planters led an immigrant church that was reaching a variety of ethno-cultural groups. The most noteworthy example was New Life Church's representation of 40 to 50 nations in its congregation and its thriving outreach to Farsi-speaking Iranians, resulting in some 700 baptisms of former Muslims over the past few years.

Additionally, the churches in my study were reaching Germans with the gospel and seeing them become assimilated into their churches. Most of the Germans I interviewed expressed that they felt quite at home in the immigrant church of which they were a part. On average, the Germans I interviewed had been a part of the church for five to ten years. Akebulan Church and Jesus For All People had Germans in positions of leadership in their churches. Finally, two of the churches in my study (Jesus For All People and New Life) had been instrumental in planting and overseeing multiple churches in Germany.

Especially notable was the fact that this missionary identity was passed on to the children of the church planters in my study. Each of the church planters had a child, or children, serving in the churches that they had planted. The most pronounced example was Jerod, one of Tony and Sarah Ibarra's three children. Jerod shared how he regularly ministered in a street evangelism team (made up of four people representing four different nations!) involved in distributing food, playing music, and sharing testimonies. The contributions of Jerod and the other children in helping their parents in their missionary task perhaps cannot be overstated.

Diaspora Christians in Germany as Transcultural Mediators

This dual identity suggests that diaspora believers can be – to use the nomenclature of Paul Hiebert – *transcultural mediators*. Transcultural mediators, according to Hiebert are 'persons whose norms can transcend national and monocultural boundaries [and who] ... build intercultural bridges'.[27] In transcending these boundaries, such persons mediate between immigrant

---

[27] Paul G. Hiebert, *The Gospel in Human Contexts: Anthropological Explorations for Contempory Missions* (Grand Rapids, MI: Baker Academic, 2009), 198.

cultures and the dominant culture of the host country. They also mediate between the gospel and non-Christian belief systems.

Mediators Between Immigrant Cultures and German Culture

As transcultural mediators, diaspora Christians in Germany manifest the characteristic of *liminality*. French anthropologist Arnold van Gennep coined the term 'liminality',[28] which has been described as an 'in-between', 'hyphenated', or 'neither/nor' space.[29] Immigrants often find themselves in this liminal state. Liminality has both challenges and possibilities. On one hand, because immigrants have left their place of origin, they feel disconnected from their homeland. And because they are foreigners, they often do not enjoy a strong cultural connection to their host country. This sense of disconnection can be both psychologically stressful and limiting.[30] On the other hand, liminality has its advantages. There is a sense in which those in diaspora can be 'both/and'.[31] They can be 'bridge people, bicultural people who, because of their dual ethnic identities, fit in both their home countries and their new locations'.[32]

Researchers have noted the key role 1.5/2.0 generation immigrants play as connectors, or bridges. Steven Ybarrola pointed out that '1.5 and subsequent generations ... often take on more of a hybrid identity [both/and] which ... can be used as a way to bridge the cultural gap between their diaspora community and the larger host society'.[33] Peter Penner added that these individuals are 'a bridge not only in the society but also between local and immigrant churches'.[34]

The role of transcultural mediators will become more needed as our urban centres increasingly become places of cultural hybridity. According to Jan Pieterse, cultural hybridity is:

A wide register of multiple identity, cross-over, pick-'n'-mix, boundary-crossing experiences and styles, matching a world of growing migration and diaspora lives,

---

28 Arnold van Gennep, Monika B. Vizedon, and Gabrielle L. Caffee, *The Rites of Passage*, reprint edition (Chicago: University of Chicago Press, 1961).

29 Steven Ybarrola, 'An Anthropological Approach to Diaspora Missiology', UReach Toronto, March 2011, http://www.ureachtoronto.com/content/anthropological-approach-diaspora-missiology, 8.

30 Ybarrola.

31 Ybarrola.

32 Payne, *Strangers Next Door*, 157.

33 Steven Ybarrola, 'Diasporas and Multiculturalism: Social Ideologies, Liminality, and Cultural Identity', in *In* Sadiri Joy Tira (ed), *The Human Tidal Wave* (Manila, Philippines: Lifechange Publishing, Inc., 2013), 135-49.

34 Peter Penner, 'John Called Mark: The Role of a Second Generation Christian in Mission', in Peter F. Penner (ed), *Ethnic Churches in Europe: A Baptist Response* (Schwarzenfeld, Germany: Neufeld Verlag, 2006), 120.

intensive intercultural communication, everyday multiculturalism and erosion of boundaries.35

Gary McIntosh and Allen McMahan described many of the world's urban centres as places 'where the culture compresses the numerous homogeneous groupings closely together'.36 Cultural hybridity is happening in today's global cities, where cultures are closely layered on top of each other. In such contexts, the boundaries between cultures are no longer represented by a solid line because they are always being negotiated.37 As liminal, transcultural people, diaspora Christians can be like the Apostle Paul in 'becoming all things to all people'38 in today's increasingly multicultural urban centres.

Mediators Between the Gospel and Non-Christian Belief Systems

Diaspora Christians can be transcultural mediators who serve as bridges between the gospel and a culture in Germany that is increasingly separated from its Christian heritage. Jehu Hanciles made the point that, 'New Christian immigrants … come from centres of vibrant Christian growth and embody a brand of Christianity that is strongly evangelistic or conversionist.'39 While Philip Jenkins shared a sense of pessimism about the institutional church of 'Europe's old-stock white populations', he viewed immigrant churches established by Christians from the Global South as 'thriving new churches [that] represent an exciting new planting, even potentially a kind of re-evangelization'.40

Andre and Stefanie, German attendees of Akebulan Church, bore witness to the observations of Hanciles and Jenkins. As Andre put it,

> The Lord will use the foreign people, cultures, to come here to Germany, to Europe, to bless the Germans. I am a German. I was born in Berlin. There are many people who come from different countries who have come to Germany and they are anointed to pray, to intercede for the Body of Christ.

Stefanie likewise expressed her perspective that immigrant believers coming to Germany are being used as mediators between the gospel and a secular culture:

---

35 Jan Nederveen Pieterse, *Globalization and Culture: Global Melange* (Lanham, MD: Rowman & Littlefield Publishers, 2003), 221.

36 Gary McIntosh and Alan McMahan, *Being the Church in a Multi-Ethnic Community: Why It Matters and How It Works* (Indianapolis, IN: Wesleyan Pub. House, 2012), 119.

37 John S. Leonard, 'The Church between Cultures: Rethinking the Church in Light of the Globalization of Immigration', *Evangelical Missions Quarterly* 40, no. 1 (January 2004): 62-73.

38 1 Corinthians 9:22.

39 Jehu J. Hanciles, *In the Shadow of the Elephant: Bishop Crowther and the African Missionary Movement* (Oxford, England: Church Mission Society, 2008), 14.

40 Jenkins, *God's Continent*, 87.

And we believe that it's not for nothing that Africans are coming here. The African community – so many of them are Christians – and we believe that this a blessing that they bring, and also to society in Germany, which is mainly secular. And most people in Germany don't go to church at all. So, we believe that this spirituality that these people have brought with them is something that can bless and help Germans.

When diaspora Christians in Germany are committed to Jesus' commission to make disciples, they embody great potential to reach indigenous Germans with the gospel. They can be like those Jewish Christians in the diaspora referred to in Acts 11:20 – the 'some of them' who 'began to speak to Greeks also'. Some of these Jewish Christian immigrants went beyond just proclaiming the gospel message in Hebrew to fellow Jews; they also began to spread the message to indigenous Syrians in the Greek language.

Diaspora Christians in Germany can also be transcultural mediators between the gospel and the beliefs and practices of Islam. I witnessed this first-hand in my field visits to the immigrant churches in my research. During a fellowship meal after the church service of Jesus For All People, a Turkish man introduced himself to me. He reported how he had recently converted to Christianity from Islam and had become a part of the congregation. Especially striking was New Life Church's ministry in reaching Muslims with the gospel. I had the opportunity to participate in a Tuesday evening prayer meeting for Muslim-background believers and seekers who were considering following Christ. As mentioned previously, Pastor Richard Aidoo shared with me that New Life had seen an estimated 700 ex-Muslims baptised over the previous eight years.

Researchers have pointed out that Christians from the Majority World may have an advantage over Western Christians when it comes to reaching Muslims. J.D. Payne argued:

> Due to the history of the Crusades and to much of the secular and ungodly cultural expression of Western society well-known throughout the Islamic world, the predominately Anglo [white] churches of the West are likely to continue to experience many challenges to reaching the Muslim context. However, much anecdotal evidence seems to support that many Hispanic, Asian, and African peoples are overcoming these barriers because they lack the cultural history in which many such problems exist.[41]

Jehu Hanciles added: 'The most significant counterforce to Islam in Europe is likely to come less from secularism or from Europe's homegrown, fairly moribund Christianity than from the steady influx of Christian immigrants [from Africa, Latin America, and Asia].'[42] Lamin Sanneh likewise proposed that post-

---

41 Payne, *Strangers Next Door*, 156.
42 Hanciles, *In the Shadow of the Elephant: Bishop Crowther and the African Missionary Movement*, 14.

Christian Europe needs help from the frontier Christians of Africa and Asia in engaging Muslims with the gospel.₄₃

Implications for Indigenous Believers and Diaspora Believers

What does all this mean to believers – both indigenous and immigrant – living in Germany? In the final section of this chapter, I would like to suggest some appropriate responses for both indigenous and immigrant believers in Germany (and beyond, as these responses can be applied to contexts outside of Germany).

Implications for Indigenous Believers

Recognise the spiritual receptivity of immigrants. As already mentioned, those in diaspora find themselves in an in-between, liminal state. People who have been uprooted from their home culture and social structure are often more open to the gospel than nationals of the host country.₄₄ According to Enoch Wan, 'People in transition are more receptive to the gospel, thus providing us with opportunities … in mission.'₄₅

A personal anecdote supports this assertion. A few years ago, I made a trip to the immigration office in Berlin in order to have my son's resident visa transferred into his new passport. After waiting in line for two hours in a sea of fellow foreigners, I was finally able to get my task accomplished. Upon leaving the office, I spotted a German missionary colleague who was manning a Christian literature table. Throughout the morning, he sought to have conversations with, and give literature to people coming and going from the immigration office. I asked my friend, 'Do you notice a difference in the level of spiritual receptivity between foreigners and Germans who pass by your table?' Without hesitation, he said, 'Absolutely. Most Germans have no interest at all, whereas many foreigners want to talk with me and take Christian literature.'

₄₃ Lamin Sanneh, 'The Church and Its Missionary Vocation: The Islamic Frontline in a Post-Christian West', in A. Walls & C. Ross (eds), *Mission in the 21st Century: Exploring the Five Marks of Global Mission* (Maryknoll, NY: Orbis Books, 2008), 144.
₄₄ Ybarrola, 'An Anthropological Approach to Diaspora Missiology', 8.
₄₅ Enoch Wan, *Diaspora Missiology: Theory, Methodology, and Practice* (Portland, OR: Institute of Diaspora Studies – U.S., Western Seminary, 2012), 132. It should be mentioned that there *are* cases in which those in diaspora are quite closed to the gospel. Craig Ott points out, "Diaspora communities are often more rigid in their beliefs and practices in an effort to preserve their religious and cultural identity." (Craig Ott, 'Impetus for Witness in the Early Church', in E. Wan (ed), *Diaspora Missiology: Theory, Methodology, and Practice* (2012), 87. This is especially true when the diaspora community is large and has its own social institutions in place. This would be true, for instance, of the Turkish diaspora community in Berlin, which, at this time, is not known to be open to the gospel.

Welcome and engage immigrants. There is a tendency to succumb to what Cody Lorance termed, the 'Babel Complex'.[46] He described this as a centripetal pull to stay clustered among people of our own cultural identity. Part of the creation mandate that God gave to Adam and Eve was the command 'to fill the earth' (Gen. 1:28). Within only a few chapters into the Genesis narrative (Chapter 11), people had largely disregarded this mandate. Rather than carrying out the Lord's agenda to fill the earth, they clung together and attempted to 'make a name for themselves'. Lorance observed that what was true then, is true today, even among Christians:

> The Babel Complex continues to plague humanity today. In the Church, it is the most significant obstacle to our faithful engagement in diaspora missions. The centripetal Christian resists God's outward call to cross national borders and cultural barriers, preferring instead the safety and familiarity of home.[47]

Christian nationals of the host country must avoid 'the urge to cling to [their] own culture as superior to all others and ... reject any semblance of diversity'.[48]

One of the discoveries of my research was the example of three indigenous German pastors who did not succumb to the Babel Complex. Peter Arthur, Tony Ibarra, and Richard Aidoo each shared how a German pastor had brought them in under his wing and gave each one the opportunity to minister in his church. This connection to a German pastor no doubt contributed to each one of the immigrant pastors' success in adapting to German culture and becoming effective transcultural mediators.

It should be added that each of the immigrant churches in my study was welcomed into indigenous German church denominations. Akebulan Church is part of the Mülheimer Association of Churches. Jesus For All People is a member of the Association of Pentecostal Free Churches (the BFP), and New Life Church is part of the German Baptist Union (the BEFG).

Be sensitive to immigrant marginality. German believers must not overlook the fact that many immigrants in their country live in a state of marginality. They find themselves on the edges of society, due to racial and/or socioeconomic differences that separate them from mainstream German culture. Immigrants are sometimes exploited by those with nefarious intentions. According to Ted Rubesh, marginality and exploitation are the shared experience of many diasporas:

---

46 Cody Lorance, 'Reflections of a Church Planter among Diaspora Groups in Metro-Chicago: Pursuing Cruciformity in Diaspora Missions', in E. Wan (ed), *Diaspora Missiology: Theory, Methodology, and Practice* (Portland, OR: Institute of Diaspora Studies – U.S., Western Seminary, 2012), 272.
47 Lorance, 273.
48 Lorance, 272.

Whether they are underpaid Mexican migrant workers in the United States or sexually exploited Filipino housemaids in the Middle East, physical abuse and political and economic exploitation have often been hallmarks of the diaspora experience.[49]

Indigenous believers have the opportunity to reach out to immigrants in compassion, hospitality, and even advocacy, where needed.[50]

Jung Young Lee made the point that *all* Christians (whether they are immigrants or indigenous) are the 'marginal people of God'.[51] In reality, all Christians are strangers and sojourners in this present world. In a state of marginality themselves, national believers should be sensitive to the marginalized migrants who live nearby, remembering the Lord's command to the Israelites:

> When a foreigner resides among you in your land, do not mistreat them. The foreigner residing among you must be treated as your native-born. Love them as yourself, for you were foreigners in Egypt. I am the LORD your God.[52]

Implications for Diaspora Believers

Embrace liminality. As pointed out earlier, in a state of liminality one can feel limited and weak in a neither/nor, in-between, hybrid space. Yet, liminality can be a strength to be embraced. Along with the Apostle Paul, diaspora believers can say, 'When I am weak, I am strong.'[53] As seen with the examples featured earlier, diaspora believers have the potential to be effective multicultural missionaries. Their dual identity enables them to be transcultural mediators who serve as bridges between immigrant and indigenous cultures, and between the gospel and non-Christian belief system.

Believers in diaspora have an edge as spreaders of the gospel. They are people on the move; thus, the 'go' of the Great Commission does not seem as daunting to them as it does to the person tied to his or her home culture. Furthermore, their adaptability to new languages and cultures can give immigrant Christians the edge when it comes to communicating the gospel cross-culturally.[54]

That said, it is of course possible for diaspora believers to fail to integrate into German society. How sad to think that immigrant Christians could squander their

[49] Ted Rubesh, 'Diaspora Distinctives: The Jewish Diaspora Experience in the Old Testament', in E. Wan (ed), *Diaspora Missiology: Theory, Methodology, and Practice* (Portland, OR: Institute of Diaspora Studies – U.S., Western Seminary, 2012), 56.
[50] Wan, *Diaspora Missiology*, 271.
[51] Jung Young Lee, *Marginality: The Key to Multicultural Theology*, 1st ed. (Minneapolis: Fortress Press, 1995), 173.
[52] Leviticus 19:33-34.
[53] 2 Corinthians 12:10
[54] Wan, *Diaspora Missiology*, 140.

opportunity to be effective transcultural mediators by failing to make a serious effort to learn the German language and adapt to the culture of their host country.

Those who do adapt to German culture need not give up their core identity. According to Hiebert, transcultural mediators 'develop a metacultural mental framework that enables [them] to live in different worlds while keeping [their] core identity secure'.55 They follow the example of their Jewish forbears. The Jewish exiles in Babylon 'became "Jewish Babylonians", proactively engaging in the socio-cultural milieu of their day'.56 Yet, those in the Jewish diaspora never completely lost their cultural and religious distinctives: they remained 'Babylonian Jews'.57

Follow the lead of the 'migrant God'. As God reveals himself through the pages of scripture, he shows himself to be the 'migrant God'.58 This can be seen in each person of the triune God. God the Father came to his people, the Israelites, and 'dwelt among them' in the tabernacle (Ex. 29:45). As the Israelites travelled through the wilderness, he moved with them. The God who cannot even be contained in the highest of heavens (2 Chron. 6:16) chose to dwell among his people and tabernacle with them in their wanderings through the wilderness. This same nature is revealed in God the Son as he left his home in heaven and 'made his dwelling [literally, "tabernacled"] among us' (John 1:14). Finally, the Son sent the Spirit (John 15:26) to take up residence within the body of each believer (1 Cor. 3:16). It is the *missio Dei* of the triune God to move and come to humanity in order to redeem us.

Diaspora believers in Germany take their cue from the *missio Dei*. If God became the migrant God in order to redeem humanity, then his followers imitate his example. They become, as Andrew Walls put it, 'migrants for Christ's sake'.59 The 'go' of the Great Commission (Matt. 28:18-20) necessitates that Christians 'scatter and … bear the good news to all nations',60 and diaspora believers can uniquely and effectively live out this commission.

---

55 Hiebert, 198.

56 Ted Rubesh, 'Diaspora Distinctives: The Jewish Diaspora Experience in the Old Testament', in E. Wan (ed), *Diaspora Missiology: Theory, Methodology, and Practice* (Portland, OR: Institute of Diaspora Studies – U.S., Western Seminary, 2012), 63.

57 Rubesh.

58 Darrell Jackson, 'Europe and the Migrant Experience: Transforming Integration', *Transformation: An International Journal of Holistic Mission Studies* 28, no. 1 (January 1, 2011), 22.

59 Andrew Walls, 'Christian Mission in a Five-Hundred-Year Context', in In A. Walls & C. Ross (eds), *Mission in the 21st Century: Exploring the Five Marks of Global Mission* (Maryknoll, NY: Orbis Books, 2008), 197.

60 Wan, *Diaspora Missiology*, 124.

Conclusion

Echoing the Jewish diaspora in the days of old, people are on the move, and human migration shows no signs of abating. We are living in what seems to be a *kairos* moment in mission, and Germany is no exception. Diaspora believers from the Global South are changing the face of Christianity in Germany. Some have taken on a dual, multicultural missionary identity and are reaching people from a variety of ethno-cultural backgrounds with the gospel. They are transcultural mediators who serve as bridges between diverse cultures and disparate spiritual beliefs. May they be welcomed by indigenous believers, and may they live out their unique and needed role as multicultural missionaries in the land in which they sojourn.

References

"Berlin Wächst Im Ersten Halbjahr 2016 Weiter, Vor Allem Durch Zuzug Aus Dem Ausland" [Berlin Grows in First Half of 2016 through Influx of Foreigners]." *Amt Für Statistik Berlin-Brandenburg [Office for Statistics Berlin-Brandenburg]*, September 27, 2016. https://www.statistik-berlin-brandenburg.de/pms/2016/16-09-27.pdf.

Bulkeley, Andrew. "Berlin's Population Growth Continues; Germans, Refugees." *Newsfeed.BERLIN* (blog), February 26, 2017. http://newsfeed.berlin/berlin-population-growth-continues.

Castles, Stephen, and Mark J. Miller. *The Age of Migration*. 4th ed. Basingstoke, UK: Palgrave Macmillan, 2009.

Connor, Phillip. "International Migration: Key Findings from the U.S., Europe and the World." *Pew Research Center* (blog), December 15, 2016. http://www.pewresearch.org/fact-tank/2016/12/15/international-migration-key-findings-from-the-u-s-europe-and-the-world/.

Dye, Stephen. "Mission in the Diaspora: Multicultural Churches in Urban Germany Initiated by Church Planters from the Global South." PhD diss., Biola University, 2017.

Gennep, Arnold van, Monika B. Vizedon, and Gabrielle L. Caffee. *The Rites of Passage*. Reprint edition. Chicago: University of Chicago Press, 1961.

Hanciles, Jehu J. *In the Shadow of the Elephant: Bishop Crowther and the African Missionary Movement*. Oxford, England: Church Mission Society, 2008.

Hiebert, Paul G. *The Gospel in Human Contexts: Anthropological Explorations for Contempory Missions*. Grand Rapids, MI: Baker Academic, 2009.

"Immigrant Churches in Berlin." *Prayer for Berlin*, December 2010. http://gebetfuerberlin.files.wordpress.com/2010/11/gfb89e.pdf.

Jackson, Darrell. "Europe and the Migrant Experience: Transforming Integration." *Transformation: An International Journal of Holistic Mission Studies* 28, no. 1 (January 1, 2011): 14-28. https://doi.org/10.1177/0265378810386416.

Jenkins, Philip. *God's Continent: Christianity, Islam, and Europe's Religious Crisis*. New York, NY: Oxford University Press, USA, 2007.

Jongeneel, J A B. "The Mission of Migrant Churches in Europe." *Missiology* 31, no. 1 (January 2003): 29-33.

Kisskalt, Michael. "Cross-Cultural Learning: Issues of the Second Generation of Immigrant Churches." In Peter Penner (Ed.), *Ethnic Churches in Europe: A Baptist*

Response, 134-52. Schwarzenfeld, Germany: Neufeld Verlag, 2006.

Lee, Jung Young. *Marginality: The Key to Multicultural Theology*. 1st ed. Fortress Press, 1995.

Leonard, John S. "The Church between Cultures: Rethinking the Church in Light of the Globalization of Immigration." *Evangelical Missions Quarterly* 40, no. 1 (January 2004): 62-73.

Lorance, Cody. "Reflections of a Church Planter among Diaspora Groups in Metro-Chicago: Pursuing Cruciformity in Diaspora Missions." In E. Wan (Ed.), *Diaspora Missiology: Theory, Methodology, and Practice*, 263-87. Portland, OR: Institute of Diaspora Studies – U.S., Western Seminary, 2012.

McIntosh, Gary, and Alan McMahan. *Being the Church in a Multi-Ethnic Community: Why It Matters and How It Works*. Indianapolis, IN: Wesleyan Pub. House, 2012.

"Mehr Als 10 Millionen Ausländer in Deutschland" [More than 10 Million Foreigners in Germany]. Statistisches Bundesamt [Federal Statistical Office], June 30, 2017. https://www.destatis.de/DE/PresseService/Presse/Pressemitteilungen/2017/06/PD17_227_12521.html.

"Merkel: 'Multiculture Has Failed.'" *BBC*, October 17, 2010. http://www.bbc.co.uk/news/world-europe-11559451.

Pantoja, Jr Luis L., Sadiri Joy B. Tira, and Enoch Wan, eds. *Scattered: The Filipino Global Presence*. Manila, Philippines: LifeChange Publishing, 2004.

Payne, J. D. "Missions in Reverse?" *Missiologically Thinking* (blog), December 8, 2010. http://www.jdpayne.org/2010/12/08/missions-in-reverse/.

– – –. *Strangers Next Door: Immigration, Migration and Mission*. Downers Grove, IL: IVP Books, 2012.

Penner, Peter. "John Called Mark: The Role of a Second Generation Christian in Mission. In Peter F. Penner (Ed.)." In *Ethnic Churches in Europe: A Baptist Response*, 113-33. Schwarzenfeld, Germany: Neufeld Verlag, 2006.

Pieterse, Jan Nederveen. *Globalization and Culture: Global Melange*. Lanham, MD: Rowman & Littlefield Publishers, 2003.

Pollock, David C., and Ruth E. Van Reken. *Third Culture Kids: Growing up among Worlds*. 2 edition. Boston, MA: Nicholas Brealey, 2009.

Rubesh, Ted. "Diaspora Distinctives: The Jewish Diaspora Experience in the Old Testament." In E. Wan (Ed.), *Diaspora Missiology: Theory, Methodology, and Practice*, 39-72. Portland, OR: Institute of Diaspora Studies – U.S., Western Seminary, 2012.

Sanneh, Lamin. "The Church and Its Missionary Vocation: The Islamic Frontline in a Post-Christian West." In A. Walls & C. Ross (Eds.), *Mission in the 21st Century: Exploring the Five Marks of Global Mission*, 130-47. Maryknoll, NY: Orbis Books, 2008.

Sarrazin, Thilo. *Deutschland Schafft Sich Ab [Germany Is Destroying Itself]*. München, Germany: DVA Dt.Verlags-Anstalt, 2010.

Simon, Benjamin. *From Migrants to Missionaries: Christians of African Origin in Germany*. Frankfurt am Main, Germany: Peter Lang, 2010.

"Vielfalt" [Diversity]. Berlin.de, March 16, 2016. http://www.berlin.de/berlin-im-ueberblick/hauptstadtleben/vielfalt/index.php.

Währisch-Oblau, Claudia. "Getting Ready to Receive? German Churches and the 'New Mission' from the South." *Lausanne World Pulse Archives*, no. 7 (2008). http://www.lausanneworldpulse.com/themedarticles-php/971/07-2008.

– – –. "Missions in Reverse: Whose Image in the Mirror?" *Anvil* 18, no. 4 (2001): 261-67.

Walls, Andrew. "Christian Mission in a Five-Hundred-Year Context." In A. Walls & C.

Ross (Eds.), *Mission in the 21st Century: Exploring the Five Marks of Global Mission*, 193-204. Maryknoll, NY: Orbis Books, 2008.

Wan, Enoch. *Diaspora Missiology: Theory, Methodology, and Practice*. Portland, OR: Institute of Diaspora Studies – U.S., Western Seminary, 2012.

Ybarrola, Steven. "An Anthropological Approach to Diaspora Missiology." UReach Toronto, March 2011. http://www.ureachtoronto.com/content/anthropological-approach-diaspora-missiology.

– – – . "Diasporas and Multiculturalism: Social Ideologies, Liminality, and Cultural Identity." In Sadiri Joy Tira (Ed.), *The Human Tidal Wave*, 135-49. Manila, Philippines: Lifechange Publishing, Inc., 2013.

(3) Reflections of a Second-Generation African Christian in Britain

Tope Bello

Introduction

This chapter focuses on the experiences and upbringing of a second-generation African Christian, born and raised in the UK. It will engage with some of the identity issues that come from having a dual identity – issues that arise from being Nigerian in terms of culture, tradition and values, while also being British.

The church plays a significant role in Nigerian circles, so this chapter explores the different ways in which disputes were navigated, the subsequent effects on personal faith, and the journey to spiritual maturity. The chapter, then, concludes with a discussion of social initiatives that are considered important as a result of the aforementioned identity battle.

In recent years, I have longed to read about experiences that reflect my own upbringing. Often, frustration has settled in when I have found nothing that mirrors or helps me navigate my dual-identity as a Christian. By this I mean my ties to British and Nigerian culture. Throughout this stage in my development as part of the diaspora, my reckoning with cultural values and identity have increased exponentially. This chapter will seek to explore the journey I have been on as a second-generation African Christian born and raised in the UK. It begins with my journey to coming to know the grace of God throughout the formative period of my childhood. Then it will examine the questions that infiltrated my experience: how my church interacted with the numerous issues that attended my teenage years. Finally, it will discuss initiatives I am a part of which are important to me as a result of my formative Christian years, as well as the reasons for which I decided to study theology academically.

How Did I Come to Faith?

My journey of coming to Christ does not begin in 2011 or 2012, when I began to become aware of my sin and standing before Jesus Christ, but rather in 1997, when my mother (who was Muslim) acknowledged her need for a Saviour. This sparked a change in direction not only for her, but also for her family. She was very intentional about bringing my brother and me up in the way of the Lord, and we were definitely beneficiaries of her heartfelt prayers. I was five years old at the time of her conversion. Unbeknownst to me, her new commitment to the Lord would be instrumental in my own coming to the faith.

Despite being brought up in a Christian home and being very familiar with Christian values and Bible verses, I knew nothing of the work of the Holy Spirit in regeneration. It was not until my college years in 2011 that I began to reckon with my apparent faith. There was not a time where I professed to be an atheist or agnostic; I believed that God was real from a young age, but did not care about this, nor did I consider that He cared for the way I conducted my life. God, to me, was distant and uninvolved in my life. I also subconsciously thought that Christianity would be something I would grapple with or become more serious about in my adult life, foolishly assuming that only those who were 21 or older would be called to give an account before God.

I grew up in a vibrant Pentecostal mega-church in east London, and as I grew older, I became more and more involved in the church life. My interest in drama and music led me to join the respective departments within the 'youth church'. Although I was yet to be converted, I found this extracurricular activity to be engaging, and that it made me excited to attend church on a weekly basis. I thoroughly enjoyed the community that came with being a part of the church, as well as the motivational insight that I received from the youth leaders from time to time. This acted, without a doubt, as a tool of the Lord in restraining me from sin.

We Move forward now to the summer of 2011, when I left college and embarked on (what seemed like) adult life in university. I began struggling with a particular sin. It was grievous, and foolishly, though I was not a believer at the time, I never anticipated that this would be a struggle of mine. I was fully aware of how it looked in the sight of God, but had not yet been confronted with the profound grace and mercy that is to be found at the foot of the cross of Jesus Christ. I spent many months in a low state of constantly indulging in this sin, but wanting to stop. I placed numerous 'boundaries' and preventatives in place, yet nonetheless, I simply found new ways to engage in the same sin. This led me to a dark place of hopelessness and guilt. I was almost certain that I was bound for hell and saw no viable way out.

Nevertheless, I spoke with a close Christian friend at the time and he directed me to the word of God. He instructed me to read the words of Paul in Romans 7 and to finish my reading at Verse 1 of Chapter 8. Eventually I did so. My initial reading compounded my frustration, and I wondered how on earth this was meant to bring me comfort and freedom. On another night, when I was low and lamenting this sin I was enslaved by, I once again picked up my Bible to read the words of Paul. As a regular church-goer, I was familiar with Romans 8:1, but on this night, I read it with fresh and new eyes:

There is therefore now no condemnation to those who are in Christ Jesus (Romans 8:1a NKJV).

The words of this verse leaped off the page and into the depths of my heart. After being riddled with guilt and shame for most of the year, I finally read the words of liberation, grace, and mercy. In Christ Jesus, there is no condemnation! However, this assurance was reserved for a particular group of people.

... [to those] who do not walk according to the flesh, but according to the Spirit. (Romans 8:1b NKJV).

I immediately realised that I was walking according to my own flesh, not just concerning the sin I struggled with, but also with what I felt to be the solution.

Reading this passage also marked my introduction to Reformed Theology. A close friend of mine, in one of many lengthy conversations, laboured to communicate to me the doctrines of grace. They are usually expressed with the acronym T.U.L.I.P.[1] As he explained the meaning of 'T' (Total Depravity), I was immediately captured by the biblical evidence for it, and how it explained my own life, my struggles, and the world around me. This introduction to Reformed Theology not only presented me with doctrine I had not been aware of before, but also to new Bible teachers. John Piper, Paul Washer and John MacArthur were instrumental in my growth as a Christian and in directing me on how to read the scriptures for myself.

I have enjoyed the last six years walking with the Lord; it has presented me with many challenges and bumps in the road, but as I sit here now and write, I know that there is no other state in which I would rather be than under the care of the Lord. I am grateful for my introduction to Reformed Theology because it has given me a great framework to understand how to interpret the Bible, and it has revealed to me that Bible studies are not to be approached as a lazy task; instead, we must endeavour to know what God has purposed in His word. I am also grateful for my upbringing within Pentecostal circles. Reflecting on my time there, I am challenged by their commitment to prayer and their unwavering faith in the power of God. Now, I seek to marry the positives from both circles, and to do away with the things I believe to be inconsistent with the God revealed to us in the Bible. This, therefore, will involve a lifetime of growth, learning, correction and change: a journey that I look forward to and that I expect, with the Lord's help, will be a blissful one.

Questions I Wrestled with as I Was Growing Up

Growing up, I barely wrestled with any questions concerning the Christian faith, for on one level I believed I was already a Christian, and on another level, I never thought too deeply about the things of God. As I began to take my walk with the

---

[1] 'T.U.L.I.P.', sometimes referred to as the 'doctrines of grace', are the doctrines pertaining to salvation as articulated within Reformed Theology. T – Total Depravity. U – Unconditional Election. L – Limited Atonement. I – Irresistible Grace. P – Perseverance of the Saints. The acronyms and headings help to highlight what people in the Reformed tradition accept as a biblical understanding of soteriology.

Lord more seriously, and took part in church life more often, I started to encounter questions about Christianity.

I recall sitting in a youth service on Sunday, the topic of which was the gift of speaking in tongues. The teacher took us through sections of 1 Corinthians 12 and 14 to explain the importance and the necessity of this gift in the life of every believer. At some point during this teaching, there was an aspect of what he was trying to explain that I did not understand. And so, I continued reading past the scriptural passage upon which he was focusing. As I read on, I came to 1 Corinthians 14:27-28:

> If anyone speaks in a tongue, two – or at the most three – should speak, one at a time, and someone must interpret. If there is no interpreter, the speaker should keep quiet in the church and speak to himself and to God (NKJV).

Now, at the time, I was not a scholar in hermeneutics, yet the meaning of these two verses was clear to me. However, it caused me further confusion. The Pentecostal church I grew up in did not practise the gift in this manner ('two, at the most three'), and in every occasion on which I was present for a service, I never once heard an interpretation of what was spoken. I began to question the gift itself: its purpose and how it should be conducted in a church service, as well as in private.

This fuelled more questions in my mind. When looking at the different understandings of the gift of tongues, how can I know which interpretation of the scriptures is the 'correct' one. I began to dive into the world of biblical hermeneutics. As I attended subsequent Sunday services, I was extremely suspicious of the teachings that I was hearing, especially when I read for myself the passage of scripture that was being quoted and found that the teaching did not reflect the broader context of the chapter. Matters of interpretation became pressing for me, as I struggled with knowing how to read and understand the Bible.

Current pertinent questions on my mind have had to do with what it means to be a black British Christian. As a second-generation African, I have the privilege of being very aware of two cultures, the British and the Nigerian. The older I get, the more I recognise the importance of being fluent in the Nigerian culture. This was further wrought within me when I came to the uncomfortable realisation that Christianity has been largely whitewashed over the last hundred years, and that an idea has been pushed forward that to look like an authentic Christian you must sing, worship, and act in a way that is Western. Recently, I have started to perceive that this attitude is pervasive in Christianity, and that it affects our understanding of forms of Christianity that look and are expressed differently to what is accepted as the norm. Joseph Solomon and Jamaica West explored this idea in a spoken word piece,[2] in which they succinctly captured this dichotomy within Christendom with these few lines:

> I'm so black Christian, I got escorted out to a room, where they wouldn't let me love the Gospel and Gospel music. Had to bottle my culture of praise and prayer, walk it down the aisle, lay it on the altar of false dichotomies and proper doctrine … like you can't love John Piper *and* John P. Kee, Paul Washer *and* Paul Morton. Like Keith & Kristyn Getty are the only ones who write and sing hymns. You can't be black and love the puritans …[3]

Most of the time, the unspoken attitude is that to love Reformed Theology and its doctrine means that one listens to the type of music that is regularly seen in Reformed churches. Gospel music is seen as 'black music', while Christian Contemporary Music (CCM) is found in many white circles. While there are a lot of Reformed pastors and churches who would denounce CCM due to the apparent lack of sound theology in the lyrics, the style seems to be most palatable to white evangelical churches. Often times the mere vibrancy of 'black Gospel music' results in it being looked upon as irreverent and not fit for worship.

My last two years studying theology gave me a greater affinity for ministry in the black context. It started off with an interest in the African American experience. This was heightened by the problems that America began to face from 2012, with the shooting of Trayvon Martin and the subsequent acquittal of his killer, George Zimmerman. Race relations became a polarising topic, within and outside the church. Frequently the history of the church and the black community was brought into the frame, with questions being asked about the present-day church and its lack of involvement in the modern-day civil rights movement and Black Lives Matter (BLM). As I began to develop my historical knowledge, I recognised that there was a disconnect, at times, with the experience of African Americans. This, therefore, led to a desire to want to know more about the historical experience of black people. More specifically, it led me to approach Christians in Britain for help in understanding some of the issues being faced in the present day.

How Did My Church Help or Not Help on this Journey?

At the beginning stages of my Christian walk, I was attending a Pentecostal 'mega-church' of about 5000 members. As a member of this church I found it extremely difficult to access church leadership with the questions I had. Although there was a structure in place for this (deacons, local pastors and

---

2 'Spoken word' is a performance-based art form. It is quite closely linked to poetry, but is generally thought of as being more dramatic in terms of actions and vocal inflections.
3 Joseph Solomon, 'I'm So Black Christian', Filmed [April, 2016], YouTube video, 4:48. Posted [April, 2016], https://www.youtube.com/watch?v=ujn0lG1VV90 (Accessed 5th August 2017).

stewards), I still found it tiring seeking answers. This often set me back along my journey of discovering and understanding the Bible.

In hindsight, I am also aware of the cultural traditions that I was not willing to transgress. Within Nigerian culture, it is often taken as an insult to have a young person question anything that has come from someone older or in a position of authority. Therefore, even when I asked questions, they met with hostility, for they were taken as a sign of insubordination. This reduced the amount of trust I had for my church and its leaders at the time, for I felt as though my genuine questions were being avoided for the sake of tradition.

Finding the church I am a member of now, Evangelical Reformed Church (Hackney), was a breath of fresh air for me as I was encouraged to ask questions, and even when the answers were not known, this was clearly acknowledged. A mistake is made when it is assumed that questions are asked as an act of defiance, rather than from a candid desire to gain knowledge and to understand.

Mission and Social Initiatives and Why They Matter to Me

Black Berea

Black Berea is an organisation I am part of that launched in February 2017 with The Black Berea Podcast. It consists of six young black Christians in London who seek to see the word of God rightly or properly explained in our local context. After many meetings and discussions with our church leaders, we found it appropriate to brand ourselves as Black Berea.

'Black' – because this is who we are. This is not to be understood in a way that corresponds to stereotypical terms and sentiments that are often associated with black culture.

'Berea' is taken from the narrative of Paul in Acts 17, where we found the Bereans to be people that we desired to emulate, and that we desired in turn for other people to seek to be like. The Bereans were a people who heard the teachings of Paul and searched the scriptures for themselves to see if the things Paul taught were true. By doing this, they showed themselves to be diligent students of the Word of God, and committed to understanding the teaching. They did not ignorantly consume what they were taught, but knew that if God had not said it in his Word, then it was of no use believing it.

Why It Is Needed

In August 2011, England was set alight (literally) after the killing of Mark Duggan[4] in Tottenham at the hands of the police. Violence was sparked across

---

4 Patrick Barkham, and Jon Henley, 'Mark Duggan: profile of Tottenham police shooting victim', 8th August 2011, Online:
https://www.theguardian.com/uk/2011/aug/08/mark-duggan-profile-tottenham-shooting (Accessed 2nd March 2017).

the UK, including Manchester, Nottingham, and West Bromwich.[5] Nevertheless, the greatest damage was done to properties in London. The riots extended beyond north London to Brixton, Orpington (Kent), Romford (Essex) and many other areas.[6] The reported unlawful killing of Mark Duggan ignited public outcry over the use of excessive force on ethnic minorities in the UK,[7] and was the beginning of heated race debates that persist to this day. Less than a year later, Trayvon Martin, a 17-year-old black male, was fatally shot by George Zimmerman, who was the neighbourhood watch captain.[8] His subsequent acquittal of second-degree murder in 2013 led to the inception of the Black Lives Matter (BLM) movement.[9] It is often viewed as a modern day civil rights movement, although it has made efforts to be distinct, and unlike the Civil Rights movement there is no single leader.[10] In the following years, the movement grew rapidly, responding to several injustices in the African American community, including injustices done to Michael Brown, Eric Garner, Sandra Bland, Philando Castile, Keith Lamont-Scott, and countless others in the context of the United States. In 2016, the BLM movement extended to the UK, with protests taking place in London, Birmingham[11] and Manchester,[12] yet the marches were not met without question of whether a UK Black Lives Matter movement is legitimate.

---

[5] Sebastian Payne, and Conrad Quilty-Harper, 'London riots: incidents and suspects mapped in the UK', 9th August 2011, Online:
http://www.telegraph.co.uk/news/uknews/law-and-order/8689355/London-riots-all-incidents-mapped-in-London-and-around-the-UK.html (Accessed 2nd March 2017).
[6] Payne and Quilty-Harper, 'London riots'.
[7] Bryn Phillips, 'I was one of the London rioters in 2011 we didn't know how to express our anger', 11th March 2015, Online:
https://www.theguardian.com/commentisfree/2015/mar/11/london-rioters-2011-anger-inequality-distrust-police (Accessed 2nd March 2017).
[8] CNN Library, 'Trayvon Martin Shooting Fast Facts', 28th February 2017, Online:
http://edition.cnn.com/2013/06/05/us/trayvon-martin-shooting-fast-facts/ (Accessed 7th March 2017).
[9] Laura Flanders, 'Building Movements Without Shedding Differences: Alicia Garza of #BlackLivesMatter', 24th March 2015, Online: http://www.truth-out.org/news/item/29813-building-movements-without-shedding-differences-alicia-garza (Accessed 6th March 2017).
[10] Elizabeth Day, '#BlackLivesMatter: the birth of a new civil rights movement', 19th July 2015, Online: https://www.theguardian.com/world/2015/jul/19/blacklivesmatter-birth-civil-rights-movement (Accessed 13th March 2017).
[11] Annette Belcher, 'Watch Black Lives Matter protesters lying in busy Birmingham Road', 5th Aug 2016, Online: http://www.birminghammail.co.uk/news/midlands-news/watch-black-lives-matter-protesters-11708792 (Accessed 2nd March 2017).
[12] Sam Yarwood, 'Black Lives Matter march to take place on fifth anniversary of shooting which sparked riots', Online:
http://www.manchestereveningnews.co.uk/news/greater-manchester-news/black-lives-matter-march-take-11708279 (Accessed 2nd March 2017).

Is the UK the Same as the US?

There is no doubt that the African American experience is different to that of black British people. African Americans have a culture that was established within the histories of racial segregation and black slavery. However, looking at the modern migration of black British people in the diaspora, they 'came to Britain in the years immediately after 1945' but never 'intended to settle permanently in a cold, austere, post-war country. They came to earn wages freely, determined to then return home.'13 Many ethnic minorities living within the UK identify a different place of origin. Home is not the UK but rather Africa, Asia or the Caribbean, as 'black people from different parts of the world, from different cultures and with different languages, have added to the cosmopolitan population which now constitutes modern Britain'.14 Although there are shared experiences and commonalities, there are a variety of cultures that are fundamentally different. The history of slavery in America has meant that the relations between the white and black communities have often been hostile. After the abolition of the trans-atlantic slave trade in the nineteenth century, the hostility continued with the Jim Crow laws,15 Brown vs. Board of Education,16 Montgomery Bus Boycott,17 and the assassination of two significant black leaders – Malcolm X and Martin Luther King Jr.18

While the United Kingdom played a major part in the slave trade, white and black relations have taken a different form. Black people still felt inferior to their white counterparts – an idea that was encouraged by the natural selection theories put forward by Charles Darwin and by the growth of the British Empire across the world (including Africa). Black people across the Western world have long been viewed as second-class citizens, yet the rise of movements such as Black Lives Matter and the notable success of some from within the black community (such as the 44th President of the United States of America) have generated positive thinking among black people concerning their identity. With this new vitalisation, many in the black community have made efforts to reclaim their identity, which have led to research into the historical contributions of black people to Western civilisation.

Stay Woke

Affirming these aspects of black identity and history is often labelled as being 'woke'. It is hard to trace the origin of the term; however, it is used to denote

---

13 Joel Edwards, and David Killingray, *Black Voices: The Shaping of Our Christian Experience* (Leicester: Inter-Varsity Press, 2007), 17.
14 Edwards and Killingray, *Black Voices,* 18.
15 This was a state and local law which held that white people and black people were to be segregated.
16 This was a Supreme Court Case which ruled that the separation of white and black students was unconstitutional.
17 This was related to protests over racial segregation on the public transport system.
18 It is worth noting that these both took place within a span of three years.

someone who is, or the act of being, 'self-aware, questioning the dominant paradigm and striving for something better'.[19] This description points to a state of enlightenment in which one's eyes are open and one is paying attention to and challenging 'problematic norms, systemic injustices and the overall status quo'.[20] It is therefore not enough merely to know; the knowledge gained must lead to action. Often, those who adopt the 'woke' label view organised systems through a pessimistic lens, and for this reason, 'it requires an active process of deprogramming social conditionings focusing on consistent efforts to challenge the universal infractions we are all subjected to'.[21] Human beings (especially the black community) are constantly viewed as victims and are encouraged to fight against structural and systemic oppression.

Christianity and Black Britain

Christianity has long been charged with being a religion of the oppressor (i.e. white people). Malcolm X alludes to this in his autobiography:

> The greatest miracle Christianity has achieved in America is that the black man in white Christian hands has not grown violent. It is a miracle that 22 million black people have not risen up against their oppressors – in which they would have been justified by all moral criteria, and even by the democratic tradition! It is a miracle that a nation of black people has so fervently continued to believe in a turn-the-other-cheek and heaven-for-you-after-you-die philosophy! It is a miracle that the American black people have remained a peaceful people, while catching all the centuries of hell that they have caught, here in white man's heaven! The miracle is that the white man's puppet Negro 'leaders', his preachers and the educated Negroes laden with degrees, and others who have been allowed to wax fat off their black poor brothers, have been able to hold the black masses quiet until now.[22]

He speaks of the black man being neutralised at the hands of white Christian men, and goes on to speak as though black people have no place in Christianity as it is something that belongs to another. With rhetoric such as this, it is no surprise that young black Christians are finding it hard to find their place within a church that does not speak on these issues.

Nevertheless, the charge that Christianity is the white man's religion is an indictment against Christians in all places. It might be that the fact that Christianity is overwhelmingly viewed as Western (despite having started in the

---

[19] Since this is a recent, colloquial term, the definition and history could only be found online: https://www.merriam-webster.com/words-at-play/woke-meaning-origin (Accessed 20th September 2017).

[20] Raven Cras, 'What does it mean to be "woke?"', 8 months ago, Online: https://blavity.com/what-does-it-mean-to-be-woke/ (Accessed 17th July 2017).

[21] Cras, 'Woke', 8 months ago.

[22] As cited in: Lisa Jones and Spike Lee, *Do The Right Thing: A Spike Lee Joint* (New York: Simon and Schuster, 1989), 120.

Middle East) is owed to laziness, a lack of foresight, and a disregard for the charge and commission of our Lord Jesus Christ. In Matthew 28, Jesus commands His disciples to take the gospel to all nations; therefore, Christianity only being prominent in the Western world could very well be evidence of our failings in this area. Finally, black Christians must be able to wrestle with what it looks like to be Christian and black, recognising that their citizenship is in heaven. And so, while earthly affiliation with countries or race is not intrinsically sinful, black Christians must guard their hearts from being ethnocentric. Christ is our peace, and He has broken down dividing walls of hostility (Eph. 2:14); so, whether one is black, white or brown; whether one is rich or poor; Christ is all in all (Col. 3:11).

The responsibility of the church, especially black Christian leaders, is to helpfully contextualise Christianity. God is not met solely through Western expressions; cultural diversity is a reality in eternity (Rev. 7:9). Therefore we must strive to see a picture of that diversity here and now. This is not about idolising blackness or whiteness, but rather about bearing the image of God within our own cultures.

Black Berea seeks to discuss the matters that are affecting the black community and to help listeners and readers to view events in the world through a biblical lens. It also seeks to engage with the more difficult discussions in the public square on the history of race and Christianity. Some of our podcast episodes have included topics ranging from knife crime, race and the gospel, and even a review of Stormzy's debut album 'Gang, Signs and Prayer'.

Daylight Prison Ministry

At the age of sixteen, I started working in youth centres and sought to work with the less fortunate in society. In 2015, I began volunteering with a Christian organisation in the UK which goes into prisons across Britain for Sunday services and during the week to conduct Bible study with the prisoners. These activities have allowed me to get an insight into the various types of people that need to be met with the message of the gospel. I was engaged in youth work for a number of years and always felt frustrated with the limitations of the support we were able to give. Solutions were often remedial but temporary.

Volunteering with Daylight allowed me to combine the work of the gospel with work with those to whom my heart is drawn. I believe the church has a duty of care to those who are in prison; yet sadly, I have more often witnessed the neglect of, and judgmental attitudes towards, prisoners or ex-convicts. This may be due to a lack of engagement with those who are in, or have been to, prison.

My compassion towards those incarcerated began when many friends I knew growing up were imprisoned for a serious crime. All of a sudden, they were no longer regarded as human beings, but were instead labelled by the acts they had committed. This attitude is not exclusive to the church, but is prevalent within society at large. It is my desire to show that this disposition is both unhelpful and unnecessary.

Why Did I Decide to Study Theology?

The desire to study first arose in my college years when I began to think about the areas I was passionate about and would want to commit considerable time and energy to in order to gain a degree. As time went on, I came to appreciate the need for young black women to be involved in the task of theology and biblical scholarship.

Young

The consumerism culture of today's climate is changing the way young people take in and respond to almost everything. With the introduction and development of social media and technology, the manner in which information is absorbed has radically changed, and thus, the way in which information is communicated has also taken on a new face.

I believe that the faith of young people in London hinges upon the willingness of the church to discuss the difficult areas of Christianity. It is not enough to assert that the claims against Christianity and Christians in antiquity are false; we (the global church) must also be able to engage with and dispel the falsehoods in order to exalt Christ and ultimately see men and women of all ages, tribes, and nations saved to the glory of God.

The church must care about these issues, for they are providing many people with an avenue out of the faith. This is particularly important given that the church exists as the pillar and ground of truth (1 Tim. 3:15).

Black

I grew up as a second-generation African in Britain, and while I was aware of my ethnicity growing up, it was not until my college years, when I attended a predominately white, middle-class sixth form, that I became more cognisant of my 'difference'. Being on the receiving end of racial slurs and ignorant forms of banter alluding to my hair, upbringing, and vocabulary made me consider the racial and cultural tensions that exist today and their history. I then began to survey Christendom and the resources that were available to me to speak into my experience. I came up short and found nothing.

During my years studying theology, I found that this struggle continued. One module in particular caused me to wrestle with the issue of race and the Christian faith. It was titled Global Theology, and explored what theology looks like in other parts of the world. I was disheartened by some of the Western arrogance towards other forms of contextualisation, but was nevertheless encouraged to find works by men of African background speaking to issues that affect their people (African Theology).

Woman

Sadly, the ministry to women that I have experienced has been idealistic and limited in the scope of conversation. Without denigrating these roles and callings, women's ministry has often put excessive focus on modesty, motherhood and marriage. While every woman should be concerned about what the Bible has to say about modesty and reflect this in their own life, not all women will experience the joys of motherhood or the gift of marriage. Motherhood and marriage are not the sum of a woman's existence; there is more to be spoken about or taught than just the idea that women are called to be keepers of their homes.

Potentially, in Reformed and orthodox circles, the fear may be that the more women are theologically trained, the more they will attempt to blur biblical gender roles and undermine the idea of the man being the spiritual leader of their home.

Theology is undoubtedly a male dominated domain. Most of the literature we have within our reach has been written by white men. This is not necessarily problematic or unusual, especially given that pastors are men and therefore it is expected that they will be involved far more in the work of creating Christian literature. However, women should be involved in the training and cultivating of mature Christian women and men.

Final Thoughts

Sadly, I am not overly enthusiastic about whether I will be able to shed the nomadic sense that has characterised my recent years; but is this not what the Christian life is – belonging yet disconnected; at home, yet knowing heaven is our eternal home? Some days, an optimistic outlook spurs me to hope and believe that there will be more resources that delve into the many complexities that are part of the diasporic narrative. Other days, I can do no more than to look to eternity for my ultimate sense of belonging; and in these moments, the declaration of Paul in Philippians 3 is a great comfort:

> For *our citizenship is in heaven*, from which we also eagerly wait for the Saviour, the Lord Jesus Christ, who will transform our lowly body that it may be conformed to His glorious body, according to the working by which He is able even to subdue all things to Himself (NKJV).

References

Barkham, Patrick and Henley, Jon "Mark Duggan: profile of Tottenham police shooting victim"
Belcher, Annette "Watch Black Lives Matter protesters lying in busy Birmingham Road"
CNN Library, "Trayvon Martin Shooting Fast Facts"
Cras, Raven "What does it mean to be 'woke?'"

Day, Elizabeth "#BlackLivesMatter: the birth of a new civil rights movement"

Edwards, Joel and Killingray, David, *Black Voices: The Shaping of Our Christian Experience,* Nottingham, England, IVP, 2007.

Flanders, Laura "Building Movements Without Shedding Differences: Alicia Garza of #BlackLivesMatter"

Jones, Lisa and Lee, Spike *Do The Right Thing: A Spike Lee Joint,* Simon and Schuster, 1989.

Olusoga, David, *Black and British: A Forgotten History,* London, Macmillian, 2016.

Payne, Sebastian and Quilty-Harper, Conrad "London riots: incidents and suspects mapped in the UK"

Phillips, Bryn "I was one of the London rioters. in 2011 we didn't know how to express our anger"

Solomon, Joseph "I'm So Black Christian"

Yarwood, Sam "Black Lives Matter march to take place on fifth anniversary of shooting which sparked riots"

(4) When Strangers Meet: Encounters and Identities in Twenty-First Century Europe
Rosalee Velloso Ewell

Introduction

The first task of the Christian community is to praise and worship God – Father, Son and Holy Spirit. The second task is to make this God known to the whole world through our words, deeds and character. Sometimes such witnessing to the gospel of Christ is referred to as 'mission' or as 'evangelism', and these are closely related to the terms 'discipleship' and 'spiritual growth'. All of these terms, however variously defined, involve some kind of encounter – encounter with God, encounter with another person, encounter between communities or social groups, encounter with difference. Encounters can be challenging and lead to growth and change; they can also create fear and lead to radicalisation.

The focus of this chapter will be on certain encounters (i) as they appear in the biblical narratives, (ii) how these encounters lead to new understandings of identity and (iii) how encounters shape our understanding of God's call on his people to witness to their societies and cultures. In particular, the role of the Holy Spirit in guiding and shaping these encounters can offer Christians in Europe today alternative ways to think about mission and our participation in God's work in the twenty-first century.

Encounters on the Margins:
Learning from Jeremiah to See God amidst Challenges

Jürgen Moltmann once asked, 'Why are most Christians in the West, whether they be Catholics or Protestants, really only "monotheists" where the experience and practice of their faith is concerned? Whether God is one or triune evidently makes as little difference to the doctrine of faith as it does to ethics.'[1] What difference does belief in the Holy Trinity make for the life and work of churches today?

It is a crucial question to consider because it has everything to do with how we might think about the unity, the diversity and how we encounter others in societies today. How can we celebrate and learn from encounters with those who are very different from us, encounters with Christians from another tradition or

---

[1] Jürgen Moltmann, *The Trinity and the Kingdom: The Doctrine of God* (London: SCM Press, 1981), 1.

with non-followers of Christ? What is the place of truth and tolerance in today's world? Why does practicing a Trinitarian faith matter in order for such questions to lead us to good answers?

All theologies and scriptural interpretations are contextual. Whether one's theology challenges consumerism in Tallinn or Turin, poverty in Budapest or Birmingham, Paul's letter to the Romans in Moscow or Madrid – we must always keep in mind the limits of our own language and viewpoints. In 1 Corinthians 13:12 Paul says, 'we see through a glass dimly …' (Lighthouse Bible 2006). 'But we do see Jesus' (Lighthouse Bible 2006), states the author to the Hebrews (Heb. 2:9). 'We see through a glass dimly' – this means learning humility and knowing that we do not have God's view of things, that we do not have all the answers or the plans or necessarily the best interpretations of scripture. Whether we are from the North or South, East or West, the scriptures' constant reminder, made succinct in the creed's affirmation that Jesus is Lord, is that we are not lords, not little gods who seek to control with knowledge or power. Power and knowledge are truly only seen in the triune God and the ways in which this God has been revealed to all of creation in Jesus and the Spirit at work in the church.

There has always been diversity and a plurality of theologies, of lifestyles and perspectives. Let us not pretend that there was once a time when Christians in Europe were unified. Perhaps there was a time when European ears were less tuned in to divergent voices, when those in power in the church were also those whose voices were loud within the general society; but the history of God's people, in every time and every age, is not one of unity. Maybe in our contemporary world diversity is just more in our faces, front and centre in the courts of law and in political and moral debates. Maybe the church and religious organisations are finally listening to the voices of young people, of excluded minorities or people on the margins whose voices had previously been silenced.

Perhaps the prophet Jeremiah is an unlikely candidate for a discussion about mission encounters, diversity and the Holy Trinity, but ours is a God of surprises. Jeremiah's story illustrates diversity, power and the ways in which the Trinity has to do with our understanding of God's call on each of us to work towards justice and the witness of God's reign. Jeremiah illustrates a kind of obedience that God demands of God's people and the implied politics of being a faithful community. Surely one goal for the churches today is to be a faithful community that embodies the good news of the gospel whatever the context. We cannot separate fidelity and obedience to God from unity. Being faithful to God's call results in participation in the divine plan for the redemption of all of creation – participation in the life of the Trinity that is being in communion and that challenges the structures of power and politics of this world.

As the story of God's activities with a particular people within creation, the scriptures often contain conflicting sub-stories. There are narratives that suggest competing ways in which God's people listen to and understand the divine calling. One example of diversity is seen in the book of Jeremiah, which recounts the final days of Israel-Judah under Assyrian domination and the bloody transition to domination under Nebuchadnezzar of Babylon. The expanse of the Babylonian empire led to the destruction of Jerusalem, with its temple and the king's palace burned to the ground in 587 BCE, and with most of the city's prominent citizens taken into exile. The Old Testament scholar R. E. Clements describes the state of affairs in Judah thus:

> At one stroke the year 587 witnessed the removal of the two institutions – the temple and the Davidic kingship – which had stood as symbolic assurances of God's election of Israel. Their loss was far greater than the loss of national prestige and left the entire understanding of Israel's special relationship to Yahweh in question. What happened demanded total reappraisal and rethinking of Israel's self-understanding as the People of God.2

Is this where Europe is today? Disunity and collapse are not new. The question is how will we respond. Is what is happening now demanding a total reappraisal of our self-understanding as Christians in the twenty-first-century world?

Christopher Seitz suggests that Jeremiah reflects 'to a greater degree than other prophetic books a situation of conflict'.3 The conflicts are numerous – they are within the community in Judah, and also within the communities who were exiled to Babylon. They are conflicts that last decades and are multi-valent. It is precisely the situation of exile and the diversity within it that is the focus of the conflicts. Where is the revelation of God in the exile? Where is the revelation of God in diversity? Jeremiah was enabled to hear the voice of God's Spirit and to proclaim, even to his own harm, the type of obedience God demanded of God's people in their situation as exiles and refugees. Thus, there are significant lessons about mission and diversity for Christians today from this tragic story in the Old Testament.

By the time of the Babylonian exile, the people of Israel had learned to confess and to repent for the sins of idolatry and syncretism that had characterised most of their life since the giving of the law at Sinai. In Jeremiah we have accounts of the diversity of the people's response to this new crisis.

In a book entitled *Reading in Communion*, the authors use Jeremiah's story to show how the Christian life must be embodied in particular practices that are shaped by such virtues as patience, hope, and faith.4 The situation in Judah demanded an immediate response – something had to be done. We hear these same cries from different corners of Christianity today – 'something must be

---

2 R. E. Clements, *Jeremiah* (Interpretation Series. Atlanta, GA: John Knox, 1988), 6.

3 Christopher R. Seitz, *Theology in Conflict: Reactions to the Exile in the Book of Jeremiah* (Berlin and New York: Walter de Gruyter, 1989), 2.

4 Stephan E. Fowl and L. Gregory Jones, *Reading in Communion: Scripture and Ethics in Christian Life* (Grand Rapids, MI: Eerdmans, 1991), 91.

done' – for the society, for the environment, for the young people, for the elderly, etc.

The diverse voices claiming to have the answer in Jeremiah's time were the following: on one hand there was Hananiah, the false prophet, calling the people to join Egypt in a revolt against Babylon and arguing that in doing so the Lord would bring Israel through the war and restore peace to Jerusalem. On the other hand, there was Jeremiah, telling the people that subjection under Babylon would last a long time and that they needed to learn to live with it, to be faithful to God in spite of their desperate situation. He instructs them to plant gardens, build houses, marry, etc. However, the people were not ready or trained to hear the words of God as spoken through Jeremiah – they had not been engaging in faithful practices that would shape them into faithful people who would be willing to understand and obey Jeremiah's call.

Jeremiah's story does not end in 587 BCE. After the siege of Jerusalem, Judah's king Zedekiah is blinded and taken into exile. Nebuchadnezzar leaves a remnant in Judah, including Jeremiah. For a short period, it looked as though the people would finally heed Jeremiah's call. Gedaliah, the governor, attempted to implement some of the policies suggested by Jeremiah and to follow the prophet's words: 'Fear not to serve the Chaldeans: dwell in the land, and serve the king of Babylon, and it shall be well with you…' (Jer. 40:9-10 ERV). But this brief turn to obedience was short-lived. Led by Ishmael, a descendant of David, the people react against Gedaliah and assassinate him along with others who had sought the welfare of the city on Jeremiah's terms.

After Gedaliah's death, Ishmael and his cohorts rebel against Babylon, but they are overthrown by Nebuchadnezzar with equal violence. Then, in fear of further reprisals from Babylon, the rest of the people decide to immigrate to Egypt (Jer. 41:16-18). Once again, they ask Jeremiah for a word from God, but again he utters words they are not prepared to hear. He tells them not to go to Egypt but to remain in the land where they will prosper. For his pronouncements against Israel's unfaithfulness and against Israel's kings and its warfare, Jeremiah is mocked, imprisoned, and suspected of treason. The people reject his word and turn toward Egypt. And, as Karl Barth so poignantly wrote,

> [So Israel] returned to the place from which Yahweh has once called and led their fathers by the word of Moses. The difference is that this time the prophet does not lead … And so they disappear and Jeremiah with them. They for their part are given the lie by events. And he is silenced by them as he had been all his life.[5]

Jeremiah had the eyes of the Spirit of God to see and to know the type of obedience God demanded of his people and the particular ways in which God invited the people to participate in God's liberation of them. But the political

5 Karl Barth, *Church Dogmatics IV/I*, ed. G. W. Bromiley and T. F. Torrance, transl. G. W. Bromiley (Edinburgh, Scotland: T. & T. Clark, 1958), 474.

implications of Jeremiah's prophetic vision included the loss of power, the submission to foreign domination, and the work towards justice at the local, community level. This was not the kind of God the people wanted to obey or the kinds of practices in which they wanted to engage.

The diversity that characterised the society in which Jeremiah lived is quite similar to Europe today. Comings and goings of people displaced by wars elsewhere; comings and goings of people seeking a better life or people who move because of a job, or for education. Corruption, scandals and divisions at all levels; society tending towards excluding and closing its ears to those they consider 'other'.

The unity of the church does not depend on agreement or a shared understanding of all theological matters. The people in Judah during the time of Jeremiah had the same theology: proper evangelical, monotheistic theology. They were not doubting God or worshipping idols. They just did not like the loss of power or the call to be patient while God worked things out with the Babylonians. Their unity depended on listening to the prophetic voices among them and living out their faith in that context. In a desperate attempt to hold onto their power, they chose disunity. They chose to splinter and to return to Egypt.

A Brazilian theologian once wrote that when speaking of the Trinity we need to recover the proper language – the grammar of our faith – and affirm the ongoing work of the Trinity in our daily lives. If we divorce the Trinity from life, we have given up on justice, peace, love and salvation:

> The Trinity has to do with the lives of each of us, our daily experiences, our struggles to follow our conscience, our love and joy, our bearing the sufferings of the world and the tragedies of human existence; it also has to do with the struggle against social injustice, with efforts at building a more humane form of society, with the sacrifices and martyrdoms that these endeavours often bring. If we fail to include the Trinity in our personal and social odyssey, we have failed … in evangelization.[6]

To be a missionary people in the twenty-first century – encountering one another as people; encountering one another online; encountering difference and diversity – we must not forget our Trinitarian faith. We must remember that the love between the Father, Son and Spirit offers us a framework for how to think about our own lives and our participation in God's life. Another word for this type of living is 'discipleship' – living into God's calling of God's people, both as individuals and collectively as church. This also means being the prophetic voice within our contexts. That is, the prophetic voice is intimately tied to what it means to live as God's people in the world, enabled by the Spirit to be witnesses for Jesus Christ.

---

[6] Leonardo Boff, *Trinity and Society*, 157.

The revelation of God as Trinity happened in the life of Jesus and in the work of the Spirit in the community. This does not mean there was no previous communication of the Trinity, 'because any true revelation of God's self must be Trinitarian'.[7] Through Jesus of Nazareth and the Spirit at Pentecost, God takes on human history as God's own and dwells among us in our dwelling place.

Jeremiah had the eyes to see what God was doing and to see the link between God's revelation to him and his own participation in God's mission in creation. Being obedient entails participating in the liberating work of God as God is revealed in history. Too often we turn the Trinity into an academic discipline, discussed only by theologians. The proposal here is that we cannot separate learning to live as disciples of Christ from the triune God's work in the world today.

To talk of diversity and unity we need to make Jeremiah's story our story. It means learning that the same Spirit that inspired the prophets is at work in the church today and enables the church to have that prophetic voice in whatever context she finds herself. We cannot have unity in diversity without that prophetic voice.

God as Trinity is revealed fully in Jesus and at Pentecost. But in our classrooms and sermons, what Jesus are we teaching? In Latin America there are many faces, many types of Jesus – from the revolutionary Che Guevara to the cute, white, plump little baby in Mother Mary's arms. The doctrine of the Trinity demands that we learn to see Jesus with the eyes of the Spirit so that our own prejudices and politics do not blind us to the obedience to which the Father calls all his people.

Encountering Jesus Today:
Learning from Corinth to See the Spirit's Work

The church at Corinth suffered from the same self-absorption and prejudices as did the people with Jeremiah. The manifestations of the Holy Spirit in Corinth – dramatic by comparison to most Sunday services in Europe – did not automatically make them more holy or wise. And yet, despite the limitations and sin of the Corinthians, the triune God was made real within that community. How? Why? Part of the answer lies in the fact that God is a missionary God and that the Spirit enables God's prophets to bear messages that relate directly to the people's witness in whatever their context:

> God sent his prophets to expose the wickedness of his people and to warn them of
> its dire consequences ... the major features of the message of those earlier prophets,
> sent by God's Spirit, were the fundamental requirements of God's law: to do

---

[7] Boff, *Trinity and Society*, 10.

justice, to show mercy and compassion, and to reject the exploitation of the needy… the prophetic Spirit of *truth* is also the Spirit of *justice*.[8]

And it is the Spirit of unity – it is God that holds the church together, not us, not our theologies or our attempts to control.

These themes of justice, truth and unity are the ones that Paul takes on when writing to Corinth. Like Europe today, Corinth had challenges with the diversity among its church members: different social and economic levels, different ethnicities, different religious backgrounds. Though the particularity of the issues of that Corinthian congregation might be different from those experienced by the people living at the time of Jeremiah, the call to be God's faithful people remains the same for them and for us now. This call has everything to do with our participation in the triune life of God.

Father, Son and Holy Spirit exist in perpetual relationship:

> It is an energetic and dynamic relationship that inevitably is centrifugal in that it is outward looking. The metaphor is not exact, but it suffices here in that the very act of creation displays a fundamental aspect of God's nature: God is missionary. The creative urge, also given to all life, is to create something new whether it be a baby or a piece of art. So it must be with God's people in community: the creative urge is the basis for mission and evangelism, to see God re-create humanity one story at a time.[9]

The metaphor of new birth is very apt, for God is both creator and re-creator. If the church is to learn how to be missionary amidst the diversity of today's world and learn to see Jesus with the eyes of the Spirit, it must embody the prophetic call to justice and truth. In such living we reflect something of God's creative nature and we will be missionary-oriented. It is our calling to be caught up in the Trinity's work of making all things new.

But we need equipping for this task: the Father calls, the Son commissions and shows the way and the Spirit empowers and comforts:

> This can be seen in the rather muddled and messy Corinthian church as Paul highlights the missionary nature of God, embodies the prophetic role in his own ministry, and teaches about the essential nature of the Son's work, especially the central importance of his death and resurrection and the need the Corinthian's had (and we have today) of God's Spirit.[10]

Paul's correspondence with Corinth displays the urgency of their calling: they must sort out their common life, from sexual ethics to how they share their food,

[8] Christopher J. H. Wright. *Knowing the Holy Spirit through the Old Testament* (Downers Grove: IVP Academic, 2006), 82-83.

[9] John Baxter-Brown, 'Evangelism through the eyes of Jesus: Reflections on the Trinity', unpublished notes. Salisbury, UK, 2013.

[10] Baxter-Brown, 'Evangelism'.

so that their witness within that pagan context is one of truth and justice. Encountering Jesus with the eyes of the Spirit means learning to live as a particular community that embodies the love of the persons of the Trinity and displays this love to neighbour, friend, stranger or enemy.

We are created in the image of God and as we live in Christ through the power of the Spirit, we echo the relationship that God as Trinity is. 'Human beings exist only in community ... we are formed by language, which is by definition social.'[11] Understanding our place in community is fundamental to being made part of God's life and receiving God's revelation. In his debates with the Corinthians, Paul is making the same point. They must understand that how they live as a community has huge implications – in fact, life and death implications – for how they exist as God's people. Having the eyes of the Spirit means, for them, seeing Jesus of Nazareth and living according to that revelation. If their encounters with one another are less than adequate, they not only fail to see Jesus, but they fail to show Jesus to those around them. They run the risk of failing at mission and evangelism.

At the beginning of 1 Corinthians 3, Paul shows the Corinthians that their jealousy, quarrelling and many divisions are directly tied to how they live in the Spirit. Indeed, those who are not spiritual will not receive the gifts of the Spirit (1 Cor. 2:14), though Paul has already affirmed in 1:7 that they are not lacking in any spiritual gift; and how does he know this? He knows because their testimony of Christ has been strengthened in speech and knowledge (1:5-6). It is a dangerous game they are playing, and the apostle is trying his hardest to persuade them again to live lives worthy of Christ.

Like the church in Europe (and all around the world), there are issues of power and greed that threaten to break apart the community in Corinth. Paul plays on popular conceptions of wisdom and honour to show that the ways in which the world conceives of such power are very different from the ways of God's Spirit, and it is with the eyes of the Spirit that they must relearn to orient their individual and their collective lives. In the history of God's dealings with creation, God has called the most unlikely people to be his voice and his instruments in a broken world. It is no different with Corinth – some might be wise, but not all; some might be powerful, but not all (2:26-31). God's Spirit rests on very unlikely and often unwilling prophets, asking them to show the world what it means to follow Jesus. For Paul, the Corinthian church is in this great line of people called to challenge the world's wisdom, strength and might so that the world might know God's justice and be drawn into God's wisdom and into God's kingdom.

The dynamics of the narrative of 1 and 2 Corinthians and the reports of Paul's ministry in the book of Acts show both how the apostle is called to be a prophet – calling the people back to justice, truth and unity, and to living as the missionary people they are meant to be – and how those who listen to the prophet

---

[11] Timothy J. Gorringe, *Discerning the Spirit: A Theology of Revelation* (London: SCM, 1990), 74.

become prophets themselves. The people of God are called to be a missionary people because in so doing we participate in God's life. Such participation requires and is enabled by the Spirit, who guides and teaches so that the life of Jesus is made real in whatever context the community finds itself. Being part of the life of the triune God means witnessing to Jesus in words, deeds and character wherever we are.

Encounters with 'Otherness':
Learning to Follow Jesus with Those Who Are Different

In his book entitled *Spirituality According to Paul: Imitating the Apostle of Christ*, Rodney Reeves explores the themes of biblical spirituality through Paul's life and his letters. In particular, Reeves looks at what it means to 'follow me as I follow Christ', a theme which turns up often in Paul's letters to the churches. Part of a missionary expression of the faith entails participation in the triune God and going to places where the Spirit leads. For Christian leaders today, how many have the boldness to say, 'follow me as I follow Christ' as part of their witnessing lives?

Paul promotes a cross-shaped spirituality for fools making their way through life's trials. Paul, following Jesus' own life, realised that images of crucifixion, burial and resurrection would never be popular images in society or in the missionary life. Still, he encourages his fellow travellers, who are spiritually united with Christ, to 'follow me as I follow Christ'. In so doing, Paul is teaching the early church lessons about discipleship and witness in the way of Jesus.

The Spirit of God empowers and leads those early Christians to encounters with others whom they were not prepared to meet. In any age, but especially at its origins, Christianity revolves around the distinctive experience of the person of Jesus Christ. The New Testament is the early church's considered reflection on encounters with Jesus of Nazareth and through Jesus with others. Such narratives lead us today to consider the implications of such encounters for the life of discipleship and the character of our Christian witness.

In all the gospels, but especially in Luke, and in the book of Acts, Peter serves as one significant testimony of such transformative encounters. In Luke 5 we read about the calling of the first disciples. Jesus is by a lake and he calls to two brothers to go fishing. A couple of amazing things happen: firstly, they catch lots of fish; secondly, after taking the boats ashore, the brothers put down their nets, leave everything and follow Jesus. Simon Peter and Andrew, James and John leaving everything – father, home, means of income – means leaving who they are to become followers of Jesus.

There are basic themes in the text of Luke 5 which echo and shape discipleship and mission in twenty-first-century Europe: themes of boundaries, borders, and of who is in and who is out; themes of identity and belonging. There always seems to be a lot of boundary-building in the history of the church. In this Gospel there is lots of 'us' and 'them' language, lots of power plays (i.e.

who needs healing and who does not; whose sins need forgiving and who gets to forgive). Throughout the narratives, the things that kept the people together – the boundaries that defined their identities – are disrupted in all sorts of ways by the arrival of Jesus and his fishermen friends.

Luke 5 begins with Peter and his friends witnessing the healing of a leper and of a paralytic, and then they are confronted with a huge challenge. After the fishermen follow Jesus, the text takes them immediately to a house in which a man comes in through the roof and is healed, and Jesus gets into one of his first arguments with the religious leaders.

Peter had to explain a broken roof and a paralytic man who walks – where would he have learned how to explain such events? In Luke 5:26, all that the disciples manage to say is, 'we have seen strange things today'. Immediately following these events, Jesus calls the next disciple: Levi, the tax collector.

In their society, culture and religion, this was not possible. Fishermen and tax collectors belonged to two very different groups, two very different social levels. There was nothing normal, nothing natural about Peter and Levi being put into the same little band or following the same rabbi together. Fishermen were at the bottom of the social scale; they were part of the family business and they tried to survive as men under the rule of a foreign power. Though poor, they were devout Jews, they tried to live by the book, to go to prayers, to follow the Mosaic laws and to respect the words of the law-keepers, the Pharisees. Fishermen were exploited by people like Levi. The tax collector was the one who served the evil empire, the corrupt official who took money from his own people to give to the Romans, while pocketing some for himself. This man was not just bad because he had money, but he was religiously an outsider, too. There was no way Peter and Levi could ever be friends, let alone brothers. How could Jesus expect devout fishermen to go on a journey with a tax collector? And yet we know that Levi, like Peter, also accepted Jesus' invitation to come and to follow. So, if Peter wanted to be near Jesus, he would also have to be near Levi.

Peter, who had given up his livelihood and even his name – his identity – to follow Jesus, was very quickly asked to welcome Levi into the newly formed little group of disciples. Luke does not tell us how Peter reacted to the calling of Levi. We do see in Luke 5:30 that the scribes and Pharisees complain to the disciples, asking (they might have asked Peter), 'Why are you eating with sinners and tax collectors?' Interestingly, Jesus is the one who answers them, not Peter or the other disciples. We also know of later struggles about money, about who is the greatest, and about such disputes of power between the disciples.

Learning to be part of Jesus' kingdom, to be a disciple, to go where the Spirit calls and to embody a people that cares for the vulnerable, the oppressed, the widow and the orphan meant learning to encounter and to be with those with whom Peter did not get along with or like. More than that, it meant learning a new kind of friendship, for which Peter (and Levi) were completely unprepared! Sometimes, loving one's neighbour is the same as loving one's enemy. Sometimes, those are exactly the encounters to which Jesus calls us.

As we get closer to Jesus, we get closer to one another, and this is usually quite challenging. It is difficult because Jesus is the one choosing those who join the band. It is easier for most Christians, like Peter, to choose their own friends and brothers and sisters, rather than having Jesus determine who will be on the discipleship journey with us.

Jesus calls us to be one so that the world will know (John 17:21). By our love we are known, he says in the Gospel of John – this is a key part of that missionary calling of the people of God. Yet so much of the energy and focus of Christian communities throughout history has been on building boundaries and walls – divisions that keep people apart and that determine who is inside and who is out. Boundaries are safer; they respect the power dynamics that give us our identity.

But the frightening lesson of the gospels is that if one wants to be close to Jesus one will end up going on a journey with people who look, feel and smell different than you do. It is complicated and scandalous today, just as it was for Peter and his friends. Mission in twenty-first-century Europe has to include learning the hard lessons of friendship and learning to love one's neighbours in the encounters of everyday life. If we are to be united by Jesus and in Jesus, then we are going to have to be with others who are also called to be close to Jesus.

Peter and Levi had to learn to be brothers, to be together in community in a society, in a culture, and in economic and religious systems that told them over and over again: you are not friends, you should not be together. Their encounter and friendship, their sharing in ministry and learning to be disciples was only possible because of Jesus.

Throughout the New Testament narratives, God's Spirit is compelling those whom God calls to encounter difference, to encounter and be with people who are radically different from themselves. Such encounters are about breaking down the boundaries of who is in and who is out. These are encounters of inclusivity, but also of transformation; both Peter and Levi are changed. Being close to Jesus, they are not made the same, but they are together. These narratives beg the question of the church today: who are we together with? Who is our neighbour, and why does that matter for our witness in the twenty-first century? In Luke 10, when Jesus is asked by the lawyer, 'Who is my neighbour?', he tells a story about those religious leaders who did not cross the boundary to help the wounded man, and the story of the Samaritan who did.

In the gospels we observe a pattern in Jesus' ministry. The gospels evince a character of Christian mission based on the stories of encounters with Jesus. Jesus himself is constantly creating a space around his own body where these conversations, these encounters, and this listening to the other can emerge. Wherever he goes into ministry – to Galilee, to Samaria, etc. – or even when he is invited to the more socially acceptable places, like the synagogue or the home of the religious leader (the table of a Pharisee), Jesus brings with him other people that challenge those divisions and that upset the paradigms. So, by being close to Jesus, people's religious and cultural expectations, their understanding of what is acceptable behaviour, and what is an acceptable embodiment of being God's people – all of these things are being challenged.

What would it have felt like for Peter to be enmeshed and embedded with a tax collector like Levi/Matthew because of his commitment to rabbi Jesus? Why would that have been a difficult practice to live out? What would it have felt like to be a Christian leader in Jerusalem listening to Paul and Barnabas talk about the inclusion of those horrible gentiles (Acts 11 and 15)? Such encounters were scandalous and created great challenges to the emerging churches. Yet through the prophetic voices and the testimonies of those empowered by the Spirit, we have examples of how those first communities learned that it was precisely in these encounters that they would learn and receive the gifts of the Spirit. Moreover, they learned that participation in God's mission entailed creating spaces where such encounters could take place, and, in so doing, acted as witnesses to the cultures around them that another world was possible with the coming of Jesus of Nazareth.

Jesus changes the conversation and creates spaces for these conversations and encounters around himself. It is a challenge to the boundaries not merely for the sake of being progressive. Rather, it is about following Jesus and participating in the mission he has given the church to act upon, both then and now.

Learning to be close to Jesus, to love our neighbour and to grow in discipleship and Christian witness is about learning to say and to live out what Peter says in Acts 10:34: 'Now I truly understand that God shows no partiality.' That is a profoundly missional statement. Peter had learned through his encounters with Levi, the Samaritans, and Cornelius the Gentile that God's Spirit compels God's people into mission through the meeting of strangers. Followers of Christ grow in their Christ-likeness in such encounters, and in the gifts the Spirit lays upon each one as they seek to follow Jesus on difficult journeys.

The encounters and call to mission are not about making everyone the same in the kingdom of God. Rather, the joy and wonder of what Christ does in bringing us together is that we hold onto our distinctiveness. Just as the Spirit made itself known in the diversity of languages at Pentecost, so the Spirit empowers and works through the diversity of peoples, languages and cultures in Europe today. God's mission is not about everyone becoming the same, but it is about being together.

Too often we are more concerned with understanding the distinctiveness of our identities and our different missions because it is too hard to be with others who are so different. The challenge both from Jeremiah and from the New Testament is this: have Christians in Europe for too long been more concerned with maintaining the purity of their group or their tribe than with crossing the boundaries that Jesus himself crossed and thus encountering others? A robust mission theology is one that trusts not in the purity of our tribe, but in the power of the Holy Spirit and in the surprising ways in which God calls God's people to encounter himself and others.

Christians are called into something far greater than anything we could have imagined. This is the work of God and not something the church can control. True Christian mission is necessarily Trinitarian – it is rooted in the very triune God, where act and being cannot be separated or divorced from one another, and where there is constant encounter and fellowship.

God as Trinity is at work in the world, whether one's church participates in this work or not. God is at work in all communities and in all the diversity and messiness of the twenty-first century – in the many acts of justice and commitments to love one's enemy; in the diversity of voices with which the church today has been called to be a prophetic voice, a voice for justice and peace that cannot be divorced from the life and teachings of Jesus. Insofar as we listen to the Spirit, we are able to see Jesus even in the least of these, and to embody in our encounters and in our relationships obedience to the Father that has called us to himself through the sacrifice of the Son and the gift of the Spirit.

References

Araya, Victorio. *God of the Poor*. Maryknoll: Orbis, 1987.

Barth, Karl, *Church Dogmatics IV/I*, ed. G. W. Bromiley and T. F. Torrance, transl. G. W. Bromiley Edinburgh, Scotland: T. & T. Clark, 1958.

Baxter-Brown, John, "Evangelism through the eyes of Jesus: Reflections on the Trinity", unpublished notes. Salisbury, UK, 2013.

Boff, Leonardo. *Holy Trinity, Perfect Community*. Maryknoll: Orbis, 2000.

___. *Trinity and Society*. Maryknoll: Orbis, 1998.

Bonino, José Miguéz. *Faces of Latin American Protestantism*. Grand Rapids: Eerdmans, 1997.

Clements, R. E., *Jeremiah*, Interpretation Series. Atlanta, GA: John Knox, 1988.

Cloke, Paul and Pears, Mike (eds.). *Mission in marginal places: The theory*. Milton Keynes: Paternoster, 2016.

Costas, Orlando E. *Liberating News: A Theology of Contextual Evangelization*. Eugene: Wipf & Stock, 2002.

Ezigbo, Victor I. *Introducing Christian theologies: Voices from global Christian communities, volumes I and II*. Eugene: Cascade, 2013 and 2015.

Fowl, Stephan E. and Jones, L. Gregory, *Reading in Communion: Scripture and Ethics in Christian Life*, Grand Rapids, MI: Eerdmans, 1991.

Gallagher, Robert L. and Hertig, Paul (eds.). *Mission in Acts: Ancient narratives in contemporary context*. Maryknoll: Orbis, 2004.

Gorringe, Timothy J. *Discerning the Spirit: A theology of Revelation*. London: SCM, 1990.

Kärkkäinen, Veli-Matti. *The Trinity: Global Perspectives*. Louisville: Westminster John Knox, 2007.

Moltmann, Jürgen, *The Trinity and the Kingdom: The Doctrine of God*. (London: SCM Press, 1981.

Seitz, Christopher R., *Theology in Conflict: Reactions to the Exile in the Book of Jeremiah*, Berlin and New York: Walter de Gruyter, 1989.

Wright, Christopher J. H., Knowing *the Holy Spirit through the Old Testament*, Downers Grove: IVP Academic, 2006.

(5) Migration, Mission and Music: Valuing the Legacy of African Caribbean Pentecostalism
Dulcie Dixon McKenzie

Introduction

The rise of African Caribbean Pentecostalism (hereafter ACP)[1] as a movement in Britain is one of the most pioneering moments in the history of Christian mission. Its growth has contributed to the spread of Pentecostalism as the fastest growing division of Protestant Christianity and has reignited and enriched British Christianity. In the discourse of World Christianity or global Christianity in the world,[2] however, ACP (in the Caribbean and Britain) receives partial attention. Note, for example, the investigative studies of Pentecostalism globally, where explorations of ACP are customarily brief,[3] associated with other experiences of Pentecostalism such as Latin America,[4] or ignored.[5] In Britain, the import of African Indigenous Churches (AICs) and African Pentecostal churches receives abundant attention as African scholars write about 'Black Majority Churches' and mission using case studies featuring mostly African churches and their leaders.[6] Recent publications have tended to merge the historic rise of ACP with

---

[1] Or ACPs, referring to African Caribbean Pentecostals.
[2] For an interesting observation about the difference between world Christianity and global Christianity, see Lamin Sanneh, *Whose Religion Is Christianity? The Gospel Beyond the West* (Grand Rapids, MI: William B. Eerdmans, 2003), 208. World Christianity, notes Sanneh, denotes Christianity arriving in places where it was not found previously, whereas global Christianity is where Christianity is replicated in different forms and patterns in Europe and is an expression that parallels economic globalisation.
[3] Allan Heaton Anderson, *An Introduction to Pentecostalism* (Cambridge: Cambridge University Press, 2014).
[4] Vinson Synan, Amos Yong, and Miguel Alvarez (eds), *Global Renewal Christianity*, vol. 2, Latin America (Lake Mary, Florida: Charisma House, 2016); Allan Anderson, *Spreading Fires: The Missionary Nature of Early Pentecostalism* (Maryknoll, New York: Orbis Books, 2007).
[5] See, for example, William K. Kay, *Pentecostalism* (London: SCM Press, 2009). This is a core text on Pentecostalism that explores its growth in Asia, Africa and four countries of South America (i.e. Argentina, Brazil, Chile, and Columbia); however, it omits Caribbean Pentecostalism and its spread amongst Caribbean migrants in Britain. Allan Anderson et al. (eds), *Studying Global Pentecostalism: Theories and Methods* (London: University of California Press, 2010).
[6] Israel Oluwole Olofinjana, *Partnership in Mission: A Black Majority Church Perspective on Mission and Church Unity* (Herts: Instant Apostle, 2015); Israel

historiographies of African Christianities or diasporan dialogue.[7] As an example, the recent publication in *Pentecostals and Charismatics in Britain,* edited by Joe Aldred,[8] there is a historical overview of *African and Caribbean Pentecostalism in Britain.* Contributor Babatunde Aderemi Adedibu presents a broad historical outline of African and African Caribbean churches, and states that 'African and Caribbean churches are diverse but intertwine historically, theologically and practically'.[9] Whilst the 'two churches' may intertwine, the overall approach here is to present a historical account by uncritically merging ancestral trajectories as a single narrative. Adedibu acknowledges the early beginnings of collective African Caribbean churches and the subsequent arrival of African churches in Britain, before concluding with details of emerging congregations that are primarily new African churches in Britain. If scholars and observers advance this methodology, there is a risk of endorsing the idea that distinctive historical experiences are not important. By consistently integrating the African Caribbean and African churches as a grand narrative there is a danger that historical, social, cultural and theological particularities of both African and ACP churches will become abridged, obscured, or ignored.

Concerned that missiological investigative interest in the formative years of ACP in Britain is in decline or in danger of being replaced; and using earlier empirical data and a selection of historiographic literature, this chapter describes aspects of the formative years of ACP in Britain. The ensuing discussion will be guided by a central question: what are some of the features of an ACP past that current and future descendants might seek to investigate further, and claim as their ACP heritage? This chapter will incorporate three themes related to the experience of the first generation of ACPs during the post-war years in Britain – namely, Migration, Mission, and Music – as it seeks to encourage more cognizance of the past so that the current and future generations may find empowerment from embracing an ACP heritage.

Olofinjana, *Reverse in Ministry and Missions: Africans in the Dark Continent of Europe – An Historical Study of African Churches in Europe* (Milton Keynes: Author House, 2010).

[7] See Babatunde Adedibu, *Coat of Many Colours: The Origin, Growth, Distinctiveness and Contributions of Black Majority Churches to British Christianity* (Gloucester: Wisdom Summit, 2012); Clifton R. Clarke, *Pentecostalism: Insights from African and the African Diaspora* (Eugene, Oregon: Cascade Books, 2018).

[8] Joe Aldred (ed), *Pentecostals and Charismatics in Britain: An Anthology* (London: SCM Press, 2019).

[9] Babatunde Aderemi Adedibu, 'African and Caribbean Pentecostalism in Britain', in Joe Aldred (ed), *Pentecostals and Charismatics in Britain: An Anthology* (London: SCM, 2019), 19.

My African Caribbean Heritage

The lack of attention to the historical and cultural particularities of ACPs is of personal concern to me. I was raised as a daughter of Pentecostal migrants who travelled from Jamaica to Britain after the second world war. My parents, like many other Caribbean migrants, arrived in the country as British citizens, just before the 1962 Commonwealth Immigration Act determined that Commonwealth citizens holding a passport that was not issued directly by the UK government would be subject to immigration control. Thus, my parents arrived in Britain in 1961 under the British Nationality Act 1948 as British subjects: citizens of the United Kingdom and Colonies, with the right to live and work in the UK. As young, single, 'born again' Christians, on arrival in Britain, only two things were on their minds: find a job and a church. They already had accommodation arranged before they arrived in Britain, so initially, they did not directly experience the signs on the doors and windows where there might have been vacancies for accommodation that said 'no Blacks, no Irish, no dogs' – that came later when they were looking for accommodation to start married life. Finding a job was easy. My father spoke much about being able to go to one job in the morning, and then being able to move on to another job the next day. My mother, on the other hand, could have done the same, but she stayed in her initial job for a few months making shoes in a factory. Finding a church, however, was much more difficult, and this is where the theme of this chapter reverberates. My parents were among the many migrants who were not given a warm welcome in the host churches in Britain during the post-war years, and memories of those tales live on in the minds of their children.

My parents had five children and raised us to love God and to love all people. They also became Pentecostal ministers and took us (their children) to church and taught us how to be actively involved in church. Thus, my mind is filled with memories of my formative years attending many church services and spending a lot of time with the first generation of ACPs who were passionate about their faith. As they juggled working full time, raising their children and faithfully serving in church, I have an abiding memory of a generation that hardly complained; instead, they took their troubles to the Lord in prayer. I heard many of those prayers in church and in the countless prayer meetings. Looking back, their prayers were packed with emotions and reflected a lot of pain, but details of their pain were always vague. They were a generation who took their troubles to the Lord in prayer. Consequently, details of their experience are stored in a treasure box of prayers and memories, and perhaps a key to that box is in the conversations yet to be had with the first generation of ACPs. How did my parents and other Pentecostal migrants overcome their challenges? What might be the lessons learned from their experience that future generations might ingest? This discussion provides support for folks who are keen about heritage.

Heritage and the ACP Movement in Britain

This discussion balances notions of the past with the present, proposing that there could be information about the formative years of ACP in Britain that could be helpful to the present and future generations. This line of enquiry sits within the discipline of Heritage and Heritage Management. Heritage scholars agree on one basic premise that defines heritage, and the following statement perhaps captures a range of the available definitions:

> Heritage is present-centred and is created, shaped and managed by, and in response to, the demands of the present. As such, it is open to constant revision and change and is both a source and a repercussion of social conflict.[10]

Thus, heritage is a contemporary use of the past, and how the past can be used in the present will determine the desired effect. Some may use the 'practice' of heritage for community development, perhaps to inspire and empower activism; some may use it for education – to provide important knowledge linked to the past; whilst others might use it for cultural identity – to affirm, or instil confidence in a disadvantaged group. The list of uses and reasons is countless. The ensuing discussion, however, seeks to stimulate the idea of interrogating the past concerning the developmental of ACP as a movement in Britain for use today and in future generations. Heritage scholars will affirm that heritage management requires identifying *tangible* and *intangible* objects of the past.[11] Tangible heritage is identifiable by something palpable and solid that can be touched, such as buildings, landscapes, artwork, and artefact.[12] Intangible heritage might seem vague or ambiguous, but it does exist, such as in beliefs, music, songs, and ceremonies.[13] What might show up in an ACP past that could be treated as tangible or intangible objects of the past for use today and in future generations? In sum, what might be lying latent for interrogation to provide encouragement, information, or perhaps affirmation for ACP inheritors today and in the future?

African Diaspora of Black Pentecostals

Pentecostalism is a global movement, and it is important to note that it is not monolithic. It has been described as a 'complex social movement with many

[10] G.J. Ashworth, Brian Graham, and J.E. Tunbridge, *Pluralising Pasts: Heritage, Identity and Place in Multicultural Societies* (London: Pluto Press, 2007), 3.
[11] Regina F. Bendix, *Culture and Value: Tourism, Heritage and Property* (Indiana: Indiana University Press, 2018).
[12] Gerard Corsane (ed), *Heritage, Museums and Galleries: An Introductory Reader* (London: Routledge, 2005).
[13] Cecilia Lizama Salvatore, *Cultural Heritage Care and Management: Theory and Practice* (London: Rowan & Littlefield, 2018).

strains',[14] which is a perceptive way of designating it as a Christian movement that has many contesting expressions, distinguishable by the classifications of race,[15] theology,[16] and location.[17] Research and surveys so far have yielded studies and dictionaries showing how various names of leaders and assemblies of Pentecostalism can be distinctively collated.[18] A close look at the surveys of Pentecostalism shows that it has advanced globally in a variety of locations, organised as denominations, independent congregations, and fellowships.

Most relevant to this discussion is the growth of Pentecostalism as a movement that has evolved amongst people of African ancestry. Examining notions of a connection by heritage within an African diaspora, British born black theologian Robert Beckford refers to black congregants within the historic Pentecostal congregations founded by African Caribbean migrants, 'Black Pentecostals.'[19] In his observation of the milieu of denominations and churches, Beckford recognises connecting theological tenets that represent shared values as well as differences that divide. Beckford, however, emphasises the importance of observing black identity within an African diaspora and concedes that it is difficult to define what is meant by 'diaspora'; and he is open to change and adaption of his working definition. Beckford confidently utilises three parts of a six-point definition of 'diaspora' formulated by Professor Emeritus of Political Science, William Safran[20] in his own discourse about politics and black churches in *Dread and Pentecostals*.[21] A black diaspora of Pentecostals, Beckford suggests, could be defined by 1) those dispersed from any original centre to at

---

14 Donald E. Miller and Tetsunao Yamaamori, *Global Pentecostalism: The New Face of Christian Social Engagement* (London: University of California Press, 2007), 1.

15 See Iain MacRobert, 'The Black Roots of Pentecostalism', in Timothy E. Fulop and Albert J. Raboteau (eds), *African-American Religion: Interpretive Essays in History and Culture* (New York: Routledge, 1997). Arlene M. Sanchez Walsh, *Latino Pentecostal Identity: Evangelical Faith, Self, and Society* (New York: Columbia Unversity Press, 2003).

16 See Keith Warrington, *Pentecostal Perspectives* (Carlisle, Cumbria: Paternoster Press, 1998); Wolfgang Vondey, *Pentecostal Theology: Living the Full Gospel* (London: Bloomsbury T & T Clark, 2017); Christopher A. Stephenson, *Types of Pentecostal Theology: Method, System, Spirit* (Oxford: Oxford University Press, 2013).

17 See Anderson et al., *Studying Global Pentecostalism: Theories and Methods*; Harold D. Hunter and Neil Ormerod, eds., *The Many Faces of Global Pentecostalism* (Cleveland, Tennessee: CPT Press, 2013).

18 See for example, Estrelda Y. Alexander (ed), *The Dictionary of Pan-African Pentecostalism, Volume 1: North America* (Eugene, Oregon: Cascade Books, 2018); Stanley M. Burgess and Eduard M. Van Der Maas (eds), *The New International Dictionary of Pentecostal and Charismatic Movements: Revised and Expanded Edition* (Michigan: Zondervan, 2003).

19 Robert Beckford, *Dread and Pentecostal: A Political Theology for the Black Church in Britain* (London: SPCK, 2000).

20 William Safran, 'Diasporas in Modern Societies: Myths of Homeland and Return', *Diaspora: A Journal of Transnational Studies* 1, no. 1 (1991).

21 Beckford, *Dread and Pentecostal*.

least two peripheral places; 2) those who have a memory, vision or myth about their original homeland; and 3) those who believe they are not, and perhaps cannot be fully accepted by their host country.[22] If these criteria were to be applied to ACP migrants, then it is possible to see that ACP are descendants of Africans who were transported from Africa to the Caribbean and Americas. In the Caribbean, Africans were enslaved for centuries, though maintained cultural memories and practices of homeland through an oral tradition. African descendants in the British Caribbean were subjects of the British empire, thus, were able to migrate from the Caribbean to Britain. In terms of a Black diaspora then, African Caribbean migrants in Britain have a history of being twice removed from 'home' – detached and displaced from their ancestral home of Africa, and then migrated from the Caribbean to Britain as British subjects. Thus, it is possible to define ACP migrants that entered Britain as British citizens and the first generation of Black Pentecostals, though, as evidenced by their social experience as new arrivals, were not fully accepted in British society.

The term 'Afro Pentecostals' is also of relevance here. In an edited collection of essays, Pentecostal scholars Amos Yong and Estrelda Alexander, with others, examine the ways of African-American Pentecostalism,[23] centring on its early history, the relationship between Afro-Pentecostals and black denominations, missionary activities, gender issues, and the distinctive theologies.[24] Yong and Alexander identify the 'collective organisation' of black Pentecostals as 'Afro-Pentecostalism',[25] and there is an acknowledgement of 'Afro Pentecostals' as black Pentecostals outside of America. In Britain, however, a common term used to identify the collection of congregations, churches, and denominations that refers to ACP (and African) churches is 'Black Majority Churches' (BMC), which includes black Pentecostal churches as a collective and other denominations with a congregation with a black majority. The term has been interrogated elsewhere,[26] and its contentious use continues to be unresolved.[27]

What is significant here is that 'Black Pentecostalism' worldwide is not monolithic, rather, it is complex due to a diversity in theological traditions and

---

22 Safran, 'Diasporas in Modern Societies: Myths of Homeland and Return'."
23 Used interchangeably with Afro-Pentecostals
24 Amos Yong and Estrelda Y. Alexander (eds), *Afro-Pentecostalism: Black Pentecostal and Charismatic Christianity in History and Culture* (New York: New York University Press, 2011).
25 See Yong and Alexander, *Afro-Pentecostalism: Black Pentecostal and Charismatic Christianity in History and Culture.*
26 Arlington Trotman, 'Black, Black-Led or What?', in Joel Edwards (ed), *Let's Praise Him Again* (Eastbourne: Kingsway, 1992). Republished in Mark Sturge, *Look What the Lord Has Done: An Exploration of Black Christian Faith in Britain* (Milton Keynes: Scripture Union, 2005).
27 Anthony Reddie, 'Churches', in David Dabydeen, John Gilmore, and Cecily Jones (ds), *The Oxford Companion to Black British History* Oxford: Oxford University Press, 2007).

cultural heritage; and the complexities of Black Pentecostalism as a movement in Britain have been meticulously examined by German theologian Roswith Gerloff, in *A Plea for British Black Theologies*.[28] Gerloff shows how Black Pentecostalism flourished amongst African Caribbean and West African adherents in its first twenty years in Britain.[29] As the title suggests, Gerloff makes a plea for an understanding of the rich diversity of theological traditions and cultural inheritance that shapes the spiritual experience of an African diaspora. Some twenty years after Gerloff, Mark Sturge, in *Look What the Lord Has Done*,[30] explored aspects of doctrines and practices relevant to black Pentecostals in Britain. Both publications are examples of the diversity of Pentecostalism amongst African descendants, and in a global context, this discussion recognises an African diaspora of Pentecostals. However, it distinguishes between cultural traces reflected in the lived experience of different black Pentecostals in Britain.

Since the concern in this discussion is the potential decline in recognition of the contribution of the generation of Pentecostals that initiated Pentecostalism as a movement in Britain, this analysis recognises them as migrants from the Caribbean located in a host country that did not fully accept them. They have ancestors from Africa who were enslaved by Europeans in the Caribbean; thus, in this chapter, the use of 'African Caribbean' corresponds with that complexity.[31]

The Arrival of African Caribbean Migrants in Post-War Britain

There is literature that helpfully describes the different types of migration,[32] while also proffering knowledge of the plight of individuals and groups of people.[33] Perhaps less known in contemporary literature is the historical experience of African Caribbean Pentecostals as migrants who arrived in Britain with social, economic and religious needs. They arrived as British citizens who were approved by the British government and had appealed earlier for members of the Commonwealth to assist in rebuilding their country after the Second World War. Britain's cabinet Manpower Working Party required a workforce of

---

[28] See Roswith I. H. Gerloff, *A Plea for British Black Theologies: The Black Church Movement in Britain in Its Transatlantic Cultural and Theological Interaction*, 2 vols., vol. 1 (New York: Peter Lang, 1992).

[29] Gerloff, *A Plea for British Black Theologies*.

[30] Sturge, *Look What the Lord Has Done*.

[31] For another perspective, and for an explanation of the term 'Caribbean British', see Joe Aldred, *Respect: Understanding Caribbean British Christianity* (Peterborough: Epworth, 2005).

[32] Susanna Snyder, *Asylum-Seeking, Migration and Church: Explorations in Practical, Pastoral and Empirical Theology* (New York: Routledge, 2012).

[33] See https://www.nationalgeographic.org/activity/introduction-human-migration/ (Accessed 26th June 2019).

at least 940,000 additional workers to address a labour shortage,[34] and a landmark event in this historical development occurred on 22nd June 1948, when a ship called *Empire Windrush* docked at Tilbury docks near London, transporting some 492 passengers from the Caribbean. The name of this ship has been used to refer to this group of migrants and others that would follow within the subsequent 12 years: the Windrush generation. Far more has become known about the experience of the Windrush generation since the summer of 2018, as a result of the news coverage of what has been coined 'the Windrush scandal'. In this scandal, men and women were wrongly detained and, in some cases, deported back to the Caribbean.[35]

From the outset, nonetheless, the arrival of this first wave of passengers from the Caribbean in the summer of 1948 caused unwavering anguish within the government at what was perceived as something that might inspire more unwanted arrivals in Britain.[36] Of note, a good number of the passengers had previously been in Britain during the war,[37] and so, many in this group of migrants could have been thought of as returnee migrants, returning to Britain to contribute again. Historic accounts highlight that many of the passengers came with the hope of a short-term stay to earn money, and others sought to gain additional education.[38] However, migrants' financial commitments towards living expenses did not allow for such goals to be realised.[39] Many migrants resigned themselves to the notion of settling down and seizing opportunities to work. In terms of numbers, the inflow of African Caribbean migrants was believed to have been 260,000 between 1955 and 1962,[40] and by then, the British public routinely expressed contempt towards black migrants. This was evinced in a widespread social rejection demonstrated in various places – on the job, in housing, in education and on the streets, which was wholesale and palpable, characterised by verbal and physical attacks directed towards migrants. As newcomers, they constantly had to find ways to navigate racism.

---

[34] David Olusoga, *Black and British: A Forgotten History* (London: Macmillan, 2016), 491.

[35] See https://www.bl.uk/windrush/themes/the-windrush-generation-scandal (Accessed 23rd August 2019).

[36] Olusoga, *Black and British*, 493.

[37] Olusoga, *Black and British*, 494.

[38] Winston James and Clive Harris (eds), *Inside Babylon: The Caribbean Diaspora in Britain* (London: Verso, 1993).

[39] See Mike Phillips and Trevor Phillips, *Windrush: The Irresistible Rise of Multi-Racial Britain* (London: HarperCollins, 1998).

[40] Olusoga, *Black and British*.

African Caribbean Migrants of Faith

How migrants survived as a community is helpfully documented elsewhere,[41] with examples of how they devised their own forms of social activities and entertainment. By contrast, the migrants arriving with faith have received less attention in the literature so far. This is a mysterious lapse because many arrived in Britain with religious beliefs that they assumed they would be able to share in the host churches as they had been able to do in the Caribbean. Many were previous members and worshippers in the colonial churches in the Caribbean, such as Anglican, Methodist and Catholic congregations, and similarly, the Baptist Church in Jamaica. Thus, it would seem reasonable for migrants to assume comparable participation in the associated congregations upon arrival in Britain.

Finding a church was important because church attendance was an indication of good social character and social standing.[42] However, they wrongly assumed that they would enjoy ongoing participation and membership within the host churches in Britain. Earlier writings describe the personal experiences of Anglicans,[43] Methodists,[44] and Baptists.[45] Believing that they were fellow brothers and sisters in Christ, African Caribbean migrants of faith visited the host churches. They realised, though, that irrespective of earlier denominational allegiance, there was not a warm welcome for them in the congregations. Many were turned away, whilst others stayed and continued to experience impolite reactions from church leaders and congregants.[46] For many, it was a painful experience, and perhaps giving space to hearing more of these narratives might help to raise awareness and support the current efforts in tackling the serious lack of diversity within the longer-established denominations.[47] Of importance to this present discussion, however (covered in the discussion that follows), is the experience of the Pentecostal migrants who, upon arrival, could not find a Pentecostal church of their own to attend.

---

[41] Phillips and Phillips, *Windrush.*

[42] Doreen Morrison, *Ruled Britainnia: Jamaican Christianity's Interregnum 1866-2016* (CreateSpace: 2018), 79.

[43] Mukti Barton, *Rejection, Resistance and Resurrection: Speaking out on Racism in the Church* (London: Darton, Logan and Todd, 2005); John L. Wilkinson, *Church in Black and White* (Edinburgh: Saint Andrew Press, 1993).

[44] Heather Walton, *A Tree God Planted: Black People in British Methodism* (London: Ethnic Minorities in Methodism Working Group, 1985).

[45] Morrison, *Ruled Britainnia.*

[46] Clifford S. Hill, *West Indian Migrants and the London Churches* (London: Open University Press, 1963).

[47] See for example 'I too am CofE' video presentation to Synod: https://www.churchofengland.org/more/policy-and-thinking/our-views/race-and-ethnicity (Accessed 23rd August 2019).

A Church Vacuum for African Caribbean Pentecostal Migrants

African Caribbean migrants of 'Pentecostal persuasion' arrived in Britain rightly assuming that they would not find their particular 'brand' of Christianity readily available in their new location. However, on arrival, they initially sought to participate in the host churches that they recognised from their experience in the Caribbean. Many attended; however, they had a poor experience. Pentecostal migrants gave accounts about the church services, indicating that it lacked vibrancy and that the liturgy was too repetitive. Most alarming was the response of the church leader and members of the congregation. Pentecostal migrants experienced overt rejection and did not feel encouraged to continue visiting. Since they were committed 'disciples' and regular churchgoers in the Caribbean, the reality of having no 'church home' was a disappointment and evoked feelings of frustration. It is the way in which the migrants of Pentecostal persuasion responded that is of significance here. Despite the social rejection from the host churches and the low appeal of their church services, Pentecostal migrants nonetheless had a strong sense of who they were and sustained a resilient desire to continue their Christian faith as newcomers.

Racism and rejection would not be a deterrent to their faith; yet in more ways than one, Pentecostal migrants faced a double dilemma. Their race and style of Christian worship were going to be immediate barriers to the expression of their faith. Put another way, being black and Pentecostal was a double disadvantage. When it proved difficult to visit the host churches, many Pentecostal migrants had little choice other than to abandon ideas of joining the worship services there. If they were not going to receive 'spiritual nourishment' from host churches, they would need to find another way. Hence, many found it necessary to create their own alternative spaces for worship. Thus, private living spaces such as bedsits and front rooms became places for worship. Pentecostal migrants hosted the gatherings and invited others to come and share in Christian fellowship. Word of mouth and personal invitations were the main ways of recruiting others, and as the small groups grew, congregations were being formed, and it became necessary to seek out public venues such as school halls and social clubs to accommodate worship.

Church Planting as Mission

The rise of ACP in the post-war years in Britain is significant to Diaspora Missiology. This is because Britain became a mission field for ACPs. Much of this episode of history is known through the existing scholarship and narratives of social scientists,48 through autobiographies,49 and through the writings of Christian authors and academics.50 There is, however, one notable exception:51 most of the denominational histories and literatures have thus far been produced by men. This raises questions about whose voices and perspectives are providing reflections about the past. Would historic writings produced by more women unearth new perspectives on the past? In the meantime, the rise of ACP churches engendered new churches and church leaders, and the growth of both inspired the need to formally organise the congregations. Although an exhaustive historic directory of the variety of early congregations, churches, and denominations that emerged in the post-war years does not exist, the denominational histories that became available helpfully explain early beginnings.52

The first known African Caribbean Pentecostal congregation to start in Britain is understood to be the Calvary Church of God in Christ (CCOGIC), which began in 1952 in the home of Mother McLachlan and her family in Hackney, London. The authorised history of CCOGIC has been thoughtfully documented by one of its contemporary members, Norma Thomas-Juggan.53 Shortly after the founding of CCOGIC, other gatherings were taking place in different locations in Britain. For instance, in 1953, the Church of God of Prophecy (COGOP) began in Bedford.54 In the same year, Oliver Lyseight was founded as the first overseer for the New Testament Church of God (NTCG) in England and Wales,55 which would become the largest of church denominations representative of ACP congregations during the post-war years in Britain. Another church denomination that emerged with strength was the Bethel United Church of Jesus Apostolic (BUCJA), founded by Sydney Alexander Dunn.56 In

---

48 Hill, *West Indian Migrants and the London Churches*; Malcolm J.C. Calley, *God's People: West Indian Pentecostal Sects in England* (London: Oxford University Press, 1965).

49 Curtis Grey, *So I Send You* (Cleveland, Tennessee: Pathway Press, 2014); Fitz. G. Johnson, *Born for a Purpose: Autobiography of Bishop Sydney Alexander Dunn* (Surrey: Grosvenor House, 2016); Oliver A. Lyseight, *Forward March: An Autobiography* (Sedgley, West Midlands: George S. Garwood, 1995).

50 Joe Aldred and Keno Ogbo, *The Black Church in the 21st Century* (London: Darton, Longman and Todd, 2010); Joel Edwards, *Let's Praise Him Again* (Eastbourne: Kingsway, 1992); Ira Brooks, *Where Do We Go from Here?* (London: Charles Raper, 1982); Adedibu, *Coat of Many Colours*.

51 Io Smith and Wendy Green, *An Ebony Cross: Being a Black Christian in Britain Today* (London: Marshall Pickering, 1989); Norma Thomas-Juggan, *Story of the Calvary Church of God in Christ: History, Organisational Structure and Doctrine* (Enfield: Norma Thomas-Juggan, 2000).

52 See for example Brooks, *Where Do We Go from Here?*

53 See Thomas-Juggan, *Story of the Calvary Church of God in Christ.*

54 See B. A. Miles, *When the Church of God Arises: A History of the Development of the Church of God of Prophecy in the Midlands and More Widely in Britain* (Warwickshire: History into Print, 2006).

55 See Brooks, *Where Do We Go from Here?*

56 Johnson, *Born for a Purpose.*

1961, the New Testament Assembly (NTA) would become another church denomination to grow and flourish at a vibrant pace with congregations primarily in London; Melvin Powell and Donald Bernard were the founding leaders.[57] These denominations are some examples of churches that were initiated by African Caribbean migrants in various locations and which grew into a primary locus and a designated place for ACP worship during a critical time in history.

Central to the faith of migrant Pentecostals was the great commission to evangelise all nations,[58] and the theological directives and missionary priorities for ACP congregations were influenced by this command in their approach to church planting and ministry. In assessing church growth and mission, it is difficult to underestimate the role of the spirituality that empowered them, which will be considered later. This brief look, however, at the inauguration of the historic beginnings of the ACP congregations shows that many migrants embraced the new fellowship groups as alternatives spaces, and there were some who arrived as migrants with ideas to plant churches themselves.[59] Some migrants had a clear mandate, a 'divine directive' to address what was believed to be a spiritual void in Britain that was potentially detrimental for Pentecostal migrants.[60]

African Caribbean Pentecostal Congregational Worship

This section considers the important role of congregational worship for ACP congregants. Significantly, congregational worship has been contributory to the growth of ACP churches as the worship event was the place where congregants would seek to meet with God corporately. Despite the importance of congregational worship, systematic research and interpretations is so far scarce. To think that ACP congregations have come of age with only fleeting analysis of its worship is baffling as congregational singing and music is perhaps the most externally visible aspect of ACP, particularly as it has extended beyond the church walls into wider society, recognisable by the formation of 'Black gospel music', a point that I have made elsewhere.[61] Social anthropologist Malcom Calley, in *God's people: West Indian Pentecostal Sects in England,* was perhaps the first to record detailed descriptions of ACP worship based on his observations of the emerging ACP congregations that he visited in the early 1960s.[62]

---

[57] See Richard S. Reddie, *From an Acorn to an Oak Tree: The History of the New Testament Assembly* (London: New Testament Assembly, 2012).
[58] See Matthew 5:15
[59] See Aldred, *Respect*.
[60] See these two autobiographies of pioneers concerned about the spiritual survival of Pentecostal migrants leaving the Caribbean for Britain: Lyseight, *Forward March: An Autobiography*; Johnson, *Born for a Purpose*.
[61] Dulcie Dixon McKenzie, 'Toward Teaching Black Theology through Black Gospel Music in Britain', *Discourse* 8, no. 2 (2009).
[62] Calley, *God's People*.

Significantly, congregational worship has contributed to the growth of ACP churches, for corporate worship in ACP congregations was deemed crucial for the Pentecostal individual and Pentecostal community – it was the place where congregants could meet with God and others.

Looking back, congregational worship was often 'dramatic, performative and transformative'. It was *dramatic*, since there was often, if not always, a series of actions characteristic of theatre that would unfold in stages, such as congregants speaking in tongues (*glossolalia*), a minister or congregant announcing a word of wisdom or knowledge (prophecy), or a few folks 'slain in the Spirit' (to use the Pentecostal language). It was *performative*, since congregants would be encouraged to participate and 'perform' expressively. For example, a song leader, a minister or the preacher would encourage the congregation to 'lift your hands and praise the Lord', or would exclaim: 'somebody shout hallelujah.' Congregational worship was also *transformative*, since there was always time given for prayer requests for healing or a conversion experience. Thus, congregational worship provided an ongoing, consistent and reliable opportunity for individual and communal spiritual encounters.

Congregational worship was, in the main, vibrant, spontaneous, and highly participatory, and there were various services and gatherings scheduled for worship and Christian fellowship: Sunday services (morning and evening), Sunday school, mid-week prayer meetings, Bible studies, fellowship groups, ministry groups, youth services, and special services, which will be considered more broadly in the next section. Singing and praying was key to each gathering, and an important observation is that there was not then, nor is there now, a centrally-agreed liturgical text or hymn book for ACP congregational worship. An assembled or composed 'hymnbook' does not exist. This has perhaps been the case partly because of the range of congregations and denominations that primarily operated with an oral tradition of singing, preaching, praying, and testifying as the core features of their liturgy and theology. ACP congregational worship nevertheless had an informal, yet essential 'singing uniformity' that was distinctive to the collective congregations in Britain, and congregations used designated hymnbooks that were popular in Euro-American congregations in the United States, featuring hymns and gospel songs. Key to the hymnody of the formative years of ACP congregational worship are choruses, which were and continue to be deposited in an oral tradition.[63] Although an agreed hymnbook did not exist for special services, congregations generated their own local 'orders of worship' that included songs. In many cases, as time went on, the production of sophisticated internal programmes and booklets occurred regularly, with a selection of hymns, gospel songs and choruses organised by a theme for each

---

[63] See my PhD dissertation, which makes a case for the preservation of choruses as folksongs. Dulcie A. Dixon McKenzie, 'The Future of the Past: Forging a Historical Context for Black Gospel Music as a Tradition Amongst African Caribbean Pentecostals in Post-War Britain' (PhD, Birmingham, 2014).

event or special service. In terms of 'liturgy', although worship was characterised by an oral tradition, there was, nevertheless, a discernible knowledge of an oral liturgy, evidenced by a collective anticipation of what was to come next. Thus, there was a shared understanding of an oral liturgy that provided an apparent structure and sequence.[64]

Congregational Worship and Fundraising

Some congregational worship services had an emphasis on singing and music for participatory-performance[65] by congregational members, and these services were instrumental in raising funds for church building projects. Funds were raised by visitation and support from fellow church leaders and congregations to special worship services that were held. Visiting leaders and congregations would attend and would also come with plans to participate by preparing an 'item' to share with the congregation. The 'item' for participation would come in different forms, such as songs to be performed by choirs, groups, duets and solos, and 'non-musical contributions' such as skits, poems, Bible readings, testimonies, and sermonettes. The 'items' of worship would shape the liturgy for the various services, such as annual and periodic conventions, frequent crusades, revival meetings, building programs, and rallies. Raising funds at these services was a liturgical act, seen as an opportunity to bring monetary gifts and offerings towards church building funds.

Also of significance here is how these special services played a major role in nurturing the musical talents of congregants. For many, such services were the first place in which they were exposed to other churches outside of their congregation.[66] Initially, music in church services was carried out by congregants who brought their own tambourines, shakers and cymbals, and they played as they worshipped. Some congregants were aspiring musicians and had their own musical instruments, such as a banjos, acoustic guitars and piano accordions. In these cases, the instrument-players became the designated church musicians. This would change dramatically once the second generation became the church musicians, which is another fascinating area for a future research project.

---

[64] Edwards, *Let's Praise Him Again.*

[65] Using the word 'performance' in this context is possibly problematic. A preferred term would be 'ministry', e.g. to minister in song.

[66] For more on this, see my unpublished PhD thesis: McKenzie, 'The Future of the Past: Forging a Historical Context for Black Gospel Music as a Tradition Amongst African Caribbean Pentecostals in Post-War Britain'. Also the forthcoming book, *Black Gospel Music in Britain,* Dulcie Dixon McKenzie

African Caribbean Pentecostal Spirituality

In a short book that introduces Black Pentecostal spirituality, *The Reason Why We Sing*,[67] British born Pentecostal scholar, Clifton Clarke, helpfully outlines some of the features of spirituality characteristic of ACPs. Clarke is careful to point out that for ACPs, spirituality is not cerebral and intellectual; rather, it flourishes within songs, dance and folklore.[68] The emphasis here is upon the sources that stimulate spirituality, with the Holy Spirit being most central, acting as an inner friendly force as the Pentecostal adherent is encouraged to pursue a personal encounter with the Holy Spirit.[69] This implies an expectation for the ACP adherent to maintain a personal relationship with the Holy Spirit in order to sustain power for ministry and mission. Looking back at the post-war years, ACPs pursued a personal spirituality that helped them to survive life's various challenges, and, primarily, to live a life of Christian discipleship that was key to their understanding of an ongoing process of sanctification in their lives; this was the requirement of holy living as they understood it. They recognised the role of the Holy Spirit purifying them as believers, and were uncomfortable with the notion of a spirituality that was not transformative.[70] Key to this, then, was an ongoing pursuit of personal spiritual growth; and guidelines and encouragement for a sanctified life and godly living would be found in the Bible. As keen readers of the Bible, they used personal daily Bible readings to search for direction and consolation, and memorised verses that they could quote when needed throughout the day.[71] In short, ACPs strived for a 'lived experience of faith.'[72]

Whilst personal spirituality was an individual pursuit and responsibility, ACPs also adhered to a communal spirituality, also referred to as 'The Pentecostal Community'.[73] This meant that they had a strong accountability and connection to their church congregation. Congregants received teachings of doctrinal guidelines from their church. Although accountability was ultimately before God, should the church teachings be contravened, church members were faced with exclusion or expulsion from the congregation. What is referred to as 'Pentecostal community' perhaps translates to a church denomination or congregation serving as a tool for accountability or enforcement to help maintain a sanctified life, cohesion and conformity to the processes followed by the majority of believers.[74] Accordingly, members strived to live a holy life – one that revolved around church, doing activities that would include members of

---

[67] Clifton Clarke, *Reason Why We Sing: Introducing Black Pentecostal Spirituality* (Cambridge: Grove, 1997).
[68] Clarke, *Reason Why We Sing*, 4.
[69] Clarke, *Reason Why We Sing*, 11.
[70] Keith Warrington, *Pentecostal Theology: A Theology of Encounter* (London: T & T Clark, 2008), 210.
[71] Warrington, *Pentecostal Theology*, 208.
[72] Miller and Yamaamori, *Global Pentecostalism*.
[73] Warrington, *Pentecostal Theology*, 208.
[74] Warrington, *Pentecostal Theology*, 208-09.

their church community, and with discretion expected of them in their friendships with 'unbelievers' who, it was feared, might influence them inappropriately. For example, activities associated with unbelievers or people of 'the world' included smoking, drinking alcohol, going to the cinema, dancing, and gambling. In sum, there was a strong emphasis on morality and abstinence from certain activities – a striving for a 'lived experience of faith'.[75]

Concluding Reflections

This chapter has aimed to paint a picture of the circumstances for African Caribbean migrants as they pioneered ACP as a movement in post-war Britain. The descriptions were employed to bolster appreciation and/or curiosity about their experience, knowledge and spirituality. At the heart of this discussion is a concern that there appears to be an implicit lack of cerebral interest in the intricate details of the formative years of ACP, which itself emerged at a difficult time in British history. The fact that a collective group of enthusiastic, passionate and Spirit-filled individuals overcame racism and intolerance to defy obstacles to their spiritual wellbeing would seem to mark it a worthy phenomenon of the past for deep interrogation. The growth of the movement in Britain is also significant to global Christianity; and yet, by examining the literature that has so far been produced about the movement, the attention globally is startlingly partial, and where ACP is discussed in British literature, material is either comparatively brief (merged as a narrative with other Pentecostal experiences) or included in wider discussions around mission and Black Majority Churches. Christian writers have so far provided official versions of denominational histories, and notably, all accounts regarding ACP history appear to have been written by men (with one known exception). This raises questions about what has been recorded, and about what might yet to be recovered concerning the past and about ACP as a movement, which, it must be said, involved the experience of men, women and children.

In short, maybe there are more details of ACP history yet to be recovered and recorded. Thus, the main purpose of this chapter is to encourage scholars, church communities and observers to identify areas of interest or concern regarding the formative years of ACP, and to interrogate the past for the benefit of the present and future generations. The main reason for encouraging more cognizance of the past is to empower the current and future generations with the heritage of ACP. This issue combines three important areas concerning Christian mission – namely, history, heritage and theology. To be specific, and as this chapter concludes, it might be helpful to frame the three areas as a thought-provoking question: How might all members of this current generation be encouraged to recover more details of the past (history) in order to use these historical details

---

[75] Miller and Yamaamori, *Global Pentecostalism.*

today (heritage) to develop a deeper understanding of God's actions in the past, and to strengthen faith in the present and future (theology)?

References

Adedibu, Babatunde. *Coat of Many Colours: The Origin, Growth, Distinctiveness and Contributions of Black Majority Churches to British Christianity*. Gloucester: Wisdom Summit, 2012.

Adedibu, Babatunde Aderemi. "African and Caribbean Pentecostalism in Britain." Chap. 2 In *Pentecostals and Charismatics in Britain: An Anthology*, edited by Joe Aldred, 19-33. London: SCM, 2019.

Aldred, Joe, ed. *Pentecostals and Charismatics in Britain: An Anthology*. London: SCM Press, 2019.

Aldred, Joe. *Respect: Understanding Caribbean British Christianity*. Peterborough: Epworth, 2005.

Aldred, Joe, and Keno Ogbo. *The Black Church in the 21st Century*. London: Darton, Longman and Todd, 2010.

Alexander, Estrelda Y., ed. *The Dictionary of Pan-African Pentecostalism, Volume 1: North America*. Eugene, Oregon: Cascade Books, 2018.

Anderson, Allan. *Spreading Fires: The Missionary Nature of Early Pentecostalism*. Maryknoll, New York: Orbis Books, 2007.

Anderson, Allan, Michael Bergunder, Andre Droogers, and Cornelis van der Laan, eds. *Studying Global Pentecostalism: Theories and Methods*. London: University of California Press, 2010.

Anderson, Allan Heaton. *An Introduction to Pentecostalism*. Cambridge: Cambridge University Press, 2014.

Ashworth, G.J., Brian Graham, and J.E. Tunbridge. *Pluralising Pasts: Heritage, Identity and Place in Multicultural Societies*. London: Pluto Press, 2007.

Barton, Mukti. *Rejection, Resistance and Resurrection: Speaking out on Racism in the Church*. London: Darton, Logan and Todd, 2005.

Beckford, Robert. *Dread and Pentecostal: A Political Theology for the Black Church in Britain*. London: SPCK, 2000.

Bendix, Regina F. *Culture and Value: Tourism, Heritage and Property*. Indiana: Indiana University Press, 2018.

Brooks, Ira. *Where Do We Go from Here*. London: Charles Raper, 1982.

Burgess, Stanley M., and Eduard M. Van Der Maas, eds. *The New International Dictionary of Pentecostal and Charismatic Movements: Revised and Expanded Edition*. Michigan: Zondervan, 2003.

Calley, Malcolm J.C. *God's People: West Indian Pentecostal Sects in England*. London: Oxford University Press, 1965.

Clarke, Clifton. *Reason Why We Sing: Introducing Black Pentecostal Spirituality*. Cambridge: Grove, 1997.

Clarke, Clifton R. *Pentecostalism: Insights from African and the African Diaspora*. Eugene, Oregon: Cascade Books, 2018.

Corsane, Gerard, ed. *Heritage, Museums and Galleries: An Introductory Reader*. London: Routledge, 2005.

Edwards, Joel. *Let's Praise Him Again*. Eastbourne: Kingsway, 1992.

Gerloff, Roswith I. H. *A Plea for British Black Theologies: The Black Church Movement in Britain in Its Transatlantic Cultural and Theological Interaction*. 2 vols. Vol. 1, New York: Peter Lang, 1992.

Grey, Curtis. *So I Send You*. Cleveland, Tennessee: Pathway Press, 2014.

Hill, Clifford S. *West Indian Migrants and the London Churches*. London: Open University Press, 1963.

Hunter, Harold D., and Neil Ormerod, eds. *The Many Faces of Global Pentecostalism*. Cleveland, Tennessee: CPT Press, 2013.

James, Winston, and Clive Harris, eds. *Inside Babylon: The Caribbean Diaspora in Britain*. London: Verso, 1993.

Johnson, Fitz. G. *Born for a Purpose: Autobiography of Bishop Sydney Alexander Dunn*. Surrey: Grosvenor House, 2016.

Kay, William K. *Pentecostalism*. London: SCM Press, 2009.

Lyseight, Oliver A. *Forward March: An Autobiography*. Sedgley, West Midlands: George S. Garwood, 1995.

MacRobert, Iain. "The Black Roots of Pentecostalism." Chap. 295-309 In *African-American Religion: Interpretive Essays in History and Culture*, edited by Timothy E. Fulop and Albert J. Raboteau. New York: Routledge, 1997.

McKenzie, Dulcie A. Dixon. "The Future of the Past: Forging a Historical Context for Black Gospel Music as a Tradition Amongst African Caribbean Pentecostals in Post-War Britain." PhD, Birmingham, 2014.

McKenzie, Dulcie Dixon. "Toward Teaching Black Theology through Black Gospel Music in Britain." *Discourse* 8, no. 2 (2009): 127-71.

Miles, B. A. *When the Church of God Arises: A History of the Development of the Church of God of Prophecy in the Midlands and More Widely in Britain*. Warwickshire: History into Print, 2006.

Miller, Donald E., and Tetsunao Yamaamori. *Global Pentecostalism: The New Face of Christian Social Engagement*. London: University of California Press, 2007.

Morrison, Doreen. *Ruled Britainnia: Jamaican Christianity's Interregnum 1866-2016*. slaverysheroes@gmail.com: Liele Books, 2018.

Olofinjana, Israel. *Reverse in Ministry and Missions: Africans in the Dark Continent of Europe – An Historical Study of African Churches in Europe*. Milton Keynes: Author House, 2010.

Olofinjana, Israel Oluwole. *Partnership in Mission: A Black Majority Church Perspective on Mission and Church Unity*. Herts: Instant Apostle, 2015.

Olusoga, David. *Black and British: A Forgotten History*. London: Macmillan, 2016.

Phillips, Mike, and Trevor Phillips. *Windrush: The Irresistible Rise of Multi-Racial Britain*. London: HarperCollins, 1998.

Reddie, Anthony. "Churches." In *The Oxford Companion to Black British History*, edited by David Dabydeen, John Gilmore and Cecily Jones, 100-04. Oxford: Oxford University Press, 2007.

Reddie, Richard S. *From an Acorn to an Oak Tree; the History of the New Testament Assembly*. London: New Testament Assembly, 2012.

Safran, William. "Diasporas in Modern Societies: Myths of Homeland and Return." *Diaspora: A Journal of Transnational Studies* 1, no. 1 (1991): 83-99.

Salvatore, Cecilia Lizama. *Cultural Heritage Care and Management: Theory and Practice*. London: Rowan & Littlefield, 2018.

Sanneh, Lamin. *Whose Religion Is Christianity? The Gospel Beyond the West*. Grand Rapids, MI: William B. Eerdmans, 2003.

Smith, Io, and Wendy Green. *An Ebony Cross: Being a Black Christian in Britain Today*. London: Marshall Pickering, 1989.

Snyder, Susanna. *Asylum-Seeking, Migration and Church: Explorations in Practical, Pastoral and Empirical Theology*. New York: Routledge, 2012.

Stephenson, Christopher A. *Types of Pentecostal Theology: Method, System, Spirit.* Oxford: Oxford University Press, 2013.

Sturge, Mark. *Look What the Lord Has Done: An Exploration of Black Christian Faith in Britain.* Milton Keynes: Scripture Union, 2005.

Synan, Vinson, Amos Yong, and Miguel Alvarez, eds. *Global Renewal Christianity* Vol. 2, Latin America. Lake Mary, Florida: Charisma House, 2016.

Thomas-Juggan, Norma. *Story of the Calvary Church of God in Christ: History, Organisational Structure and Doctrine.* Enfield: Norma Thomas-Juggan, 2000.

Trotman, Arlington. "Black, Black-Led or What?". In *Let's Praise Him Again*, edited by Joel Edwards, 12-35. Eastbourne: Kingsway, 1992.

Vondey, Wolfgang. *Pentecostal Theology: Living the Full Gospel.* London: Bloomsbury T & T Clark, 2017.

Walsh, Arlene M. Sanchez. *Latino Pentecostal Identity: Evangelical Faith, Self, and Society.* New York: Columbia Unversity Press, 2003.

Walton, Heather. *A Tree God Planted: Black People in British Methodism.* London: Ethnic Minorities in Methodism Working Group, 1985.

Warrington, Keith. *Pentecostal Perspectives.* Carlisle, Cumbria: Paternoster Press, 1998.

Warrington, Keith. *Pentecostal Theology: A Theology of Encounter.* London: T & T Clark, 2008.

Wilkinson, John L. *Church in Black and White.* Edinburgh: Saint Andrew Press, 1993.

Yong, Amos, and Estrelda Y. Alexander, eds. *Afro-Pentecostalism: Black Pentecostal and Charismatic Christianity in History and Culture.* New York: New York University Press, 2011.

Online Sources

British Library: https://www.bl.uk/windrush/themes/the-windrush-generation-scandal Windrush Scandal (accessed 23.8.19)

The Church of England website, *"I too am CofE"* video presentation to Synod: https://www.churchofengland.org/more/policy-and-thinking/our-views/race-and-ethnicity (accessed 23.8.19)

National Geographic, Introduction to Human Migration: https://www.nationalgeographic.org/activity/introduction-human-migration/ (accessed 26.6.19).

Section Two

Missional Narratives

(6) Stories of Reverse Missionaries: A Brazilian Missionary Couple in Britain
Flavio Gurattos

Background: Life in Brazil

This chapter reflects my missionary journeys in Europe, which included England, Scotland and Italy. My story is one example that serves to illustrate the reverse flow of missions from Latin America to Europe. The story challenges the notion that all migrants are economic migrants. Contrasting this idea, my wife and I came to Europe as missionary migrants responding to God's call. We left good jobs and a good life in Brazil to pursue God's call in the UK.

I was born in the fast-growing city of Uberlandia, in the south-central part of Brazil. More specifically, it is in the western part of the vast state of Minas Gerais, located between Sao Paulo (Brazil's financial capital) and Brasilia (its political capital). Today, it has approximately 700,000 inhabitants and is the fourth-largest city in the interior of Brazil, and the twelfth most populous city in the country. But Brazil is big, and Uberlandia is amongst plenty of other fast-developing cities, excepting Sao Paulo and Rio de Janeiro. It is not in the jungle as most Western people think. Uberlandia has become an important business hub over the years, not due to soccer tournaments or because it is the city where the seat of government is located, but because it has generated considerable growth in private sectors such as agribusiness, oil and gas, industries, telecommunications, IT, and ports and logistics.

Religious Background

My father came from an Italian family and moved from Sao Paulo in the 1950s to start a furniture industry there. He became one of the directors of Uberlandia's chamber of commerce in the 1960s, and one of the visionaries in the development of the city's industrial district. My mother was a very skilful wedding dress maker. I grew up in this middle-class family during Brazil's military regime, when the world was in the midst of the cold war. My family had no religious background or practice whatsoever, except my grandmother, who was a devout Roman Catholic. My friends and I tried quite a variety of spiritual experiments in spiritism,[1] candomblé,[2] Roman Catholic pilgrimages, mind control and so on.

After my father's sudden death, my life changed quite dramatically. I had to stop my studies overnight and take over the family business, which by then was not doing very well. (It was Brazil's dead economic decade, and there was hyperinflation in the 1970s and 1980s.) I thank God for this extremely challenging experience, and I am happy to say that in five years I successfully led the company's turnaround from imminent bankruptcy to a stable position of profitability and growth. This experience tested my integrity to its limits, but proved it is possible to remain ethical, yet still achieve results amid a widespread business culture of corruption.

Many things happened throughout this process. My friends and I drank quite heavily, which led to taking drugs, initially on most weekends, but it soon became regular. The fact is that binge drinking, smoking weed and taking some cocaine (or whatever else) made me feel stronger and better, even if that was short-lived. It was fun. I felt my intense stress and deep insecurity fall away for a night at least. Soon we were in the pattern of saying: 'Monday to Wednesday you tell yourself you won't do it this weekend; Thursday you feel OK; Friday you're back on form.' This went on for many years until I was really tired and empty inside, but I kept this frustration with me.

Salvation amid the Beginnings of What
Would Become a Widespread Revival in Brazil

The mother of one of my best friends was saved and started a prayer group in her house, and my friends and I were among their weekly prayer topics. At his mum's request, my friend went to a small church plant, liked it, and one day invited me to attend it with him. I refused the invitation many times, as I did not like evangelical Christians: I thought they were backward, weak, fanatical, and narrow-minded, and that anybody who joined that bunch would be stripped of everything in life that is fun. Yet he insisted so much that I finally decided to attend a Sunday morning meeting. This was a church plant from Uberlandia's Central Presbyterian Church, which was held at one of the elder's homes. I sat at the very back of the meeting, ready to leave when anything said or sung displeased me. But God had other plans, and that day proved to be the biggest and most important day of my life. The relaxed atmosphere and the environment of hospitality, love and honest friendship began to open my heart and captivate my tired soul. The message touched my heart: it was all about my inner life, my emptiness inside, my constant search for meaning and purpose, which were all

---

[1] Spiritism postulates that humans are essentially immortal spirits that temporarily inhabit physical bodies throughout several necessary incarnations for the purpose of attaining moral and intellectual improvement.

[2] This is a widespread Afro-American religious tradition in Brazil.

addressed in a way that I had never heard them addressed before. I broke down in tears and tried unsuccessfully to hide it. The invitation to be totally forgiven and to start a brand new life, with my sins forgiven, my past cleansed, and myself in total reconciliation with God won my heart completely. This was the biggest, most unexpected and unplanned turnaround of my life. That morning, I accepted Christ as my only and sufficient saviour. I was born again (I did not know these terms then).

I later came to learn that thousands of young adults like me were going through the same radical transformation. I was born again amid an unprecedented revival in our land that is still going on to this day.

I had a hunger to learn the Bible and the ways of God. Also, some of my friends and I who were saved around the same time started evangelising everyone we met. Besides our discipleship lessons, we were encouraged to explore spiritual gifts and natural abilities to share the gospel. We started a weekly program to visit secondary public schools and tell our stories. Principals of these schools did not want any religious messages, but they were desperate for anything that could encourage young people to avoid drugs. Therefore, we always started with our own stories of how we had been set free from regular drug and alcohol abuse by the power of the gospel. We saw thousands of students give their lives to Christ, and we loved it.

Early Days of Ministry

The church's group for young people founded a School of Arts and Media to equip the new converts to share the gospel through creative means. Later on, we founded a small TV studio, where we recorded 15-minute gospel programs which were broadcasted on a regional TV station. Also, a local gospel radio station and a recording studio were set up. On a monthly basis, we hired the central theatre, where we held the School of Art's presentations, followed by a testimony of gospel transformation. Then we became more ambitious and hired the theatre every week, and then every day for two consecutive years. Thousands of young adults heard the gospel through this program, and hundreds accepted Jesus publicly.

This deep passion to spread the gospel drove our church growth from about 60 people to 600 in a couple of years, mostly through radical conversions. Week after week, dozens kept giving their lives to Christ, and were baptised in the water and in the Holy Spirit. Alongside that, we started our first charity work, which looked after children at social risk and several other church planting initiatives. My first missionary trip was to Manaus, the capital of Brazil's northern state of Amazon, where we embarked on a small hospital boat and went down the majestic Negro River to start a project which provided essential medical and dental care to remote communities near the river, as well as to help missionaries with their work. This was our church's first church-to-church partnership with the Presbyterian Church of Manaus.

Around the same period, I started dating a lady named Karen (who is now my wife), and together we were encouraged to start a home group where young adults came to worship and learn the scriptures. Soon, a parallel, two-year Bible Institute program came along to further equip the growing number of young leaders.

Besides the ever-growing work in the church, I was in charge of a wood manufactory company, which, as mentioned above, had undergone a major turnaround and was now expanding. As both my ministry in the church and my company continued to expand, I knew that I had to make a tough decision between being a businessman and a full-time church leader.

Missionary Call and another Major and Unexpected Change

In 1992, my senior pastor, Paulo Borges Junior, visited some young Christians in London, and God stirred his spirit as he learned about the severe decline in church attendance, about church buildings closing down or being sold, about an increasing presence of world religions, and about the many leaders crying out for a new revival. God told him clearly that the church in Brazil is the spiritual child of the UK church, as it had sent thousands of missionaries to Brazil (as well as to many other nations in the world). In fact the first Portuguese-speaking church, *Igreja Evangélica Fluminense*, was planted by Robert and Sarah Kalley in Rio de Janeiro around 1855. Paulo felt God telling him that now was the time for the Brazilian churches to send missionaries to the UK as a token of gratitude for their missionary efforts in the past. He later met Reverend Boyd Williams, a Baptist Church pastor from Southall, west London, and invited him to come to Brazil and reveal the situation in the UK to local Brazilian pastors. Pastor Paulo sent some post cards to a few leaders of our church, challenging them prayerfully to consider becoming missionaries in London. My wife Karen and I were among the leaders that received the post cards. It is important to mention here that we had a comfortable life in Brazil at this particular time, and responding to this call was going to be a sacrifice. My wife had come from a very united family, and from a very wealthy background, having lived in a 600 square-meter house with several maids, a swimming pool, a sauna and the like. She was doing her first year of a degree programme at the Federal University, our ministry in the church was fast growing in every direction, and my company was doing very well. We had been married for three months and had no idea what a missionary was, and neither of us had any plans whatsoever to become one. There was no reason for any change, at least in our plans. But we learned to listen to our leaders, and most of all listen to the voice of God. We began to pray seriously about this, not knowing that our lives were just about to be radically changed.

At that time, Uberlandia was hosting a quarterly nationwide leader's prayer meeting. Many of the participants, like us, had been experiencing exponential growth through radical conversions. Boyd Williams came to one of these meetings later on in that year and spoke about the situation of the British church, calling the Brazilian churches represented there to 'help their spiritual fathers in the United Kingdom'. All who were present on that day knew that they were under a very strong conviction that God was calling that group to start a missionary movement, in which local Brazilian churches would send missionaries to London, and would seek to partner with UK churches and together do missionary work in other nations. A lot of prayer and pondering ensued, and the final decision was made that seven families from six churches involved in the nationwide unity movement were to be set apart, prepared and sent to Southall Baptist Church in west London. This mission movement came to be known as the Go To The Nations Movement.

Our church was one of those tasked to set apart two families to complete the pioneering group. One was to be the church's main worship leader, a former professor of IT in Uberlandia's Federal University. The other was going to be one of the leaders of the young people, either Karen and me, or another couple who led the young adults in our church, Olgalvaro and Fabiana. After praying about it for a while, Karen and I felt strongly that God was calling us to join the adventure. This was going to have huge implications for our families, my company, her studies and so on. We accepted the challenge, and our lives have never been the same.

Karen and I had no reason whatsoever to leave our beloved city of Uberlandia, our family, our friends, our work, her studies and our fast-growing church – no reason, that is, except to obey this divine call and embark on a life-changing adventure. In human terms, there was no reason to make such a move. Economically, we had well-paying jobs and access to capital; spiritually, we were in the midst of a historical revival in our country; academically, Karen was at the beginning of her long-awaited career; culturally, we were in our comfort zone. When we began to share this vision to move abroad to do Christian missionary work with our family and friends, most of whom were non-Christians, we had to answer reasonable questions like: Why would we leave all this and go to a land we do not know, and learn a language and culture we do not know? Why would we learn to live as immigrants, as foreigners? We did not have any other reason except our desire to obey God's voice, to follow his direction, and to experience a much deeper level of dependence on him. For both of us, there was a strong sense of adventure, of being pioneers in something fresh that the Holy Spirit was doing in our nation and in our local church.

Arriving in the United Kingdom as Missionaries

After a couple of months of preparation, and many very emotional farewells, we left our family, our friends, our home city, our culture and our lifestyle behind. Like the patriarchs in the Old Testament – wandering Arameans – we travelled abroad for the very first time and landed in London's Heathrow airport on 29th April 1993 to join five other Brazilian missionary families, who had arrived in January. We joined Southall Baptist Church, a small congregation totally surrounded by huge Mosques and Hindu and Sikh temples in west London. Karen and I were enrolled in the beginners' class of the church's School of Languages. Everything was so alien to us – the weather, the traffic on the left-hand side, the highly multicultural communities, living out of two pieces of luggage, sharing a house with another family, using public transport for the first time in our lives (we were given two bikes later on), the absence of friends and family, and the exciting atmosphere of revival. Despite the personal disorientation, the unfamiliar way of life, the extremely different social environment, the feelings of confusion and uncertainty, the sense of deep alienation, the initial cultural shock, and the challenges and difficulties we faced, somehow God made it feel fun and adventurous, which made us willing to go through the process of transition, adjustment and accommodation.

At that time, the internet was at its beginnings. Owning a laptop was a luxury, and there was no Google or Safari, no multi-task handsets, and no mobile GPS. We used letters and fax machines to communicate to our family and church; we navigated in the city using a book called *London A to Z*, which was basically a detailed map that included every road in London.

Our first goal was to learn the language from scratch. This was an incredibly tough job, but without doing it, our mission was not going to be effective at all.

Soon after our arrival, we learned that the church had not baptised anybody for many years – something very unusual to us – and I remember it took months before I was invited to greet the church congregation; and I was only given two minutes to do so (with translation, it became just one). In many ways, we felt as if the hand-brake of our ministry had suddenly been pushed on and we had made an abrupt stop. Our first assigned task as missionaries was to clean a hidden garden in the back of the church building. Our team spent a lot of time getting to know one another, praying and discerning our new mission field. We had come from different churches, (some of us) from different cities, and from diverse backgrounds, and we had to spend time strengthening the relationships within our team.

We were able to communicate with majority of the Christians we encountered (usually through translators). However, some people struggled to understand that missionaries were now coming from the Majority World to the UK to help British churches; some clearly were upset by the idea, and argued that the UK church had always been a sending church and did not need foreign missionaries to help – especially missionaries from the southern hemisphere. The first white English church leader to state publicly that in his view we were sent by God and that the church in England was in deep need of help was Richard Plummer from Lewisham in south-east London. He was so convinced of this point that he began devoting a lot of his time to coming from south-east to west London just to meet us, hear our story, and learn about our call, our gifts and our vision. He also began introducing us to many other pastors and leaders in London, and it was really through him that we began to feel a sense of welcome and fulfilment in our mission.

Twice a year the leaders of our churches in Brazil would come to London to bring encouragement, pastoral guidance and counselling. We would pray together and gather with the British pastors with whom we had been in contact. We also sought to discern a team strategy in line with the vision. It was an intense season of learning for us – and the learning curve was steep.

Icthus Christian Fellowship and Mission to Azerbaijan

Richard Plummer introduced us to a London-based church called Icthus Christian Fellowship, one of the Charismatic churches led at the time by Roger Foster and Roger Mitchell. This was clearly a missionary-focused church, and a good fit for our vision. After the initial introductory meetings and explanations of our mutual vision, our team was invited to join their missionary team on a trip to Azerbaijan. We promptly accepted the invitation with huge excitement. I confessed that I had never heard about that country.

Azerbaijan has a very rich history. Situated at the crossroads of south-west Asia and south-eastern Europe, it was the first democratic state in the Muslim-oriented world. The country was incorporated into the Soviet Union in 1920 and proclaimed its independence on 30th August 1991, prior to the official dissolution of the USSR. At the time, the country was at war with Armenia over the Nagorno-Karabakh region, with about 1 million refugees from the war. At the time of our trip, the country was being disputed by the forces of the USSR, Muslims who wanted it to become an Islamic Republic, democratic nations, and multi-nationals who were after its vast oil reserves. The church in the country had been suppressed by the USSR regime and was very small and accustomed to suffering and timidity. We were told by the local leaders that ours was one of the first Christian missionary teams to have come after the country's independence from the communist regime. This was our vision becoming reality. We were part of a multi-national team with people from England, Brazil, Indonesia and the USA, going together from the UK to other nations. Our mission was to take Bibles in Azeri, the local language, which were very rare at the time, and to pray and, if possible, conduct open air evangelism. This was pre-globalisation and pre- 9/11, and travelling and communication were much more difficult and expensive than they are now. We went through Istanbul, which in itself was an adventure as we went through various security checks but still managed to get the Bibles through. The trip ended up being incredibly successful. An Icthus missionary received us and organised our schedule, which basically consisted of praying for about six hours every day, meeting local Christians and pastors, attending services, and looking for evangelistic opportunities.

The first opportunity came after a Sunday service. Together with local believers, we walked to an area in the outskirts of the capital, known for high levels of alcohol consumption. We stopped at a courtyard about 100 yards from a big mosque. A small crowd gathered, and we had a very basic battery-powered sound system. The local Christians sang some songs in Azeri, a young girl read a poem,[3] and I had the privilege of sharing my story, which was translated into Turkish and Azeri.[4] About ten people came forward to receive prayer, and we were told this was likely the first open air evangelistic meeting to have taken place in the last 100 years in that nation (since it had been totally forbidden under the Communist regime). We were thrilled to hear this, and felt encouraged to look for other similar opportunities. The next opportunity came in a large public square, opposite the Turkish embassy. A bigger crowd gathered around us. This time we sang songs in English, our leader shared a message in Turkish,[5] and we prayed for people who had been sick. Two of these people witnessed to having been instantly healed after we prayed with them.

We managed to have five open air evangelism gatherings in various squares in the city of Baku. We prayed between four and five hours every day, either in our apartment or in various areas of the capital city. Our apartment was invaded by two soldiers who identified themselves as being from the KGB and asked for our passports and telephone. Our team leader arrived at this point and was able to talk to them in Turkish. We had to move from that apartment in order not to compromise our host.

There is Hope, Bill Cowie and Scotland

After our return from Azerbaijan, at the end of October 1993, we were introduced to Richard Iredale and Bill Cowie, from There is Hope and Leith Baptist Church in Edinburgh. They both came all the way from Scotland to meet us, and to explore possible partnerships between Brazilian churches and Scottish churches. This invitation changed the whole dynamic of the vision and expanded our horizon within the United Kingdom. The first Portuguese-speaking church planted on Brazilian soil around 1855 was planted in Rio de Janeiro by Robert Reid Kalley (1809-1888), a Scottish missionary known as the Wolf from Scotland. The opportunity to engage in missionary activity in Scotland therefore reflects a reverse flow of missions. My home church derived from a Presbyterian Church, and this new prospect in Scotland had a very strong appeal to my leaders in Brazil. Richard Iredale and Bill Cowie organised a conference for pastors and leaders and invited our team to be the main speakers. Five leaders from my home church attended, including my senior pastor Paulo Junior. It was the very first time my wife and I saw snow – and there was a lot of it. After the conference, three churches made official offers to receive missionaries from our team. We returned to London and shared this with the rest of the team, and after much prayer and discussion, a decision was made that part of the original team would remain in Southall Baptist Church, and the other part would to go to Edinburgh.

---

[3] This is common in that culture.
[4] I had been learning English for just six months.
[5] Most Azeris understood Turkish.

The team in London was to focus its efforts on church-planting initiatives in continental Europe, Azerbaijan and beyond, and the team in Scotland was to explore church-to-church partnerships in the United Kingdom.

Move from London to Edinburgh, Scotland

My wife and I stayed in London for another three months and moved to Scotland to work alongside Bill Cowie in Leith Baptist Church in the former port area of the city. One of the main highlights of our time in Edinburgh was our practice of gathering with pastors from a diverse spectrum of denominations and backgrounds for early morning prayer meetings on top of Carlton Hill every Thursday at 7 am. These meetings continued uninterrupted for more than ten years, which is quite remarkable considering the weather conditions in Scotland. Sometimes we had ten pastors praying; on other occasions, around 60. We had 100 people gather for prayers around the time of the so-called Toronto Blessing.

Together with the church's group of young adults, we went to Albania in 1994 – just after the end of the communist regime in that country – and to the northern Borneo Island region of Sarawak, where we spend four weeks with Sarawak's native people, the Ibans. Less than a century ago, the state was still the personal fiefdom of Sir Charles Brooke, greatest of the white Rajahs of Sarawak, who saw himself as the protector of the Ibans' way of life. Although he led ferocious punitive expeditions to eradicate headhunting, he did everything he could to preserve the Ibans' local customs and animist beliefs. In Brooke's account of the people and their practices, he makes it clear that for the Ibans, a human head was the ultimate aphrodisiac – an object which ensured the fertility of his land and the wealth of his household, and which made the murder irresistible. It did not matter who it originally belonged to – man, woman or child – once a head had been lopped off, its spirit then became the property of the hunter. What I found when I went there was completely different. After travelling many hours by plane and seven hours in a car, we finally got to the villages and find out that all of the people across the villages were Christians. This was owed to the missionary work of an Australian couple. Today there are more than 600 local churches spread all over the region, all of them pastored by locals. It is an incredible story of God's power and grace but also of immense missionary sacrifice. I had the privilege of being the main preacher of the Millennium Conference in the city of Miri, which was attended by thousands of Christians from this family of churches.

Bill Cowie became one of the important leaders of the Go To The Nations movement. He was the key leader not only in Scotland, but also in the United Kingdom and beyond. I took several teams of Scottish Christians to Brazil to visit our churches there and to build partnerships. Leith Baptist Church became the main partner of one of our congregations in the state of Goias, and a crucial supporter of a social action project called Vida Criança, which rescues vulnerable young children from the streets, places them in a house, and provides educational, financial, emotional and psychological support. This support continues to this day, and many young lives have completely turned around for good through this work.[6]

Raising Awareness, More Missionaries, and Prayer Support in Brazil

My wife and I were called by our senior pastor to return to Brazil in 1997 to strengthen this vision in Brazil by mobilizing people in prayer, developing more missionaries and equipping churches. During this time, my wife finished her university degree, and we had our daughter. I was one of five pastors of Sal da Terra's mother church, and was in charge of missions, prayer, teaching and the apostolic team. Our main strategy for spreading that vision was to organise two international conferences, one in Brazil and another one in the United Kingdom. In these conferences, a vision was cast, and church leaders were encouraged to meet one another, spend time together, and, through prayer, find out if there was something more beyond having a good time together. Several other partnerships between Brazilian and British churches were initiated and developed around that time as a result of the conferences. Churches in Hereford, Gloucester, Coventry, Birmingham, Harrogate, Leeds, Bognor Regis, Bolton, Manchester and London partnered with Brazilian churches. A lot of hard work and prayer went into these cross-cultural ventures. The October teams were successfully brought from Brazil to the UK in consecutive years from 1993 to 2012. In 1997, we managed to mobilise and bring 197 Brazilian Christian leaders and intercessors to the Go To The Nations Conference in Manchester. From there, we split into five teams, and each of them went to a different capital in the United Kingdom to pray together with the churches there. We then split them into 16 smaller teams and went to 16 European capital cities, all in partnership with Christians leaders in Europe.

These conferences in Brazil brought together thousands of leaders from various nations and from almost every region in Brazil. We also thought of spreading the vision to continental Europe, especially to Portugal and Germany. It later became possible for Brazilian missionaries to work at both of these two countries in particular as a result of partnerships between Brazilian, British and German churches.

As part of the national *Ide as Nações* (Go To The Nations) team, I travelled extensively across the country, preaching in mission conferences, seminars and Sunday services. My task (together with many others) of proving to Christian leaders that Europe was a mission field was not an easy one, but by the grace of God, from 1997 to 2002, Karen and I brought more than 250 Christian leaders to the UK and Europe on short-term mission trips. As a result, ten churches officially engaged in this process, establishing partnerships and sending missionaries to be based in UK churches.

---

6 Bill Cowie is semi-retired and is a Brazilian pastor. He was part of the Go To The Nations movement, and is the senior minister at Leith Baptist Church.

Second Mission to the UK in 2002

The year 2000 is worth mentioning in the above context because during our trip that October, I met a group of leaders from Surrey, in Guildford, who accepted our invitation to come to Brazil to visit our churches and charities. (This was how it worked in most cases.) Two remarkable things happened. First, a couple who had been struggling to have children, Phil and Gill Hawkins, were prayed for and eventually conceived – not only once, but twice. The family became missionaries, and were sent by Bookham Baptist Church to Brazil from 2010 to 2015. Secondly, Stuart Lindsell had what he describes as a visitation of the Holy Spirit in my house during his stay. In this visitation, he says, God clearly told him to invite Karen and me to return to the UK and work as missionaries with a group of five churches across Surrey. This was a pivotal event: as Stuart described this visitation to our apostolic team, they felt unanimously that it was indeed from God and that in response they should send me back to the UK. Karen and I were thus sent to the UK again in March 2002. We were based at Pioneer People Cobham, and my main – although not exclusive – role was to extend the bridge to Brazil to a group of churches under the umbrella name of Mustard Seed (namely, Bookham Baptist Church, Redhill Christian Fellowship, Guildford Community, Pioneer People Farnham and Life Community Baptist Church-Horsham). From there, we were to make further connections to other nations under the guidance of the Holy Spirit. As a result of this new partnership in Surrey, three English couples – Duncan and Jan Weird, Phil and Gill Hawkins and Ben and Liz Cole – and one single young adult, Joanna Whiteman, became missionaries to our church in Brazil. Several short-term mission teams went to Brazil every other year from 2002 to 2014. Sal da Terra also sent a team of creative evangelists to perform Brazilian cultural dance and percussion in schools, parks and churches in the whole region.

There was a lot of movement of people, projects and resources. However, due to a number of internal problems in several of the churches mentioned above, and to a divergence in the discernment of our vision, the process stalled; and after a lot of prayer, an apostolic team decision was taken in 2005 that my family and I should leave the context of the Mustard Seed/Pioneer People. The purpose here was to move to Orpington to be based at Orpington Town Church and to embark on what for me was the most audacious task of a cross-cultural partnership developer, namely, to merge the New Frontiers family of churches with the Sal da Terra family of churches and charities in Brazil. Initially, this looked challenging yet nevertheless possible, given the apparent similarities between the two movements in terms of theology, values and vision. I facilitated the coming and going of short-term mission teams, as well as several meetings of apostolic leaders in Brazil and in the UK. Moreover, every other year, Sal da Terra sent its creative evangelism groups to Orpington. There was a lot of excitement, and it looked as if the merge was definitely going to happen. However, at a crucial meeting in the city of Goiania in Brazil, the whole project collapsed abruptly due to a theological difference. The excitement became frustration and disappointment to everyone involved, but especially to my family and me, since we were in transition. We tried several avenues of dialogue between the Brazilian and British leaders, but the differences were clearly insurmountable at that point. The theologically-based values and principles that divided these groups were non-negotiable on both sides, and the process ended. My role was no longer relevant; my presence in the church became somewhat awkward, and my family and I had to pray hard in order to learn the lessons we needed to learn and to find God's answers for our future.

Mission to Italy

After several months of praying and pondering, God spoke to me quite clearly, telling me that his vision for us remained the same: we were to be a blessing to Brazil's spiritual fathers in the UK, in Europe and beyond. At this point, I was reminded that Europe had been at the heart of Sal da Terra and of the Go to The Nation movement, and that it was perhaps time to consider going deeper into the vision and to move from the UK to continental Europe – more specifically, to Italy. There were three main reasons for this Firstly, there was the history of gospel heritage in that nation. Secondly, my ancestors had immigrated from Italy to Brazil. And finally, Italy is in great need as far as the gospel is concerned. In reflecting on the history of the church in Europe and indeed the world, it only makes sense that Italy would be a part of our journey. After much prayer and preparation, my apostolic team in Brazil, my leaders and friends in the UK, and, most importantly, my wife and I were all in agreement that Italy should be our next stop. As part of our plan, we visited seven cities across the north of Italy,[7] and eventually, in August 2008, my family and I moved from Orpington to Bergamo, where we stayed for three years. Our goal was to reach Italians, start a Bible study group in our home, and eventually, plant a church. We did this by reaching out to parents at the school gate. Later on, we expanded on this work with a project of cultural exchange, in which we facilitated visits from British and Brazilian young people to perform drama and dance at Italian secondary schools. We also began an arts project called Kids in Color, which was very successful and connected us directly with 100 Italian families from our immediate community. We managed to build very strong relationships with several Italian families, some of whom we remain in touch with to this day. A few turned up at our home Bible study – some of them regularly – and they heard the gospel there. Only one of them accepted my invitation to come to a proper church service, yet only attended once. Our journey in Bergamo had to come to an end after exactly three years. This happened for various reasons which would take another chapter to explain, but in short, we were completely worn out and

---

[7] We chose the north because it is the least evangelised, and it is where my ancestors had come from.

felt too isolated and too lacking in the level of support we would have needed to take the work to the next stage.

Leading the Missions Team of an English Church

After a long season of prayer and consultation with our apostolic leadership in Brazil and with our supporters in the UK, we decided to return to the United Kingdom in 2011 for what was called an active sabbatical at Bookham Baptist Church. This congregation had been a partner of Sal da Terra since the year 2000. After a time of emotional and spiritual recovery, we were kindly invited to take over the role of Overseas Mission Coordinator of Bookham Baptist Church and to be a part of their ministry team. Bookham Baptist Church had been working with missionaries in Lebanon, Nepal, Siberia and Brazil, and supported a family of nationals in Slovenia. I preached regularly and had the opportunity to provide my own insights into these various leadership groups – local, regional and international. In the same way as I had done in other partnerships, I facilitated visits from Brazilian teams, which included visits from leaders for the purpose of exchange and mutual encouragement, as well as visits every other year from the creative evangelism team to perform in schools, churches and public areas. While in Bookham I was also a trustee of Aprender, a British educational charity to which I provided expertise in forming a partnership with Total Education and Culture, a Brazilian charity supported by our churches. At Bookham, my cross-cultural skills were developed in a multicultural direction for many reasons: perhaps most importantly, because I was no longer working exclusively with British people and Brazilians (which is in itself a challenge), but was now also working with Italians, Lebanese people, Syrians and Slovenians (and at times, with all of them at the same time). Each one of these groups had different cultural nuances, complexities, challenges and opportunities. My time in Bookham encouraged me in a distinctive way because in a sense it was the fulfilment of what God had told us prophetically at the beginning: that we would come to the UK to help the churches there to become fruitful again in the nations. Each one of these partnerships could be the subject of its own chapter, and some cases would require a whole book to explore all the challenges, joys and lessons that attended these cross-cultural relationships, and to explore how God led and sustained my family and me in each one of them.

Concluding Reflection

In hindsight, one of the things I have reflected on is that there have perhaps been too many inconsistencies in our journey, too many moves and changes. This was due to the fact that decisions about our path were taken collectively, and included my wife and me, my sending church in Brazil (which worked closely with the broader Go to The Nations apostolic team), and the leaders of the local congregations with which we were working at specific times. This decision-making model made things much more complicated for us as they involved various cross-cultural differences, diverse leadership styles and management dynamics, theological differences, and different interpretations of our collective call and (consequently) of the direction that should be taken on the ground. Nevertheless, amidst these many voices, my wife and I tried to follow a pattern closely related to our call back in 1992 – to that which God had called us to do as a couple. In every change of direction and move, we gauged our decisions in relation to what we have heard from God originally. These were:

1) To unblock the wells of Abraham our father (Gen. 28): to work in partnership with our spiritual fathers, beginning with the British churches, and to resist the temptation to start a Brazilian church in a foreign soil. This is an important challenge for today's reverse missionaries who are starting monoethnic congregations in the UK and in European cities.

2) Mutual encouragement based on Romans 1:12: 'that you and I may be mutually encouraged by each other's faith' (NIV). The word 'mutual' here has been crucial to our calling. This missionary endeavour has been a dual carriageway. It is not just a journey for Brazilians inspiring and encouraging our spiritual fathers, but a journey of mutual learning. We Brazilians have so much to learn, too. Help the local church to revitalise the passion for evangelism, unity and mission, and learn from their history, experiences, heritage, resilience, theological rigour, passion for socio-political justice, systemic transformation and transcultural missions.

3) Seek to do missions together in other nations, including taking British Christians to do missions in Brazil, and Brazilians to do missionary work in the UK. Brazilian and British Christians sharing the gospel together adds a powerful ingredient of witness to the message of the gospel.

(7) Majority World Christianity in Wales
By Jim Stewart

Background

In the summer of 2017, the Evangelical Alliance in Wales organised a two-week exhibition in Wales' capital city of Cardiff on 'Majority World Christians in Wales and their contribution to Welsh society'. The launch, in Cardiff Bay's iconic Senedd building, included worship from Nigerian Christians and the city's Eritrean Orthodox Church, with ushers from Wales' Pakistani Christian community. The exhibition itself gave an overview of, and insight into, a Christianity in Wales that is increasing in its diversity and international nature.

Four years previously, in December 2013, Revd Irfan John, a refugee from Pakistan working as Missions Enabler for the Methodist Church in Wales, organised a nativity event in Cardiff with Christians living in Wales from 55 different nations involved. In so doing, he set a new Guinness world record.

The growth in Wales of Majority World Christianity – from Asia, Africa, Eastern Europe, Oceania and Latin America – is one that has only begun to receive attention and yet is one of great richness.

Introduction

What are the drivers that have contributed to the current demographic makeup of Majority World Christianity in Wales? Wales, with a population of just over 3 million, is a constituency part of the United Kingdom with a strong history of nonconformity and political radicalism. The legacy of Wales' missionary past has produced unique spiritual connections with South Korea and the state of Mizoram in North East India, with Christians from both regions residing in Wales because of those links. There is also a special cultural relationship between Wales and the Argentinian province of Chubut in Patagonia, where Welsh settlers arrived in 1865 to establish a Welsh-speaking colony.

Migration patterns to Wales over the past century, not dissimilar to UK trends in general, have also contributed to an increased richness and diversity in Wales' Christianity. These include the growth of Tiger Bay in Cardiff as a result of the coal industry, the arrival of Jamaican immigrants of the Windrush generation in the 1950s, European Union enlargement in 2004 and 2007, and the introduction of the dispersal policy for asylum seekers in 2000, leading to growing numbers of Christian asylum seekers arriving in the Welsh cities of Newport, Cardiff and Swansea, and the town of Wrexham.

Spiritual and Cultural Connections

Spiritual Connection with Korea

Robert Jermain Thomas was a missionary from Rhayader in Wales who, in 1863, left with his wife, who he had only recently married, for China to work for the London Missionary Society (LMS). His wife tragically died three months after arriving in Shanghai while, later in 1864, Thomas left the LMS because of disagreement over the nature of mission. He had made a first trip to Korea in 1865 but it was his second trip in 1866 that would result in his martyrdom. While working as a customs officer, he met two Korean Catholic traders who were wearing crosses. They had no Bible but had catechisms from French priests. Catholicism had grown in Korea during the nineteenth century in the face of fierce persecution from the Korean government, who were opposed to all forms of foreign influence. Many Catholic Christians had been martyred. Thomas, a Protestant missionary, was motivated by a desire to help the Catholics and to spread the gospel. He joined the American trading ship, the General Sherman, which reached Korean shores in August 1866. Facing hostility from locals, Thomas and others on the ship were killed, but not before Thomas was able to distribute Christian tracts and Chinese Bibles.

Thomas' legacy grew after his death, and his martyrdom acted as a precursor to the growth of the Protestant church in Korea in the years that followed. The leaders of the North Korean church met in 1928 at Thomas' grave and said that they needed to remember that this was the seed of the Protestant gospel.[1] Christianity is now the largest religion in South Korea, with Protestants comprising 19.7 per cent of South Korea's population and Catholics 7.9 per cent,[2] and South Korean Christians remember those who lost their lives in bringing them Christianity. The interest in Thomas is particularly strong among the Protestant Christians, and thousands have come to visit Wales, with hundreds coming every year. Of those who come to visit, some decide to stay. Jacob Park, Gi Jung Song and Peter Cho are among those Koreans who are now serving as pastors in English-language churches in Wales. There is also a Korean worship tram based in Llanelli in West Wales. Stephen and Stella Price welcome Korean Christians to their home near Abergavenny, a converted manse where Robert Jermain Thomas used to live.

---

[1] Emmaus Road Ministries, 'Emmaus Road ministry report 2011-2012', https://roadmin.org/index.php/site/NewsDetail/emmaus_road_ministry_report_2011-2012/ (Accessed 16th February 2019).
[2] Korea.net, 'About Korea: Religion', http://www.korea.net/AboutKorea/Korean-Life/Religion (Accessed 26th January 2019).

Spiritual Connection with Mizoram in North East India

Sangkhuma Hmar and his wife Rini and family arrived in Wales as missionaries from the North East Indian state of Mizoram in 1998 to work with the Presbyterian Church of Wales. The state, nestled in the Khasi hills, is 90 per cent Christian and only one of three states in India with a majority Christian population. Welsh missionaries such as Rev David Jones brought Christianity to the region in the nineteenth and twentieth centuries. They were credited, not only with establishing Christianity there, but also with building schools and hospitals, transcribing the local language, and teaching the local people valuable trade skills.

The Mizoram Presbyterian Church is the largest denomination in the state, and the attachment to the 'mother church', the Presbyterian Church of Wales, and Wales itself, was augmented and intensified through the 1904 Welsh revival. The sister and brother-in-law of Evan Roberts, the 1904 revivalist, resided in Calcutta and ran a Bible school at the time. Upon hearing of the 1904 revival, they implored Christians in Wales to come to Calcutta to work as missionaries. Many arrived in the years that followed and many then made their way to North East India with its strong Welsh connection. Welsh Christians already there had heard stories of the revival through their regular correspondence, and the newly arrived visitors gave first-hand accounts of what had been happening.

Towards the end of the twentieth century, the Mizoram Presbyterian Church, hearing that the mother church in Wales was in decline, offered to send a missionary to the church in Wales. Although the Presbyterian church in Wales was initially reluctant to accept the offer, citing linguistic and cultural barriers, the Council of World Churches (CWC), of which the Mizoram Church is a member, stepped in and said that, if the Presbyterian church in Wales was ready to accept a missionary, the CWC would provide the funding.

Sangkhuma has worked for 20 years in Wales, not only for the Presbyterian church but also ecumenically for Evangelical Alliance and Cytûn. He was joined by another missionary from North East India, John Colney, who is serving as a pastor for the Presbyterian church in Ebbw Vale.

Cultural Connection with Argentina

On 28 May 1865, 153 Welsh-speaking men, women and children from all over Wales set sail from the port of Liverpool on the ship Mimosa, arriving two months later on 28 July at what was to become the city of Puerto Madryn in the Chubut region of Patagonia, the southern part of Argentina. The visionary behind the venture, Rev Michael D. Jones, had been concerned that migration into Wales was eroding the Welsh language and culture. He had purchased land from the Argentine government and dreamed of establishing a community in which every facet of life – chapel, government, commerce and schooling – could be conducted through the medium of Welsh.

For the first 50 to 60 years of its existence, Y Wladfa, 'the colony' in Welsh, was a success, with many new emigrants arriving from Wales to bolster the population and bring new skills. Chapel life was embedded into everyday life, and this was strengthened in the early twentieth century by news and first-hand accounts of the 1904 Welsh revival and its impact in Welsh society. The Welsh culture in Patagonia began to wane, however, in the first half of the twentieth century as the Argentine government sought to assimilate ethnic and cultural minorities into a stronger national identity.

The colony's centenary in 1965 rekindled the relationship with Wales and saw increasing numbers of visitors from there. Mair Davies, a missionary from Llandysul in West Wales, had arrived in Argentina in 1963 and, for 46 years until her death in 2009, she worked tirelessly among the Welsh speakers of the region – numbering around 10,000 – and people of Welsh heritage. Historian Dr Robert Owen Jones credits Mair Davies' influence for ensuring the ongoing presence of the Welsh chapels: in the twentieth century, ministers from Wales had continued to visit the region but brought liberal doctrinal ideas that were different from the nonconformity that they were used to. Mair preached a classic evangelical message, the same one that the older generation in Patagonia, the children of the 1904 revival, had heard.[3]

The relationship between Wales and Patagonia is now cemented, with ongoing financial support from the British Council and the Welsh Government. There are visitors who come from Patagonia to Wales every year to attend Welsh language classes and to compete in the Eisteddfod, while others have relocated there for reasons such as marriage and work. Among the Patagonians in Wales, some are Christians. The Presbyterian Church of Wales employs Judith Jones from Patagonia as a youth worker in North Wales. Rev Isaias Grandis is working for the Baptist Union of Wales, while Alicia Arthur and her husband Carwyn reside in West Wales, where Carwyn is a minister. The couple met in 2005 when Carwyn spent a year in Patagonia teaching Welsh classes. Nonconformist chapel culture is still a part of Welsh Patagonian identity, although nowhere near as embedded as it was.

Other Connections

The examples mentioned above represent the strongest overseas connections that impact upon Majority World Christianity in Wales, but they do not include them all.

Welsh missionaries such as Thomas Bevan and David Jones were instrumental in bringing Christianity to Madagascar in the early nineteenth century, and the 200th anniversary of their arrival in Madagascar was celebrated in 2018 with a delegation from the African country visiting Wales.

The prominence of rugby in Wales has also led to players from rugby-playing nations in the southern hemisphere coming to the UK and to Wales. In 1997, the

---

[3] In a phone Interview with Robert Owen Jones on the 20th February 2018.

Tongan national rugby side toured Wales and, from this, a number of Tongan players were recruited by Welsh clubs. A house in the south Wales valleys became a gathering point where the growing Tongan community in Wales, normally Christian, would meet for food and worship.[4] Ministries have been birthed from this community as well, including one led by Rev Singa Vunipola, whose husband Fe'ao was one of the first Tongans to come and play rugby in Wales, is a Methodist minister. Emori Katalau, who played for the Fijian national rugby team, and Llanelli are the current pastors of a church in Newport which serves the Fijian Christian community in the area as well as the wider community.

Majority World Christianity in the Methodist Church in Wales: A Case Study

Looking at Majority World Christianity in Wales through a denominational lens provides further insights into its richness.

The Methodist Church in Wales has been a cornerstone of Welsh Christianity since the eighteenth century. Despite a fall in membership in the British Methodist Church, its global membership of approximately 80 million is similar to that of the Anglican Communion.

According to Rev Dr Stephen Wigley, Chair of the Wales Synod of the Methodist Church, Majority World Methodist communities in the UK – from countries such as Ghana, Nigeria, Tonga and Fiji – represent a significant part of the British Methodist Church and are part of its future.[5] In London, the Methodist Church is black majority. In Wales, 5 out of 60 staff, roughly 10 per cent, are leaders from the Majority World. These ministers have come into their posts in one of two ways:

Firstly, the British Methodist Church is part of the World Methodist Council, representing over 80 million members and made up of 80 'conferences' in 138 countries.[6] It is a long-established practice for ministers to be sent by their conference churches to spend some time serving in the British Methodist Church. Initially, this is under the authority of the home conference, but some people, after a period of time, apply to transfer and become fully part of the British Methodist Church. Wales currently has two such Methodist ministers – Rev Dr Kofi Ammisah in Cardiff, originally from the Ghanaian conference, and Rev Professor Teddy Kalongo in Porthcawl, originally from the Zambian conference.

---

4 Wales Online, 'The ordinary Valleys house at the heart of an extraordinary Welsh rugby story', https://www.walesonline.co.uk/sport/rugby/rugby-news/welsh-rugby-faletau-house-story-14495044 (Accessed 29th December 2018).
5 In an interview with Stephen Wigley at Cardiff on the 7th February 2019.
6 World Methodist Council, 'Member churches: Our worldwide church family', http://worldmethodistcouncil.org/about/member-churches/ (Accessed 29th December 2018).

Secondly, at the same time, the British Methodist Church has other ministers who are from the global church in the broader sense. These are ordained ministers who have applied and transferred directly into the Methodist Church. In Wales, there are three such ministers: Rev Siperire Mugadzaweta in Swansea, originally from Zimbabwe; Rev Hee Gon Mon in Llanelli, who is from South Korea and is an ordained Presbyterian minister; and Rev Irfan John, an ordained Presbyterian minister who arrived in the UK as an asylum seeker with his family, fleeing religious persecution in Pakistan.

Rev Irfan John's case was a very unusual one-off situation for the Methodist Church in Wales. After arriving in the UK in 2005 as asylum seekers, he and his family were dispersed to Cardiff while their asylum claim was being processed. While staying in their Home Office accommodation, they started to attend a nearby Methodist Church, whose members made them welcome and who supported them through the asylum process. Methodist leaders recognised that Irfan was a minister with the Presbyterian church in Pakistan and, once he was given asylum status, he decided to apply to become a Methodist minister. He began the transfer process, which he completed successfully, and then attended training to orientate him to British Methodism and the Welsh culture.

The normal process for ministers being accepted into the Methodist Church would be for them to be deployed somewhere in Wales in a local church setting. In Irfan John's case, however, Methodist leaders noted his distinct skills, gifts and experience, and took the step of responding to this by creating a Wales-wide role for him as Synod Enabler for Culturally Diverse Communities. This role, which he began in 2007, was composed of two parts:

One was to work with asylum seekers and refugees, building up Methodist contacts and the development of the Trinity Project at the Trinity Centre in Cardiff; the second was to develop working links with minority ethnic and culturally diverse congregations. A primary focus was with Urdu-speaking Christians in Wales, and he founded three Urdu-speaking fellowships which now meet regularly in Wales – in Cardiff, Swansea and Haverfordwest (in Pembrokeshire). He has also forged strong ecumenical links with others such as the Chinese Christian community and the Ethiopian Orthodox Church.

In his role, now held for over ten years, Rev John has worked tirelessly to support Majority World Christians, to arrange events to introduce culturally diverse communities from the Majority World to each other, and to the host Christian communities. In 2013, he decided to try and establish a new Guinness world record by organising a Nativity play with the biggest number of nationalities taking part. His intention was to raise awareness of the diversity within the church and to bring positive press coverage of Christianity in the media. The Nativity play took place in November 2015 with 55 nationalities represented, and the record was achieved.[7]

Migration to Wales

Wales has seen regular demographic changes to its population over the centuries, while at the same time maintaining a distinct culture and language. The population of Wales in the 2011 census was 3.06 million, with roughly two-thirds living in the industrialised south and 19 per cent speaking the Welsh language. Historically an agricultural society, it transformed into an industrial one during the Industrial Revolution. The Industrial Revolution and the nineteenth century in particular saw a major change in demographics, with the exploitation of the South Wales Coalfields and the growth of the coal and iron industries. The burgeoning coal industry attracted migrants from rural Wales and the rest of the UK, as well as from other European countries such as Ireland, Spain and Italy.

The booming ports of Cardiff, Barry and Newport saw increased shipping traffic from all over the world, and many people from the Majority World began to settle in south Wales as a result, often marrying local women. Yemeni, Somali and West Indian communities began to grow, with the latter providing one of the most striking early examples of Majority World Christianity in Wales.

Apart from the coal industry, patterns of migration in Wales were in many respects no different from other parts of the UK over the past century. Chinese workers arrived and Christians from that community formed a church in south Wales in the 1960s. Wales now has three Chinese churches altogether. The arrival of the Windrush generation in the 1950s and 1960s, many of whom were Christians, has meant that churches with Christians of Caribbean heritage have now been established in Wales for many decades.

Looking at Wales through an evangelical lens, much of the international fellowship since the birth of evangelicalism in the 1730s has been between evangelicals in North America and Western Europe, rather than with the Majority World. Indeed, one of the reasons for establishing the World Evangelical Alliance in 1846 was to facilitate fellowship between evangelical Christians on both sides of the Atlantic. The many regional and national evangelical revivals that had occurred in North America and Europe in the eighteenth and nineteenth centuries had intensified a desire for increased fellowship and contact among Christians across the Atlantic. A study of Wales' national and regional revivals is notable in that, despite numerous examples of Christian leaders from North America and Europe being used by God, there are

---

[7] Guinness World Records, 'Most nationalities in a nativity play', http://www.guinnessworldrecords.com/world-records/most-nationalities-in-a-nativity-play (Accessed 19th January 2019).

no known examples of Christians from the Majority World being instrumental in initiating revivals in Wales.

A fascinating example of engagement with the Majority World, however, emerged from Colwyn Bay in North Wales, where the African Training Institute was established in 1890, training over 100 students from countries such as Cameroon, Nigeria and Sierra Leone until its closure in 1912. The centre's founder, Rev William Hughes, had preached in the Congo as a missionary from 1882 to 1885, when ill health forced him to return to Wales. He felt that African Christians were better suited to reach their fellow Africans, and that they were equal to Europeans in every way, but simply lacked education and training. According to academic Marian Gwyn, 'He cherished what was different about the people he had met in the Congo because he felt that his own Welsh language, culture and traditions had been undervalued by the English in Britain.'[8]

The Windrush Generation and West Indian Christians

The arrival of West Indian Christians in Wales followed a similar trajectory in Wales as it did in other parts of the UK. Pastor Lester Freckleton's father arrived in Newport, Wales in 1956 from Jamaica. A devout and godly Christian, he went to a British church but was told not to come back; as a result, he started a church in his front room with other West Indian Christians, and this went on to become affiliated with the New Testament Church of God denomination. Such churches served as enclaves from the rejection and indifference that had been experienced from the host Christian community. This divide would be an example of something that would need to be overcome in the future as relationships between different Christian ethnicities, cultures, national backgrounds and denominations would need to be re-imagined.

Joe Aldred, the Principal Officer of Pentecostal and Charismatic relations for Churches Together in England (CTE), has argued that there was definitely an element of racism in the experience of some Caribbean Christians, but that there were other factors involved as well: host white Christians and non-Christians were not used to the West Indian cultures, and the exuberance exhibited in worship therefore would not join these churches. There was also the mission factor in the creation of Black Majority Churches.[9]

At the same time, other West Indian Christians had begun to settle in Cardiff's City Temple Church (now City Church), an Elim Pentecostal church that was started in 1929 through the evangelical work of the Jeffrey brothers. City Temple's multicultural DNA would continue to grow, and the appointment in 1997 of Rev Chris Cartwright as Senior Pastor further strengthened this. He had

---

8 BBC News: Forgotten histories: The black missionaries of Colwyn Bay, https://www.bbc.co.uk/news/uk-wales-41777209 (Accessed 24th February 2019).
9 Joe Aldred, *Thinking Outside the Box on Race, Faith and Life* (Hertfordshire: Hansib Publications Limited, 2013), pp 65-68.

previously been on the leadership team of a thriving multicultural church in London, and, once in post in Cardiff, made visitors and church members from the Majority World feel affirmed and valued. By 2018, over 40 nationalities were represented in its congregation, an excellent example of a multicultural church whose creed is to reach every nation and language.

EU Expansion and Economic Migration

The accession of new states into the European Union in 2004 and 2007 brought a further influx of people into Wales – in this case, many Majority World Christians from Eastern and Central Europe (Catholic, Orthodox and evangelical), including a Romanian church and Roma churches.

Healthcare professionals from countries such as India and the Philippines coming to Wales for work led to the establishment of Malayalam and Tamil-speaking fellowships and Filipino Christians attending other host Welsh churches. Catholic churches in the cities of Wales were filled with Christians from Poland, Pakistan, the Philippines and India.

Asylum Policy of Dispersal

The Immigration and Asylum Act 1999 established the policy of *dispersal* for asylum seekers. The intention of this was to alleviate the burden that local authorities in London and south-east England were disproportionately bearing to house asylum seekers while their claims were being processed. Under the policy, introduced in 2000, asylum seekers were sent to participating local authorities in the north of England and other parts of the UK where there was more accommodation available and where it was cheaper. Four local authorities in Wales opted to take part in the voluntary programme – Newport, Cardiff and Swansea in south Wales and Wrexham in the north.

Over the following years, this meant that Christians from countries such as Pakistan, Iran, Eritrea and Ethiopia began to arrive in increasing numbers in these localities for the first time.

Christian asylum seekers were signposted to churches, and so, for the first time, many host churches began to see asylum seekers turning up at their services on Sunday mornings. Although many would move to the bigger cities of London, Birmingham and Manchester once they received their papers, others began to settle in Wales, having made contacts in the local community while awaiting a decision on their claim. As a result, Christian refugee communities began to grow in these localities, with some choosing to attend existing churches, but with others forming their own congregations, where they could worship in their own language and culture.

Trends

The Seeds of Wider Civil Society Engagement

According to Lester Freckleton, whose father had arrived from Jamaica in 1956, and with reference to the sons and daughters of Jamaican migrants to Wales: the first generation was often characterised by its resilience – a willingness to put up with hardship for the sake of their families and getting established. The second generation, however, were not so willing to accept such hardship and were more active in public life.[10]

The sweeping social changes in British society in the 1960s led to a greater emphasis on equality, and this led to the passing of the Race Relations Act in 1976. Local authorities around the UK were giving thought as to how they could implement their findings, and in 1978 in Gwent in south-east Wales, the Gwent Race Forum was established. Three Christians from Newport's Presbyterian church were invited by the council to be founding members. This was due to the work that the church had done in establishing Community House, a community cohesion project that sought to reach out to the communities in their immediate vicinity, in this case many South Asian Muslim communities.

Ingrid Wilson was one of the Christians who were invited to take part, and she credits this, along with the founding of a local Amnesty International branch in Newport in the 1970s, as the impetus which gave her the opportunity to engage with communities that she may never have met otherwise. Through these bodies she met Christians from the Chinese and West Indian communities who were willing to take part in different initiatives. Christians Against Torture, founded by BBC broadcaster Roy Jenkins, was another such example that brought like-minded people together and gave opportunities for Christians to meet each other.[11]

Lester Freckleton noticed in the 1980s, however, that although some Christians were getting involved, more needed to do so in order not to lose influence. More Christians from the Majority World in Wales are now engaging in public life and civil society, with a notable example being Uzo Iwobi from Nigeria, who founded Race Council Cymru and whose work has been acknowledged in many different ways.

There remain challenges, however, to alerting policy-makers, influencers and the media of the existence of Majority World Christian communities in Wales and of the need to provide them with a voice. For example, a comparison with the Muslim community is that the religious component of Muslims' identities tends to be essentialised at the expense of other aspects, such as gender, ethnicity and class; the religious component, on the other hand, of Majority World Christians, can often be masked. The exhibition organised by the Evangelical Alliance Wales, mentioned at the beginning of this chapter, sought to address

---

[10] In a phone Interview with Lester Freckleton on 5th March 2018.
[11] In a phone Interview with Ingrid Wilson on 6th March 2018.

these issues and provide a platform for Majority World Christians in Wales and to raise awareness of their existence and of the contributions that individuals and communities are making to Welsh society.

Engagement Between the Host Church and Majority World Christians

The relationship and interaction between the host church and Majority World Christians has grown over the past two decades. The racial equality forums that began in the late 1970s, as mentioned above, provided opportunities for many Majority World Christians in Wales to meet host Christians and to get involved in public life. Many of these interactions have explored themes such as racial justice, equality and community cohesion, and have included both Majority World Christians and Christians who are Welsh and British but whose roots are in the Majority World.

Evangelical Alliance Wales, for example, produced a Church Diversity Index in 2001, mapping ethnic minority churches and networks. They also coordinated the South Wales Churches' Refugee Network and facilitated a Black and Minority Ethnic (BME) leaders' network from 2005 to 2010, intended for evangelical leaders of ethnic minority congregations in Wales to meet one another and enjoy fellowship.

Cytûn (Churches Together in Wales) was formed in 1990 and has supported Christians from the Majority World in many ways. These have included: organising an annual Welcome to Wales ministry course for ministers who move to Wales; convening a quarterly Racial Justice Network that provides opportunity for black and minority ethnic Christians to have a voice on issues affecting them and to meet with denominational representatives; initiating and taking steps to make Wales a Nation of Sanctuary; and welcoming into membership churches from Germany, India, Ghana and Ethiopia.

Many Majority World Christian communities often find friends among the host community, Christian or otherwise, and these contacts can greatly assist integration and well-being. This has been true in Wales, for example, for Pakistani, Eritrean and Iranian Christians. The small Armenian Christian community in Wales, numbering only around 50, was delighted that a friendship with Eirian Williams, a sheep farmer from north Wales that began in 1998, led eventually to a plaque commemorating the 1915 Armenian genocide being erected on public land in Cardiff in 2007. This remains the only part of the UK where such a memorial has been erected, and it has brought a great degree of closure to the Armenian community in the face of an ongoing policy of genocide denial from Turkey.

Conclusion

This chapter has provided some glimpses into Majority World Christianity in Wales. This increase in diversity in Wales' Christianity is at the same time rich, complex, multi-layered and an expression of God's heart.

One of the challenges facing denominations in Wales with the inclusion of Majority World fellowships as part of their membership is this: to what degree should those communities remain distinctive, and to what extent should they integrate with the host church? What the Methodist Church in Wales has tried to do is to find ways in which those churches can be who they are but also contribute to the host church and belong to it fully.

On the other hand, there are a handful of churches in Wales that are truly international, with dozens of nationalities represented in their congregations. One such church, led by Korean pastor Rev Gi Jung Song, is Cardiff International Church, which has documented visitors to their services representing 99 different nationalities.[12]

Majority World Christians are often living out their faith both locally and globally. Many belong to diaspora groups that are dispersed around the world across different time zones, but who are nevertheless very attuned to what is happening – spiritually, socially and politically – in their country of origin. This affects their prayer lives and what they talk about, and so, can provide an opportunity to broaden the perspective of the host church.

With a decline in Christianity in the UK among the host population, the presence of Majority World Christians in Wales provides a breath of fresh air. Welsh church structures and institutions have enabled Majority World communities to be supported, and have facilitated their integration into the host church, where appropriate, and into Welsh society.

References

Aldred, Joe, *Thinking Outside the Box on Race, Faith and Life*, Hertfordshire, Hansib Publications Limited, 2013.
Freckleton, Lester. Interview by Jim Stewart. Interview by phone conversation, Cardiff, March 5, 2018.
Godding, Elfed. Interview by Jim Stewart. Personal interview, Cardiff.
Hmar, Sangkhuma. Interview by Jim Stewart. Personal interview, Cardiff, February 15, 2018.
Jones, Robert Owen Interview by Jim Stewart. Interview by phone conversation, Cardiff, February 20, 2018.
Noel Gibbard, *On the wings of the dove*. Bridgend: Bryntirion Press, 2002.
Price, Stella. *Chosen for Choson (Korea)*. Essex, MA: Emmaus Road Ministries, 2010.
Price, Stephen and Stella Price. Interview by Jim Stewart. Personal interview, Abergavenny, January 20, 2019.
Sinclair, Neil M.C., *The Tiger Bay story*. Cardiff: Butetown History & Arts Project, 1993.
Wigley, Stephen. Interview by Jim Stewart. Personal interview, Cardiff, February 7, 2019.
Wilson, Ingrid. Interview by Jim Stewart. Interview by phone conversation, Cardiff, February 6, 2018.

12 Cardiff International Church, 'Nations at CIC', http://www.cardiffinternationalchurch.org/about-us/nations/ (Accessed 26th February 2019).

(8) Pentecostal Immigrant Churches in Sweden
By Nils Malmström

Introduction

The centre of Christianity has moved today from Europe and North America to sub-Saharan Africa, Latin America, and parts of Asia, as has been noted, for example, by Philip Jenkins.[1] Some developments in these regions have meant that Pentecostalism has increased its influence during the last decade, partly through congregational growth and new native churches, but also because Pentecostal movements have influenced 'older' churches, such as the Anglican and Catholic churches.

Through migration streams in the last 20 years, these Pentecostal churches have established themselves throughout Europe, including in Sweden. The development in Sweden is likely a few years behind that of the UK and the Netherlands, but ahead of East European countries.

Starting in the 1990s (with an increase in the early 2000s), several immigrant Pentecostal churches have been established in Sweden.[2] I will discuss below some trends and typologies that can be seen, illustrating them with examples from churches that have emerged primarily in Africa, but also in Asia and Latin America.

In my previous studies in Missionsvetenskap (at Centrum för Teologi och Religionsvetenskap at Lund's University), I have discussed Nigerian Pentecostalism in Sweden, and this context is thus prevalent in my examples, although my purpose is to provide a broader picture.[3]

One can, I think, identify four types of Pentecostal immigrant churches that are active in Sweden today.

1. 'Mega Churches' from the 'Global South'

These are churches which were founded in their home countries from the 1970s onward. Several of them are leaders in the development of global Pentecostalism

---

[1] Jenkins, Philip, *The Next Christendom: The Coming of Global Christianity* 3rd edition (Oxford: Oxford University Press, 2011).

[2] This does not mean that Pentecostal immigrant groups did not exist in Sweden previously, or that they had not had an influence (e.g. Finnish and Estonian groups).

[3] This chapter is based on a previous article published in Swedish. Nils Malmström, 'Migrantkyrkor Pentekostala', in Jan-Åke Alvarsson (eds) *Pentekostalism i Sverige på 2000 talet* (Uppsala: Institutet för Pentekostala Studier, 2013).

and have several million members. They often have a dominating leader who influences the picture of the movement as perceived from the outside. Examples of such churches that have come to Sweden are Igreja Universal do Reino de Deus ('Universal Church of the Kingdom of God') from Brazil, Redeemed Christian Church of God from Nigeria, and the Jesus is Lord Church from the Philippines. Even if these churches have only attracted a few hundred members in Sweden, they are supported by their mother churches, creating a strong identity among the members as being part of a major global Pentecostal movement. They have primarily managed to reach out to compatriots in the diaspora, even though they have justified their presence in Sweden with an aim to reach all people. However, few of these churches have started in Sweden as pure missionary projects. Instead, the leaders of these churches have moved to Sweden for different reasons, and have felt the need to start a congregation. They often have an ethnic image of being a Nigerian or Brazilian church, but they have also attracted members from outside their own specific groups. In most cases, the parent churches consider it an important indicator to be able to mention in various contexts the many countries in which they operate.

2. Independent Pentecostal Immigrant Churches which Started in Sweden

This second category consists of churches started in Sweden by immigrants and which have developed there. This category includes two subgroups: those which remained independent, and those which later contacted or otherwise joined established churches. The first subgroup is exemplified by *Restoration and Fire Ministries* in Malmö. This subgroup consists of churches which started with members of an ethnic group, but have also, in many cases, attracted other immigrant groups since then.

Examples from the second subgroup include *Elim Pentecostal* and *Mevam* in Malmö.

3. Pentecostal 'Mega Churches-in-the-Making' Created in Sweden with Congregations in Several Countries

This third group contains churches which have been so successful in Sweden that they have managed to build a base here, from which to expand to other countries in Europe and the Global South. In my presentation, this group is represented by the International Mission Church, a Hispanic-speaking church which was founded in Sweden and now also has congregations in Spain and Latin America.

4. Pentecostal Immigrant Churches with Connections to Swedish Churches

The fourth group can be described as immigrant churches which started within, or became part of, an already-established church, such as Pingst-Fria

Församlingar i Samverkan (Pingst FFS), Evangeliska Frikyrkan (EFK) and also Equmeniakyrkan. This category encompasses, in particular, groups with a Latin American background. One such example is the Hispanic *Iglesia del Pueblo* in Sollentuna.

At this point, it is appropriate to compare my categories with the typologies created by Claudia Währisch-Oblau in her analysis of Pentecostal immigrant churches in Germany. She also identified four different categories:

1. Independent Local New Mission Churches: No affiliation.
2. New Mission Megachurches: Affiliation to a strong leader.
3. New Mission Church Groups: Affiliation through language, nationality or creed.
4. Denominational New Mission Churches: Affiliation to a mother church.[4]

There are many similarities here to my typologies. For example, her fourth category is similar to my category of 'Mega Churches from Global South', and her first category is similar to my 'Independent Pentecostal immigrant churches which started in Sweden' group. But my typology does not include a special category of churches in which language and nationality are viewed as the deciding marker, since I think that a majority of the Pentecostal churches I have included actually have this factor in common.[5] Her typology also does not include my category of churches with links to already-established churches. Currently, I do not know whether this is due to the differences between the Swedish and German contexts, or if these links were not included in her investigation.

The majority of the churches I studied possess a common structure for parish activities, which I think aligns closely with the weekly schedule which Werner Kahl[6] has described as being typical of African Pentecostal churches in Germany.

A weekly schedule could be simplified as follows:

* Sunday – church service
* Monday – prayer group
* Wednesday – Bible study
* Friday – evening meeting
* Saturday – musical/worship rehearsal, possibly with choir or worship team.

---

4 Claudia Währisch-Oblau, 'We shall be Fruitful in this Land: Pentecostal and Charismatic New Mission Churches in Europe', in André Droogers, Cornelius van der Laan and Wout van Laar (eds), *Fruitful in this Land – Pluralism, Dialogue and Healing in Migrant Pentecostalism,* (Boekencentrum, Zoetermeer, The Netherlands, 2006).
5 Admittedly, I have only studied one French-language church, and the language might play a more decisive role there.
6 Werner Kahl, 'Migrationsgemeinden aus Afrika in Deutschland – Zum Phänomen, zu seiner Genese und Bedeutung', in Werner Kahl and Martin Keiper (eds), *Zusammen wachsen – Weltweite Ökumene in Deutschland gestalten,* (Hamburg: Evangelisches Missionswerk in Deutschland, 2011).

In addition, there are special events, such as prayer night on Friday or Saturday, or a weekend conference with a guest speaker, often from an African country.

There are often networks between different European countries, so that the headquarters of several African missionary churches in Europe can be found in the UK or the Netherlands.

Usually, the congregations consist of small groups, rarely above 30 to 50 members. They often meet in a home or in a rented room, and frequently possess a clearly ethnic character due to the nationality of the group's leader. Above all, they are located in metropolitan areas, although some groups have also established themselves in medium-sized cities such as Eskilstuna, Kalmar and Borlänge. The situation is not static, and congregations arise, split, and disappear, often due to the conditions of uncertainty faced by migrant groups, who come to Sweden for shorter periods, whether for temporary work or for studies.

Below is a selection of Pentecostal congregations and churches that fit within my typologies. Since the typologies are quite generalised, the boundaries are not always clear, and some congregations fit into several categories, or they change categories over time. Southern Sweden is dominant among these examples, since this is where I live and work. Most of the examples come from communities whose church services I have attended at least once during the past five years.

1. 'Mega Churches' from the 'Global South'

Deeper Life Bible Church

Deeper Life Bible Church is one of the early 'big' Pentecostal churches in Nigeria. It was started in 1973 and was long considered the world's largest church (besides the Korean churches). This church is led by William F. Kumuyi. It has sometimes focused significantly on sanctification and holiness, which might explain why its membership declined in the 1980s, during which the church opposed the possession of televisions and uses of other media. Their position on this point has since changed, and today, just like other Pentecostal churches in Nigeria, they use both television and the internet to spread their message. Nevertheless, they have retained some of the features and rules that reflect their historical emphasis on sanctification, such as separating men and women at church services, discouraging the use of jewellery, and so on. Deeper Life has several churches in Europe, the majority of them in Britain. In Sweden they started their first congregation in 2009 in Umeå, and today they also have churches in Luleå, Uppsala, Västerås, Gothenburg, and Stockholm. The work in Sweden (and the other Nordic countries) is led by Dr Ogonna Obudulu, a graduate of Umeå Plant Science Centre who is presently working at Gothenburg University. Their activities have attracted the attention of Radio Sweden.[7]

The majority of the members are students. The official number of members in Sweden is 50, but more than 200 people attended their annual Christmas retreats in 2012 and 2014.

Redeemed Christian Church of God (RCCG)

RCCG is one of the largest Pentecostal churches in Nigeria, with about 6 million members in more than 80 countries worldwide. It was founded in 1952 by Joshia Akindayomi, and originated from the *Aladura* movement, a domestic Nigerian church movement that emerged in the early 1900s. Upon the death of the founder in 1980, the current leader, Enoch Adeboye, took over, and under his leadership RCCG grew from a marginal *Aladura* church into one of the leading Pentecostal churches in Africa. The number of congregations in Nigeria has grown since the 1980s, and while it previously included mainly low-skilled members, it now attracts a growing number of middle-class professionals.

RCCG has a large centre outside Lagos called Redemption Camp, where people gather for regular prayer meetings and conferences that attract large crowds. Figures from 700,000 to 1.5 million are cited in various contexts. Since the early 1990s, RCCG has expanded both to other African countries and to several countries in Europe.

The church's vision is expressed in the following points:

To make heaven.
To take as many people as possible with us.
To have a member of RCCG in every family of every nation.
To accomplish No. 1 above, holiness will be our lifestyle.
To accomplish Nos 2 and 3 above, we will plant churches within five minutes' walking distance in every city and town of developing countries, and within five minutes' driving distance in every city and town of developed countries. We will pursue these objectives until every Nation in the World is reached for Jesus Christ our Lord.[8]

They have divided Europe into two areas: in the UK and Ireland (with headquarters in London), and in what they call 'Mainland Europe' (with headquarters in The Hague). They have been especially successful in the UK, where they have about 860 congregations, most of them in London. Their annual All Night Prayer Festival of Life gathered 40,000 people in 2010. Their social work has been recognised in British media and by politicians and the royal

---

[7] http://sverigesradio.se/sida/avsnitt/114637?programid=3103. 'Missionär i Hednaland', documentary on Sveriges Radio P4 2012 about Deeper Life Church and its work in Umeå.

[8] RCCG Central Office Europe, https://www.rccguk.church/mandate/ (Accessed 19th August 2019).

family. They have also established contact with the Church of England (the contact is through their national offices working together with Church of England through Churches Together in England (CTE) instruments. The national leader of RCCG UK is the Pentecostal president of CTE and so in this capacity works with the Archbishop of Canterbury).

Mainland Europe is organised into three Regions, with headquarters in The Netherlands (Region 1), Spain (Region 2) and Sweden (Region 3).

Region 3 consists of 19 countries, including the Nordic Countries, the Baltic states and Eastern Europe.

They started their first church in Sweden in Gothenburg in 2001, and today they have 32 congregations in total throughout Sweden. The present leader is pastor Sola Oludoji, who is also a pastor of Royal Connections Church in London, but regularly visits Sweden and other countries of the region.

Despite the rather strict organisation and hierarchical leadership structure, the individual congregations seem to enjoy a lot of freedom for action, and they can even start new congregations. The oldest congregation in Sweden, Jesus Connections in Gothenburg, has become a member of Evangeliska frikyrkan (EFK).

Today, there are congregations in 18 cities in Sweden, including Stockholm (6), Gothenburg (4), Malmö (3), Uppsala (2) and Borås (2).[9] Each congregation is led by a pastor or deacon. Most of the pastors originate from Nigeria, but there are exceptions. A typical congregation probably has between 30 and 70 members.

However, there is a large flow of people coming and going, so the number of worshippers in a year in a given congregation can vary between 30 and 110. The majority are of African origin, but other groups are represented as well. For example, in 2011, the church in Karlskrona had a large group of Indian members. Most of the non-African members are married to, or have some other form of relationship with, an African member.

The language used for services is English, although some meetings include a Swedish interpretation. Swedish-language church services are held once every quarter. Once per year, they hold a 'multicultural Sunday', where members are encouraged to wear traditional clothes and sing songs from their countries of origin.

In addition to the English-speaking part of RCCG, there are three Hispanic congregations (Iglesia de Dios Redimida) in Sweden. These are located in Stockholm, Norrköping and Jönköping, and have been formed in contact with an RCCG congregation in Valencia, Spain. Their pastors originate from Chile and Bolivia, and the members mostly have Latin American roots. The congregation in Norrköping originated from an independent Latino congregation, Jesus Vive, which was founded in the early 2000s and joined RCCG in 2010.

---

9 See list in the brochure Festival of Life, Stockholm Sweden April 15, 2016.

In 2016, the church organized a Festival of Life at Stockholm Waterfront Arena with around 1,500 participants. Pastor Enoch Adeboye and Pelle Hörnmark, the leader of the Swedish Pentecostal Movement, were the main speakers.[10]

Enoch Adeboye was in Sweden for several days, and during this time visited the Swedish Parliament, where he met with a group of Christian MPs.

Mountain of Fire and Miracle

This is a Nigerian Pentecostal church led by Daniel Kolawole Olukola. It was founded in 1994 and has congregations in Nigeria and several European countries. It is best known for its emphasis on deliverance and spiritual warfare. Olukola is both a pastor and a biochemical researcher, and has published both prayer collections and articles in scientific journals.[11]

This church's activities in Sweden began in August 2009 with a small group in Hässleholm, and it currently has two congregations in Stockholm (Skanstull and Alby) and two smaller prayer groups in Malmö and Helsingborg. The work in Sweden is led by Pastor Peter Clarvel Uti, who has been specifically seconded by Olukola. According to Uti, in the early years they were in contact with Pastor Thomas Anderson, from Göingekyrkan in Hässleholm.

The church's emphasis is on prayer and deliverance, and it tends to keep strictly to its own doctrines and to keep some distance from other congregations.

Christ Embassy Sweden

The Christ Embassy Church in Nigeria is led by Pastor Chris Oyakhilome.

In 2013, the church started a congregation in Stockholm, holding meetings in Flemingsberg. According to Pastor Angela, who leads the Swedish branch, about 50 people attend the church services. They also distribute a devotional book, 'Rapsodi i Realiteten',[12] which is published every month in Swedish with a daily devotional written by Oyakhilome and his wife Anita. The book is translated from English and is printed in Nigeria. Recently, a church was started in Malmö called New Birth Embassy, which, according to its pastor, is inspired by the teaching of Oyakhilome. Christ Embassy had some publicity in the Swedish Christian newspaper Dagen, which published an article about how Oyakhilome is the richest pastor in the world.[13]

---

10 https://www.varldenidag.se/tro-och-liv/ett-ar-praglat-av-enhet-nya-initiativ-och-tillvaxt/BbbplA!GwsvGk0iPIgnCZjGnwufDw/ (Accessed 10th March 2019).

11 http://www.cesnur.org/2005/pa_adogame.htm (Accessed 20th February 2013).

12 http://www.rhapsodyofrealities.org/index.php/en/ (accessed 2013-02-20).

13 https://www.dagen.se/de-forsvarar-pastorns-450-miljoner-kronor-1.351452?paywall=true (Accessed 20th February 2013).

Manmin Church Stockholm

Manmin Church has its headquarters in Seoul, South Korea, where it was founded by Pastor Jaerock Lee in 1982. The word *Manmin* is Korean, and translates approximately to 'All creation, all peoples and nations'. Currently, the church claims to have over 9,000 churches worldwide, with 120,000 members, the majority of them in Korea. It is known for its television programmes, which are broadcast in several countries.

Activities in Sweden started in 2006 with five members in Stockholm. During my visit to the church in 2012, they claimed to have 25 members, but the service was only attended by two families. The service strictly followed a defined liturgy, which also included prayers by the leader who appeared on a computer. They distribute several books by Lee, including a 300-page biography of his life which is printed in Korea and translated into Swedish.

Jesus Is Lord Church

This is a Filipino church which was started in 1978 by Eddie C. Villanueva and is considered the largest non-Catholic Charismatic church in the Philippines today. It has a large number of members (figures vary between 750,000 and 2 million) in both the Philippines and the Filipino diaspora around the world.

The leader, Villanueva – known as 'spiritual director' – has twice entered the presidential election in the Philippines, and the church has formed its own political party.

The European headquarters of the church is located in Italy. In Sweden there are three congregations. The first was founded in Gothenburg in 2003, and there is now a second one in Gothenburg; and there was also one in Jönköping, founded in 2012. Altogether, the church has about 100 members in Sweden. The majority of members and those who visit the church services are women of Filipino origin. The services are held in English. Organizationally, the congregations are overseen as part of a region which also includes Norway. The members of Jesus Is Lord Church in Jönköping left the church in 2017 to start an independent church called Amazing Grace of Christ Church.[14]

Igreja Universal do Reino de Deus

This is a Brazilian Pentecostal church, which was founded in 1977 by Bishop Edir Macedo and is considered one of the larger Pentecostal churches in the world today. In Swedish, they are called Gudsrikets Universella kyrka.[15]

It was established in Sweden in 2007. According to Pastor Daniel Guerrero, the reason for which this congregation was started was that many Brazilians living in Sweden had heard of this church at home and had asked that one be

---

14 https://www.facebook.com/pg/Amazing-Grace-Of-Christ-
122000394824464/about/?ref=page_internal (Accessed 9th March 2019)
15 In English *Universal Church of the Kingdom of God* (UCKG). The Portuguese abbreviation is IURD.

planted in Sweden as well. Guerrero, formerly a pastor in New York and Florida, leads the work along with an assistant pastor.

The church premises are located quite centrally in Stockholm, where activities take place daily, including religious services, advisory services and activities for young people. The venue is located on the ground floor, and is open and bright, with a table for coffee and conversation, and a corner stocked with Portuguese and English books about the church and its founder. A smaller room for religious services is located further inside.

Following the pattern of IURD's work in other countries,[16] there are set themes for each week day, according to the following schedule: Monday – finance; Tuesday – physical health; Wednesday – Bible studies; Thursday – emotional health; Friday – spiritual healing; Saturday – evangelisation and youth activities; Sunday – church services with a focus on the family.

These activities involve about 100 people, most of whom are Portuguese-speaking; but meetings are also held in Spanish and English. Pastor Guerrero estimated that the number of Swedish-speakers is around 15 per cent.

The church has also used Öppna kanalen[17] to spread its message. Information brochures about the church have been translated into Swedish, in which religious terms have been deemphasised. According to Guerrero, this is deliberate, and is intended as a strategy by which to reach out to Swedes.

Zion Temple Sweden

This is a branch of the Church of Zion Temple Rwanda, which was founded in 1999 by Paul Gitwaza, and has congregations in the UK, Belgium, Denmark and Sweden.

In Sweden, a congregation was started in Eskilstuna in 2009. The majority of the members are from Rwanda, and the service is held in French. It keeps in frequent contact with the Zion Temple in Copenhagen, and regularly participates in the latter's conferences.[18]

In 2017, Paul Gitwaza visited Sweden and preached in Eskilstuna and Gothenburg. The meeting in Eskilstuna was held in a cinema, which was nearly full (mostly with Africans from many places, especially in the middle of Sweden). A short presentation was also given by the Rwandan Ambassador to Sweden. In his sermon, Gitwaza thanked the Scandinavian missionaries who had come to the Congo and other parts of Africa. Mentioning that his father became

---

16 "I have visited their church in Toronto a couple of times. Very different approach to about everything they do in terms of church. Worship 3x every day (except Sat and Sun). Each day is devoted so some aspect of life (personal, work, family, bible study, etc.)." – mail conversation with David A. Reed, Professor Emeritus from Wycliffe College, Toronto, Canada, 29th August, 2013.

17 Cable TV channel which reaches about 620,000 households in the Stockholm area, http://www. oppnakanalenstockholm.se/; (Accessed 20th February 2013).

18 Information from the web site and from discussions with members I met in Copenhagen in 2010.

a Christian through having been taught by Norwegian missionaries, he explained that he is now paying back this debt by preaching the gospel in the Scandinavian countries.

2. Independent Pentecostal Immigrant Churches which Started in Sweden

Restoration Fire Ministries

This congregation was started in the late 1990s in Malmö and is led by Pastor Rita Richmore from Nigeria (along with her husband Francis). Its emphasis is upon prayer and spiritual warfare. The leaders of the congregation come from Nigeria, but members also come from other African countries.

Before founding the congregation, the Richmores had been members in Malmö Bibelcenter (belonging to Trosrörelsen). Restoration Fire Ministries has its own venue in an industrial area in Malmö, with room for about 150 people. When I visited one of their church services in 2012, they were hosting a guest speaker from Nigeria, Bishop Francis Wale Oke, who founded Sword of the Spirit Ministries. The premises were overcrowded.

All Nations

This is a loose group of about 40 people, mostly women of African descent, who meet in the S:ta Maria church (Svenska Kyrkan) in Malmö on Sunday afternoons.

It is led by Pastor Victoria Pedersen from Kenya. She says she has been inspired by the prophet, Dr Owour[19] from Kenya, who visited Sweden in 2010.[20]

In 2013, she organised some meetings with Dr Owour in Malmö.[21]

Elim Pentecostal Church

This is a congregation in Malmö with origins in Ghana, led by Pastor Philip Boakye-Agymang. Before he founded the congregation in 2003, he was a member of the international community of Pingstkyrkan in Malmö.

Most of the members have origins in Ghana, but there are also Tanzanians in their numbers. About 110 people participate in the church services, which are held in a private room in an industrial area in Malmö. The services are held in English.

Iglesia Evangelica Asamblea de Dios-Suecia / Församlingen Den Gode

---

[19] http://nkc.be/profet-owour (Accessed 20th February 2013).
[20] Visiting, among other places, Gnarp and Stockholm.
http://www.repentandpreparetheway. org/ (Accessed 20th February 2013).
[21] https://www.youtube.com/watch?v=9ZzW8Y4C0tY (Accessed 9th March 2019).

Samariten

This is a congregation in Borås, founded in 2010 by Giorgio Pereira Rodriguez and his wife Ivonete Pereira Santana. They both studied at a Bible school in São Paulo, which was run by the Assembly of God Ministry Santos. In 2010, they were sent by the apostle Alves Corea as missionaries to Sweden. Services are held in Spanish and Portuguese, with Swedish interpretation provided. There are about 50 members, mainly with Latin American origins.

The congregation also operates the second-hand store, 'The Good Samaritan', the proceeds of which go to various projects for the homeless and the poor in Brazil. They previously hired premises from RCCG, but have recently acquired their own. The congregation is regularly visited by various guest speakers from Brazil. In 2016, they joined the organisation of churches led by Apostle Guillermo Maldonado in Florida, USA.[22]

Missões Evangeliticas Vinde Amados Meus[23] (MEVAM Malmö/Kalmar)

This congregation was started as a prayer group in September 2010 by the two Brazilian footballers Wilton Figuereido and Ricardo Ferreira da Silva, who at that time both played professionally in Malmö FF. When, after six months, the group had grown to 20 people and had started to meet in the premises of Korskyrkan in Malmö, they decided that they needed a pastor and contacted a church in Brazil called Emmanuel Church. The latter church then decided to send a pastor to Sweden, and chose Dennis Goes, who was well-suited to the task because he held a Master of Theology degree with Friends International Christian University (FICU) from the University of Florida[24] and had a good knowledge of the English language.

A further advantage was that because of his grandmother he had Italian citizenship, which solved the problem of acquiring a work permit in Sweden. Goes came to Sweden with his family in 2010. In their first year there, they were supported by his congregation in Brazil, but this then stopped. He was then approached by an acquaintance, Apostle Luiz Herminio, who leads the MEVAM church in Brazil. They were offered an opportunity to join MEVAM and to receive financial support which would pay Goes's salary and for the rent of the congregation's premises.

MEVAM was established in Brazil in 1997 by Luiz Herminio, who is a former drug addict. They have their head office in Itajaí in southern Brazil and have about 4,000 members spread across some 30 congregations. They engage in various social enterprises in Brazil, such as drug rehabilitation, while also carrying out missionary work in India through churches and orphanages.

---

[22] http://www.guillermomaldonado.org/ (Accessed 18th March 2019)
[23] Which loosely translates into, "Gospel Mission – come my beloved".
[24] http://www.ficuflorida.com/ (Accessed 20th February 2013). See also facebook.com/FriendsinternationalChristianUniversity/.

The congregation in Malmö has grown from 15 to about 40 members today. The Portuguese language is used in church services, although there are some Swedish-speaking members who sometimes provide a Swedish interpretation. Most of the members originate from Brazil.

Since 2011, they have rented premises in Wesley-Kyrkan (Equmeniakyrkan) in Malmö, where they hold services on Sunday afternoons. They also have a student group on Tuesdays and receive regular visits from Brazilian speakers. In the materials that they have translated into Swedish, they call themselves *Internationella församlingen MEVAM – Guds Rike Upprättat i Himlen och Uppenbarat på Jorden. Portugisisktalande kyrka i Malmö.*

Goes is also responsible for MEVAM's work in Europe, with congregations in Denmark, Germany, Spain and Switzerland. In 2016, MEVAM decided to change its mission strategy, and pastor Denis Goes moved to Portugal. This led to the church in Malmö closing down. A large group of these people became members of Malmö International Church.[25] They still maintain some connections with MEVAM in Brazil, and Brazilian pastors sometimes come and preach in Malmö International church.

3. Pentecostal 'Mega Churches' Created in Sweden with Congregations in Several Countries

International Mission Church

This congregation was founded in 1999 in Stockholm by Rodolfo Rojas (23 years old at the time) and his wife Leyla Alexandra, both of whom originate from Chile. Rodolfo holds a degree in theology from Teologiska Högskolan in Stockholm which he obtained in 1996.[26]

Today, about 800 people attend the church's Sunday meetings, which are held at Åsö Gymnasium on Södermalm, and the church also has about 150 cell groups. In 2013, they started two churches (in Singapore and Södertälje). The activities of the church are focused on discipleship and leadership training. Its vision is encompassed in the following words: 'Raising a generation of leaders for God which will win the nations of the earth'. According to their own estimates, they reach about 1,500 people, the majority of whom seem to be Hispanic. Outside the Greater Stockholm area, they have local congregations in Karlstad, Sundsvall, and Flen, as well as having congregations in Finland, Spain, Switzerland and Colombia.

In 2008, Rojas spoke at the Jesus Manifestation in Stockholm. Interestingly enough, he mentioned Stanley Sjöberg and Ulf Ekman as role models for his own activities.

---

25 http://malmochurch.se/ (Accessed 18th March 2019)
26 http://www.ths.se/site/ (Accessed 20th February 2013).

He also frequently travels in Latin America and the United States, and speaks at various conferences. At a ceremony in September 2010, Rodolfo and Leyla were anointed apostles by the prophet Rony Chaves, who is with the organization, Coalition of Latin American Apostles, C.L.A. In 2011, they bought the Saxenborg Training Centre (outside Grangärde, in Ludvika) and renamed it Bethel.27 It is used for training courses, congregation camps and conferences. When it was opened in 2011, 150 people were baptised in the adjacent lake. During the summer of 2012, they held a camp for more than 200 young people, who were taught and trained to do evangelism. The camp ended with practical evangelism activities in several Swedish cities. During the riots in Husby in the summer of 2013, they went out into the suburbs to offer people support and help. Currently, they meet every Sunday at Älvsjömässan (Stockholm International Fair), and gather around 1,700 people in the service.

4. Pentecostal Immigration Churches with Connections to Swedish Churches

Iglesia del Pueblo /Folkets kyrka

This is a Spanish-language church in Sollentuna, which started in 1994, and in 1997 became a part of Pingst-Fria Församlingar i Samverkan. It is led by Pastor Luis Berrios, and the director is Victor Campos. They collaborate to a certain degree with ABF28 (the Worker's Educational Association) through workshops, which have attracted the attention of ABF's journal.29 They also run community radio broadcasts in Sollentuna.

Among the immigrant Pentecostal churches with connections to Swedish churches, there are two Spanish-speaking churches that are also worth noting. These are the Ichtus,30 led by Pastor Hernan Clavijo, and Kyrka För Alla,31 led by Pastor Eduardo Hurtado. Both churches belong to Evangeliska Frikyrkan. It is interesting to note that the website of the latter church states that 'it places

---

27 This was noted in the local papers:
http://www.dt.se/nyheter/ludvika/1.3188450kristen-forsamling-koper-saxenborg; – http://www.dt.se/nyheter/ludvika/1.3203081saxenborgs-kopare-ber-om-pengar-pa-hemsida; (Accessed 20th March 2013).
http://www.dt.se/nyheter/ ludvika/1.4968477-hoga-ljudnivaer-stor-manga-boende; (Accessed 20th March 2013).
http://www.dt.se/nyheter/ ludvika/1.3726791--saxenborg-ar-herrens-boning. (Accessed 20th March 2013).
28 https://www.abf.se/distrikt--avdelningar/abf-skane/abf-malmo/english/ (Accessed 18th March 2019)
29 http://www.jvnf.org/books/Folkets_kyrka_Sollentuna_ABF_reportage_2008.pdf (Accessed 20th March 2013).
30 http://www.dagen.se/nyheter/avknoppades-till-en-egen-forsamling/ and http://www.icthus.se/contacto/ (Accessed 20th March 2013).
31 http://www.kfasweden.com/ (Accessed 20th March 2013).

itself under the protection of EFK'.[32] A third example with Equmeniakyrkan (Uniting Church in Sweden, an ecumenical umbrella for churches) is the English-speaking part of Hallundakyrkan,[33] south of Stockholm, the activities of which are led by Reverend Samuel Nweze from Nigeria. The English-language congregation, which meets on Sunday afternoons, has significantly more attendees than the Swedish-language congregation. Its form is clearly Pentecostal, which is also where Nweze positions himself theologically.[34]

Concluding Thoughts and Some Development since 2013

I created this typology for an article published in Sweden in 2013.[35] Since then, I have been following many of the churches I mentioned as well as some new ones. I will therefore end this chapter with some reflections on developments since 2013.

Mission in Sweden

When I wrote about RCCG in Sweden and the UK in 2005, I stated that their mission could be understood at four different levels.

The first concerns their mission to Europe, where the aim is to reach out to all European people. The second concerns their mission in Europe, where the focus is upon helping their fellow Africans. The third concern their efforts to establish relationships with churches and denominations in Europe, with whom there might be mutual exchange, learning and support.

The fourth concerns their efforts to bring back the supernatural aspect of Christianity to Europe, which might be accomplished through prayer, healing and deliverance.

I continue to believe that these four factors are an important part of how many migrant Pentecostals see their mission in Sweden today.

Identity in Sweden

In a study of two African congregations in Uppsala (RCCG and Deeper Life), Jan-Åke Alvarsson describes the way in which members are shifting in their identity from being emigrants to becoming immigrants, as well as the way in which the churches which are largely mono-cultural become homes away from

---

[32] Reverend Tutu Olutayo from Jesus Connections (in Gothenburg) advanced a similar argument when he said that their congregation, which is part of the Redeemed Christian Church of God, also joined the Evangelical Free Church. The reason for this was to protect themselves from being accused of being a cult. (Conversation with author Nov 11, 2012).
[33] http://www.hallundakyrkan.se/index_en.html (Accessed 20th March 2013).
[34] Interview with Reverend Samuel Nweze 29 August 2010. He has a background within the Anglican Church in Nigeria, which he says is very charismatic.
[35] Nils Malmström, 'Pentekostala invandrarkyrkor', in Åke Alvarsson (ed) *Pentekostalismen i Sverige på 2000-talet* (Uppsala: 2013).

home for Africans who are seeking to engage meaningfully in multicultural Swedish society.[36]
I believe this observation is correct. For churches in my first category, in particular, it appears to be evident that over time there is a shift in the way in which people relate to their churches in their countries of origin. This is indicated, for example, by the way in which the founder becomes less visible in the church service or in the print materials used by the church.[37]

Academic Attention
Ever since the growth in the number of migrant Pentecostals in Sweden, there has been more academic work done on this subject.
Torbjörn Aronsson, Reader in Church History at Uppsala University, has listed around 130 Migrant Pentecostal churches in Sweden, and he estimates that they influence around 20,000 people in Sweden today. Of these churches, one third are a part of RCCG and IMC.[38] He has also published some articles on this subject, and has highlighted, in particular, the growth taking place in Stockholm among Spanish-speaking and Ethiopian groups. He has also blogged about church growth, including the growth of migrant churches.[39]

Media Attention
Generally, not much attention has been paid to the migrant Pentecostal churches in Swedish media. There have been some articles in local newspapers about a few congregations and their work.[40] In some cases, there has been an observable cultural clash when a pastor has met with a Swedish journalist.[41] In the two main Pentecostal newspapers, Dagen and Världen Idag, there have been several

---

[36] Alvarsson, Jan-Åke, 'Afrikanska pentekostaler i Sverige. Kyrkans roll i skapandet av en ny identitet', in Hovdelien Achim & Kringlebotn Sodal (ed) *Kristne Migranter i Norden* (Kristiansand: 2016).
[37] This observation emerges from having followed African churches in Sweden since 2003, but the reason for this needs to be analysed with reference to more facts from interviews.
[38] Torbjörn Aronson, *Ett nytt karismatiskt landskap i Sverige* (Stockholm: 2016), 31-36.
[39] https://www.teol.se/blog/forsamlingstillvaxtbloggen/migrantforsamlingar-i-stor-stockholm/ (Accessed 9th March 2019).
[40] https://www.hallandsposten.se/familj/ny-kyrka-s%C3%A4tter-gl%C3%A4djen-i-fokus-1.7443863?noAccess=true&aId=1.7443863. (Accessed 9th March 2019). "That a service of worship can be celebrated in many different ways becomes evident when you visit The Redeemed Christian Church of God. The congregation has been in Halmstad for over a year and is now pleased to have its own premises." 1st August 2018.
[41] Phillip Alfredsson, "NWT möter IMC-pastor", *Wermlands Tidningen* 1st August 2017. This article is based on an interview with the local pastor of IMC in Karlstad about a prayer meeting they held in an area of Karlstad in which there are plans to build a mosque. You can feel the tension between the lines – a tension which was also confirmed by the journalist in an email to the author.

articles about migrant Pentecostal churches. For example, Torbjörn Aronson has written several articles in Världen Idag, and has also been quoted in Dagen.

Additionally, there are two people with connections to migrant Pentecostalism who have been popular guests in Swedish media. One of these is the former criminal and rap artist, Sebastian Stakset, who received a lot of attention after his conversion to Christianity.[42] One point that came up in some interviews with him is that he belongs to a small Spanish-speaking congregation.[43]

The other person is Annahita Parsan, whose story about her journey from Iran to Sweden and from Islam to Christianity has received much attention in the media, and has even led to a book.[44] Today, she works as a priest in the Church of Sweden (Lutheran).[45] Even though she does not belong to a Pentecostal migrant church, her message has several features in common with Charismatic Christianity, and her work is primarily among migrants from the Middle East.[46]

Ecumenical Relations

The growth of migrant churches in Sweden has also had fresh implications for the ecumenical scene. In 2013, the Christian Council of Sweden[47] conducted a three-month survey to learn about migrant churches in Sweden.[48] The results were presented at a meeting in Stockholm in April 2013. The survey reached 117 congregations of which the Christian Council of Sweden had relations with

---

[42] https://sverigesradio.se/sida/avsnitt/1049625?programid=3765
https://www.tv4.se/nyhetsmorgon/klipp/sebastian-stakset-vill-be-om-f%C3%B6rl%C3%A5telse-f%C3%B6r-vad-jag-gjort-3796052 (Accessed 9th March 2019).

[43] https://sverigesradio.se/avsnitt/1158533 (Accessed 9th March 2019).
"Q: You are member of a church called Ichtus?
A: Yes
Q: What kind of church is that?
A: It is a lot of latinos. Gloria Dios...ha ha.
Q: Are you also saying like that?
A: No I praise the Lord in Swedish really. At least for the moment. You could say I am like milk in the coffee in this church."

[44] https://www.svt.se/nar-livet-vander/annahita-har-overlevt-bade-misshandel-och-fanglager/ (Accessed 3rd September 2019).
https://www.tv4.se/efter-tio/artiklar/muslimska-annahita-blev-svensk-pr%C3%A4st-55238774fca38fe5b9000100 (Accessed 3rd September 2019).
Annahita Parshan and Craige Borlase, *Stranger No More* (Nashville: Thomas Nelson, 2017).

[45] http://www.junia.se/profilen/muslimsk-sommerska-fran-iran-blev-prast-i-svenska-kyrkan/ (Accessed 3rd September 2019).

[46] http://budbararen.nu/artikel/vackelsen-i-hammarbykyrkan/ (Accessed 3rd September 2019). Annahita Parshan and Craige Borlase, *Stranger No More*.

[47] https://en.skr.org/ (Accessed 20th February 2013).

[48] https://www.skr.org/kartlaggning-av-migrantforsamlingar-i-sverige/ (Accessed 3rd September 2019).

many, although only a few showed up at the presentation. Unfortunately, the report has not been published, and so, the exact results are not known, and the work did not proceed from there.

From 2013 to 2015, EFK (Evangeliska Frikyrkan) regularly held meetings for migrant pastors on topics such as leadership, communication with authorities in Sweden, developing a deeper understanding of Swedish Christianity, and reaching the second generation of immigrants.[49]

In local contexts, the situation varies little from place to place, but there are cities in which migrant pastors have been invited to take part in different ecumenical meetings.

Notably, the premises of other Swedish churches are also rented by these groups to be used as places of worship. In such cases, I believe it is important for Swedish churches to be generous, but also to be clear about what they want from this kind of cooperation.

In some cases, the cooperation has worked out well, but in others, there have been tensions and even difficulties caused by everything from noise complaints to theological objections to healing practices and prosperity teaching.

Challenges in Swedish Society

The immigrants in many of these churches are in a position in which they struggle to understand and fit into Swedish society. Sometimes their struggles are economic; sometimes they have to do with racism, or simply to clashes surrounding Swedish laws and values. Here, the churches play a crucial role in many individuals' lives, offering them help and support.

Pentecostal immigrant churches have only recently attracted attention from the outside, and this article represents an attempt to give a brief sketch of some of these groups. Groups that are missing in my survey include churches originating from the Middle East and from French-speaking parts of Africa where Pentecostalism is prominent, such as Congo-Kinshasa.

A more comprehensive study would be very interesting, particularly one that uses outreach-based methods such as interviews and the first-hand observation of worship services. I believe that such a study would reveal a number of groups that have not previously been identified, thus providing an even more nuanced picture of Pentecostalism in Sweden today.

References

Alfredsson, Philipe, *NWT möter IMC-pastorn,* (Nya Wermlands-Tidningen 2 augusti 2017.)

Alvarsson, Jan-Åke, *Afrikanska pentekostaler i Sverige. Kyrkans roll i skapandet av en ny identitet,* in Achim, Hovdelien, Kringlebotn Sodal(editor) *Kristne Migranter i Norden,* (Portal forlag, Kristiansand 2016.)

---

49 Talk with Markus Sand 18th March 2019. http://www.efk.se/kontakt/personal-efks-sverigekontor.html?lp-page=3 (Accessed 18th March 2019).

Anderson, Allan & Tang, Edmond (Ed), *Asian and Pentecostal – The Charismatic Face of Christianity in Asia,* (Regnum books International, 2003.)

Aronson, Torbjörn, *Ett nytt karismatiskt landskap i Sverige,* (Areopagos Stockholm 2016.)

Bosund Hedberg, Marie, *De sjunger Herrens lov i främmande länder;* (Uppdrag Mission, Nr 5., 2011 årgång 165.)

Droogers, André & van der Laan, Cornelius & van Laar, Wout (eds), *Fruitful in this Land – Pluralism, Dialogue and Healing in Migrant Pentecostalism,* (Boekencentrum, Zoetermeer, The Netherlands, 2006.)

Festival of Life – Inaugural FOL in Northern Europe. April 15 2016. Brochure distributed at Festival of Life in Stockholm 15 April 2016.

Jenkins, Philip, *The Next Christendom: The Coming of Global Christianity,* (Oxford University Press, 3 edition, 2011.)

Kahl, Werner & Keiper Martin (red), *Zusammen wachsen – Weltweite Ökumene in Deutschland gestalten,* (Evangelisches Missionswerk in Deutschland, Hamburg 2011.)

Lee, Jaerock, *Budskapet om Korset,* (Urim Books, Seoul, Sydkorea, 2012.)

Lee, Jaerock, *Mitt Liv – Min Tro,* (Urim Books, Seoul, Sydkorea, 2011.)

Macedo, Edir, *Nothing to Lose – Moments of Conviction that Changed My Life,* (Barcelona, 2012.)

Malmström, Nils, *Pentekostala Migrantkyrkor,* in Alvarsson, Jan-Åke, (Ed) *Pentekostalism i Sverige på 2000 talet,* (Institutet för Pentekostala Studier ,Uppsala ,2013)

Ojo, Matthews A, *The End-Time Army: Charismatic movements in modern Nigeria,*(African World Press Inc,Trenton NJ, 2006.)

Parshan, Annahita & Borlase Craige, *Stranger no more,* (Thomas Nelson, 2017.)

Persson, Yvonne, *Ny kyrka sätter glädjen i focus,* (Hallandsposten 1 aug, 2018.)

Suico, Joseph, *Pentecostalism in the Philippines.* i Anderson, Allan & Tang, Edmond (Ed), *Asian and Pentecostal – The Charismatic Face of Christianity in Asia,* (Regnum books International, 2003.)

Ukah, Asonzeh F-K, *A New Paradigm of Pentecostal Power: A Study of the Redeemed Christian Church of God in Nigeria.* (African World Press, Inc, Trenton, NJ, 2008.)

Wonsuk Ma, artikel *Philippines* och *Villanueva, Eddie C.* i Burgess & Van der Maas, *The new International Dictionary of Pentecostal and Charismatic Movements,* (Zondervan, Grand Rapids, 2002.)

Unpublished Material

Malmström, N., *Bringing the Gospel Back to Europe: En studie av Redeemed Christian Church of God´s mission I Storbritannien och Skandinavien.* (Unpublished Essay at Center for Theology and Religion, Lund University, 2006.)

Malmström, N., *How to Interpret a Case of African Pentecostalism: Focusing Upon Classification, Formative Processes and Characteristics of Contemporary Nigerian Pentecostalism.* (Unpublished Essay at Center for Theology and Religion, Lund University, 2009.)

Premack, Laura, *Hope and the Holy Spirit: The Global Pentecostal Movement in Brazil and Nigeria 1910-2010,* (Unpublished Phd dissertation from University of North Carolina, 2013.)

Internet Sources

http://www.deeperlifesweden.se/ (accessed 2013-02-20).

http://sverigesradio.se/sida/avsnitt/114637?programid=3103 Sveriges Radio P4 dokumentär "Missionär i Hednaland" (accessed 20130220)2012. En dokumentär om Deeper Life Church och dess arbete i Umeå.

http://www.rccgmainlandeurope.org/ http://www.centropeniel.com/ (accessed 2013-02-20).

http://www.mfmsweden.org/index.html http://www.mountainoffire.org/ (accessed 2013-02-20).

http://www.cesnur.org/2005/pa_adogame.htm (accessed 2013-02-20).

http://www.christembassy.org/hikanotes/ (accessed 2013-02-20).

http://www.rhapsodyofrealities.org/index.php/en/ (accessed 2013-02-20).

http://manminchurch.se/index.html (accessed 2013-02-20).

http://www.manmin.org/foreign/main.asp http://jilsweden.se/ (accessed 2013-02-20).

http://www.uckg.se/ (accessed 2013-02-20).

http://www.ziontemplesweden.org/index.php?option=com_content&view=article&id=8&Itemid=18&lang=sv http://www.ziontemplerwanda.org/ (accessed 2013-02-20).

http://www.restorationministries.se/ http://www.repentandpreparetheway.org/ (accessed 2013-02-20).

http://nkc.be/profet-owour/ http://www.mevam.org.br/ (accessed 2013-02-20).

http://www.bethesdastockholm.se/ http://www.ficuflorida.com/ (accessed 2013-02-20).

http://www.imcstockholm.se/ http://www.imckarlstad.se/ (accessed 2013-02-20).

http://www.varldenidag.se/nyhet/2008/05/02/Leder-forsamling-med800-medlemmar-nu-talar-pastor-Rodolfo-pa-Jesusmanifestationen (accessed 20130220)www.varldenidag.se/nyhet/2013/05/23/Pastor-vill-ge-stod-tillorosdrabbad-forort (accessed 2013-02-20).

http://www.dt.se/nyheter/ludvika/1.3188450-kristen-forsamling-kopersaxenborg (accessed 2013-02-20).

http://www.dt.se/nyheter/ludvika/1.3203081-saxenborgs-kopare-ber-ompengar-pa-hemsida (accessed 2013-02-20).

http://www.dt.se/nyheter/ludvika/1.4968477-hoga-ljudnivaer-stor-manga-boende (accessed 2013-02-20).

http://www.dt.se/nyheter/ludvika/1.3726791--saxenborg-ar-herrensboninghttp://ihcc.se/ (accessed 2013-02-20).

http://www.hallundakyrkan.se/index_en.html http://www.kfasweden.com (accessed 2013-02-20).

http://www.icthus.se/contacto/ (accessed 2013-02-20).

http://www.dagen.se/nyheter/avknoppades-till-en-egen-forsamling (accessed 2013-02-20).

https://www.teol.se/blog/forsamlingstillvaxtbloggen/migrantforsamlingar-i-stor-stockholm/ (accessed 2019-03-20).

https://www.hallandsposten.se/familj/ny-kyrka-s%C3%A4tter-gl%C3%A4djen-i-fokus-1.7443863?noAccess=true&aId=1.7443863. (accessed 2019-03-09).

https://sverigesradio.se/sida/avsnitt/1049625?programid=3765

https://www.tv4.se/nyhetsmorgon/klipp/sebastian-stakset-vill-be-om-f%C3%B6rl%C3%A5telse-f%C3%B6r-vad-jag-gjort-3796052 (accessed 2013-02-20).

https://sverigesradio.se/avsnitt/1158533 (accessed 2019-03-09).

https://www.svt.se/nar-livet-vander/annahita-har-overlevt-bade-misshandel-och-fanglager/ (accessed 2019-03-09).

https://www.tv4.se/efter-tio/artiklar/muslimska-annahita-blev-svensk-pr%C3%A4st-55238774fca38fe5b9000100 (accessed 2019-03-09).

http://www.junia.se/profilen/muslimsk-sommerska-fran-iran-blev-prast-i-svenska-kyrkan/ (accessed 2019-03-09).

http://budbararen.nu/artikel/vackelsen-i-hammarbykyrkan/ (accessed 2019-03-09).

https://en.skr.org/ (accessed 2019-03-09).

https://www.skr.org/kartlaggning-av-migrantforsamlingar-i-sverige/ (accessed 2019-03-09).

https://www.varldenidag.se/tro-och-liv/ett-ar-praglat-av-enhet-nya-initiativ-och-tillvaxt/BbbplA!GwsvGk0iPIgnCZjGnwufDw/ (accessed 2019-03-09).

https://www.youtube.com/watch?v=9ZzW8Y4C0tY (accessed 2019-03-09).

https://www.facebook.com/pg/Amazing-Grace-Of-Christ-122000394824464/about/?ref=page_internal (accessed 2019-03-09).

http://www.guillermomaldonado.org/ (accessed 2019-03-18)

http://malmochurch.se/ (accessed 2019-03-18)

https://www.abf.se/distrikt--avdelningar/abf-skane/abf-malmo/english/ (accessed 2019-03-18)

http://www.efk.se/kontakt/personal-efks-sverigekontor.html?lp-page=3 (accessed 2019-03-18)

RCC Central Office Europe, https://www.rccguk.church/mandate/ (accessed 2019-08-19)

(9) Migration and Mission: British Missionaries in Italy
Claire and Mark Ord

Introduction

Our son Lewis belongs to an improbably-named gang at school called the 'The Rubber Duckies'. It has an open and fluctuating membership, but the core of the group is made up of five 10-year-old boys, a Syrian, a Bangladeshi, a Brazilian, a Chinese and an Italian. Each speaks another language, in addition to English, and the world faiths are represented in the gang – Islam, Buddhism and Christianity. Of these boys, two were born in the UK, and the simple-sounding question, 'where are you from?', would receive some surprising answers – not least from Lewis, who was born in Italy to British parents. Migration and identity are complex issues in the UK today. It will be interesting to see if these boys remain friends over the coming years, although it is likely they will drop the tag of 'Rubber Duckies'. It is certainly the case that their opportunities and experience of inclusion and exclusion will be different and will, in large part, depend on how they are seen and the opportunities they receive.

It will also depend on what they give to those around them, which will itself, in turn, be conditioned by what their neighbours – to use the biblical term – are able to receive from them. These are political issues, though in biblical terms, where faith is always an embodied matter and God's action is intertwined with politics, economics and the dynamics of identity, they are also theological concerns – matters of faith. By telling the stories of two Christian communities in Liguria (in Northern Italy) through the 1990s and the 2000s, we will explore the dynamics of migration in the context of mission, and of the hospitality through which migrants and indigenous believers are caught up in the ambiguities and opportunities of God's gift of migrant mission.[1] These are stories of community-formation – the shaping of places and people that goes beyond the politics of embattled identities to glimpse hints of a new community; its necessity and cost. These are lived stories of migration and hospitality, so no

---

[1] We do well to be mindful when speaking of hospitality that it refers not to the one-sided provision of welcome, but to a complex and shifting dynamic of gift and receptivity, in which the blessings of God are shared. 'There is an interesting and intriguing conundrum around the Greek word *xenos* which denotes simultaneously guest, host or stranger. And the Greek word for hospitality in the New Testament, *philoxenia*, refers not so much to love of strangers but to a delight in the whole guest-host relationship and in the surprises that may occur'. Cathy Ross, 'Creating Space: Hospitality as a Metaphor for Mission', *ANVIL* Volume 25 No 3, 2008.

large claims are made. They are stories of people forming fellowship while building lives and livelihood – of brothers and sisters coming to recognise each other, as the Spirit provides the gift of sight to see beyond the reductive categories that are imposed by dominant narratives.

Migrant Workers Church:
Women's Leadership with Hospitality and Humility

'For women, their involvement in mission is often experienced from this point of weakness, sacrifice and invisibility.'[2]

We went to Italy in 1994 with Baptist Missionary Society (BMS) World Mission to work with the Italian Baptist Union (UCEBI), bringing with us our one-year old daughter. After a year of language-learning in Perugia and an initial period of orientation in Genoa, Claire found that she had been struggling to learn the wrong language. She was invited to pastor a Filipino fellowship in the seaside town of Rapallo, in Liguria, where services were conducted in a mixture of Tagalog and English. Migration was a fairly new phenomenon to Italy, but boomed in Liguria in the 1990s and has continued to grow since then. Filipino migrants were among the earliest to arrive. They were mostly women, who had left their children at home in the Philippines with their extended families and had arrived in Italy to work as domestic servants, carers, and nannies for wealthy Italian and foreign families. These migrant workers formed 'a fellowship' of around 25 people, consisting almost entirely of women, with two of these women's husbands attached to the church.

Dana Roberts has described the growth of Christianity in the Global South as a women's movement. She asks, 'what would the study of Christianity in Africa, Asia and Latin America look like if scholars put women in the centre of their research?'[3] Cathy Ross has asked what an all-female mission agency would look like. This is a good question – not because there has never been one, but because those that were formed were fruitful and distinctive, and also because they soon amalgamated into male-led mission agencies, resulting in the silencing of women at strategic and board level for many years. Cathy Ross argues that more attention to mission work as performed by women would lead to a 'missiology "from below", a more ordinary, a more personal, a more modest missiology'.[4] As Ross has pointed out, the contribution of women who are recognised as missionaries, at least within the category of 'mission units', is often less readily

---

2 Cathy Ross '"Without Faces": Women's Perspectives on Contextual Missiology', http://www.methodistheritage.org.uk/missionary-history-ross-without-faces-2011.pdf, 5 (Accessed 7th July 2014).
3 Dana Robert, 'World Christianity as a Women's Movement', *IBMR* vol 30 no 4 (Oct 2006), 180.
4 Cathy Ross, '"Without Faces"', 3.

noticed than that of men. There is, then, little chance of attention being given to a migrant worker women's church. The Filipino church in Rapallo was 95 per cent female, and leadership was, unquestioningly and almost unconsciously, female. The leadership was humble, collegiate, hospitable and effective. Letty Russell, one of the mothers of contemporary feminist theology, has reflected on renewed Christian communities where women make a large contribution. She finds that inclusiveness is central to their ministry and emphasises three mission concerns: justice, hospitality and what she terms a 'spirituality of connection's – that is, a connection with the Holy Spirit. The Filipino Fellowship would confirm Russell's findings in an intriguing way. Hospitality was at the heart of everything the church did – its leadership, its pastoral care and its evangelism. Food was always lavishly prepared and shared. Worship and discipleship were charismatic, with a concern that all had the opportunity to use the gifts that the Spirit gave. In terms of justice, through their hospitality these Filipino sisters created a place of welcome for Italian friends, for their employees and for newly arrived Filipinos. Here, although still working at cooking and cleaning, they were not domestics, but hosts and witnesses; and they reconfigured their relationships, even with their employers.

This female leadership and fellowship echoed Sarah Coakley's charting of pre-Nicaean churches, which were characterised by charismatic spirituality, female leadership and 'an explicitly prayer-based access to the workings of the divine'.6 In such contexts, Coakley states, church may 'hold vulnerability and personal empowerment together, precisely by creating the space in which non-coercive divine power manifests itself'.7

The non-coercive power that was experienced within the Filipino church was expressed as a form of humility that was tied up with all sorts of experiences of humiliation. When Claire read Mary's song with these Filipino sisters, she picked up a strong longing for the great reversal that Mary celebrates. They knew the world that Mary sang within, and they inhabited the hope she articulated:

> He has performed mighty deeds with his arm; he has scattered those who are proud in their inmost thoughts. He has brought down rulers from their thrones but has lifted up the humble. He has filled the hungry with good things but has sent the rich away empty (Luke 1: 51-53, NIV).

One day, Anna's husband collapsed with a brain haemorrhage and was in a coma in a hospital in Genoa. Claire spent a lot of time with her, and the doctor would invariably address his comments about Anna's husband to Claire, or to

---

5 Letty Russell, *Church in the Round: Feminist Interpretation of the Church* (Louisville Kentucky: Westminster Knox Press, 1993)
6 Sarah Coakley, *God, Sexuality, and the Self: An Essay 'On the Trinity'* (Cambridge: Cambridge University Press, 2014), 6.
7 Sarah Coakley, *Powers and Submissions: Spirituality, Philosophy, and Gender* (Oxford: Blackwells, 2008), 5.

her employer, despite Anna's responses demonstrating that her grasp of Italian was sufficient for the complexities of such a conversation. On the day of her husband's funeral, Anna had to work, and we had to delay the start time of the service so that she could attend. A year later, Anna's sister, Marie, who was eight months pregnant, became unwell. Her work schedule meant she delayed going to the hospital; when she finally was able to go, she was diagnosed with sepsis. Both Lina and her baby died. Anna's and Marie's employers were not wicked people, but they were the rich, and the proud.

One of the outcomes of such lives of faith and adversity was that these sisters were finally accustomed to their perception and cultivation of certain Christian virtues, such as humility and hope. This 'hope', though, was the biblical hope that is fashioned in suffering and longs inarticulately for a reversal. Humility is where grace encounters humiliation. It is not an easy antidote to pride – it is arrived at sideways, and there are no shortcuts. As Stanley Hauerwas reminds us, 'there is no humility without humiliation'.[8] Humility is not what we think it is from the vantage point of middle-class status and security. Anna once described to Claire, when discussing a pastor of long standing, that she could see his pride walking into the room ahead of him. It did not occur to Claire that she too was also among the proud and the privileged until, years later, she heard a report from two young British development workers, who had gone to the Philippines to give advice on development and receive reports on how relief grants had been spent. These young colleagues noted that when they arrived, people were surprised that such young women had come to tell them what to do. Claire only realised then how she must have seemed to the Filipino Fellowship. The trip to the Philippines was an experience of empowerment for the young women, but it may have come at the cost – on a range of registers – of further belittlement towards their hosts.

> Teachers of my early youth,
> taught forgiveness stressed the truth,
> here then is my Christian lack,
> if I'm struck then I'll strike back.[9]

Perhaps we need to look again at our definition of Christian humility both in terms of women and migrants. This poetry may be inaccessible to many Christian women who are privileged, and for whom humility is an aspiration that is disassociated from humiliation.

The Italian church in Rapallo, which was struggling in terms of numbers, had been proposing for a while to merge with the Filipino fellowship. Just after Anna's husband had died, she did not feel up to opposing it, and though some

8 Stanley Hauerwas, "Celebration," in *Minding the Web: Making Theological Connections*, edited by Robert J. Dean (Eugene, OR: Cascade, 2018), 259.
9 Maya Angelou, 'Lord in My Heart'.

objections were voiced, they were not voiced strongly enough. The Italian church benefitted from the committed membership as well as from the tithes. For some months, worship services were bilingual, though they were conducted in Italian-English, not Tagalop-English. Promises were made about leadership, but within a few months there were no Filipinos on the diaconate. A number of the Filipino sisters moved to Genoa for work, as did Claire.

There are questions about a homogenous church, but the example of the Filipino fellowship may suggest that there is an important place for monocultural migrant churches. Where mission can add misogyny to colonialism as one of its besetting sins, and in a global context in which '#metoo'[10] and '#timesup'[11] have near universal purchase, there is also a case for mono-gendered churches which offer places of refuge and empowerment to women.

Multicultural Church: Learning to See the Other Well

The Church should be the place that suspends the worry of how multiple peoples may encounter each other together, not by avoiding such complexity but through showing a collective body moving, living, and struggling to form a space of life and love. Indeed the joining of multiple peoples is born of the desire of the Spirit and enabled only as we yield to the Spirit and turn in relentless embrace to one another.[12]

Thirty kilometres away in Genoa, Mark was working with two traditional Italian Baptist churches. Mark's ministry in Genoa had started with typical problems of church decline in the secular West: two aging congregations, both with vibrant histories within the memory of older members, but few vital signs of flourishing in the present situation of the churches. Eventually one church – in Sampiederena – closed, leaving the city centre church on its own with its small, committed membership, but with few resources for growth. It was a monocultural church, with the exceptions of a Chinese family who had migrated in the 1960s and a Filipino woman married to an Italian – and now a British minister. As we have noted, in the 1990s there was a wave of migration to Italy,

---

10 https://metoomvmt.org/. "The 'me too' movement was founded in 2006 to help survivors of sexual violence, particularly black women and girls, and other young women of colour from low wealth communities, find pathways to healing." (Accessed 10th November 2018).
11 https://www.timesupnow.com/. "TIME'S UP is an organization that insists on safe, fair and dignified work for women of all kinds. We want women from the factory floor to the floor of the Stock Exchange, from child care centres to C-suites, from farm fields to the tech field, to be united by a shared sense of safety, fairness and dignity as they work and as we all shift the paradigm of workplace culture." (Accessed 10th November 2018).
12 Willie James Jennings, *Belief, A Theological Commentary on the Bible: Acts* (Louisville, Kentucky: Westminster John Know Press. 2017).

and many South Americans arrived in Genoa, from which their families had set sail several generations earlier. A few had Italian citizenship; most had not. A sign of hope and a path into the future opened when a group of Peruvians asked to use the buildings for a church plant. They were keen to engage Mark in preaching, and were open to the suggestion from the deacons that together we should aim at forming a bilingual and multicultural church.

This project took over five years to bring to fruition. There were two hectic years of separate Spanish and Italian services, which coincided with the period that Claire was pastoring the Filipino church in Rapallo. After this, the Italian and Spanish congregations joined regularly for joint bilingual services over a period of two years, before eventually combining the two congregations into one multicultural community, in which Claire and Mark shared a pastoral ministry. Very soon we decided to conduct services principally in Italian as the church had grown and was made up of people from Asia (mostly from South Korea and China), from several African countries, from Eastern Europe, and from up to ten South American nationalities.

The development of multicultural churches in Italy was, and is, taking place against a political backdrop that has been veering to the right. Italy, of course, has a history of migration and so has a communal memory that can resource the vocation of welcome. It also has a history of fascism that leads to both a fascination with and fear of political discourse and dynamics that point in that direction. Liguria is a traditionally left leaning region, but even there, local and national elections played on a cultural and economic fear of foreigners. While many of the arrivals in church were students, particularly from Cameroon and South Korea, the majority were economic migrants, and lots of them did not have the documentation to live legally in the country. The labels and the stigma of *clandestini* and *irregolari* were being attached to church members – to committed followers of Jesus. While the project of developing a multicultural church has been predicated on the practice of hospitality and the Christian virtue of welcome, we came to see that a key aspect of life within the community of faith is that of learning to see the world differently – to undergo a process whereby the Spirit of God superimposes the coordinates and the categories of scriptural story onto the imaginations of believers. In this context, we started to find that the labels of 'economic migrant' and even 'illegal immigrant' were reductive. The experience of the church was that these new sisters and brothers were, among other things, missionaries. Their impact was doubtless never reported in connection with the mission strategy of any mission agency or church denomination, though their impact on the church and its mission was crucial.

A case study could be made of Tito Figueroa. Tito was Peruvian and the oldest son of a large family. Both his parents died when he was in his teens and he had to quit school and find work to support his family. Eventually he found work in the pharmaceutical company that had employed his father, and he became involved in the union. He was quickly earmarked for a career in politics and was offered the chance to go to Cuba for training. In this period, in his early twenties,

Tito came to faith in Jesus through contact with the Baptist Church. Faith was felt to be incongruent with union politics, and Tito turned down the opportunity of a union career. As Tito's commitment to Christ and to the church grew, his gifts and calling were recognised within the church and denomination, and he was approached on three occasions to train for pastoral ministry. Since he was responsible for eight brothers and sisters, as well as grandparents, he could not take up the offer, though he did lead a growing youth ministry in his local church. By the time he arrived in Genoa, Tito was an experienced and able church leader and organiser. He was a guitarist, and formed and led an ever-increasing, diverse and skilled music group, made up of Asians, South Americans, Africans and Europeans. He also formed a Peruvian Folklore group. These groups were not simply music groups – they were discipleship- and leadership-training groups, as well as acting as a context of integration for many new arrivals in church, both Italians and those from overseas. Through this work, church worship was renewed and church outreach revitalised. Tito was not unique. Among these migrant mission workers there were those who had been worship leaders in huge churches in Asia, organised Sunday Schools, Youth Work and evangelism in thriving churches in various Global South contexts; had been part of new and fresh church plants in Eastern Europe; or had simply grown up in faith settings in which God was not the contested question of secular Europe, but the acknowledged presence of all aspects of community life.

Jonathan Ingleby notes that 'Europe has become the testing ground for a number of new missiological issues such as … witness to the gospel in a post Christian society (often by Christians who have no experience of a post Christian society!).'[13] The contextual training that these migrant mission workers received was on the hoof and relational, and their impact came about as they modelled (often in adversity) a faith that had a different texture to that of the indigenous secularised Christians. A few Baptist churches within the Baptist Union in Italy were experiencing, in their characteristically small way, what was becoming a global phenomenon. As Andrew Walls puts it,

> Christianity was once the religion of confident technological advance and rising affluence, and sometimes saw these things as a mark of God's favour. Christianity now will increasingly be associated (mostly) with rather poor and very poor people, and with some of the poorest countries on earth. And people from the non-Western world will be the principal agents of Christian mission right across the world.[14]

Within the church, the boundaries of who is really 'us' were being redrawn – sometimes painfully, sometimes heroically. A positive example was that of Nabil, a Moroccan street seller, aged ten. He would position himself outside the

---

13 Jonathan Ingleby, *Beyond Empire: Postcolonialism and Mission in a Global Context* (Milton Keynes: Author House, 2010), 116.
14 Andrew Walls, 'Mission and Migration', *Journal of African Christian Thought* 5, no. 2 (December 2002), 10.

church on Sundays to sell tissues to people coming to and from church. Theft was a regular problem in our city-centre church, and suspicion regularly fell on the Moroccan and Algerian street sellers who often ventured into the church in search of a captive market. Over the winter, Daniele, our youth leader, started inviting Nabil to join with the Sunday School rather than having to wait in the cold for the service to finish. Nabil began attending and enjoying the time of games and drawing with the other children. One Sunday, as Nabil was heading through the sanctuary a few minutes before the service was due to start, he put his backpack on a pew and opened the door that led to the Sunday School rooms. Grazia, a church member not known for her tolerance, shouted loudly to him from across the worship space: 'eh boy!' Nabil froze, looking terrified and glancing back toward the exit. The woman carried on, not noticing Nabil's fear: 'Don't leave your backpack unattended up here. Don't you know there are thieves about.' Nabil looked taken aback – puzzled – as it registered with him that he was not one of the thieves, but one of the family being looked out for. He smiled widely, grabbed his backpack and ran through to Sunday School. Grazia had not changed her view of the world, but she had moved Nabil into a different place within it, and Nabil was given, to some extent, the opportunity to see himself differently.

We now turn to a more serious episode that illustrates how small steps of welcome and the process (however uneven) of community formation can unsettle convictions and reshape the ways in which followers of Jesus both see themselves and understand how they should act in society. Many of the migrants in the church were illegally or irregularly present in Italy. Italy has a large shadow economy, and these people found work and housing there. The government had announced a number of 'moratoriums' for illegal migrants, which allowed those who could demonstrate that they had work and fixed housing to apply for the documentation that would allow them to be legally present in the country. This change in status represented the possibilities of security and flourishing for workers and their families. When the first moratorium was announced, there was rejoicing in church as, at that time, around forty members were living without legal documentation. The optimism soon changed to despair as more and more members reported that their employers had no intention of signing the necessary papers, since this would entail making tax contributions. The idea emerged that church members, who were able to demonstrate an income above the required level for an employer, could sign for these sisters and brothers, claiming to be their employers. The issue was risky, as it was clearly illegal and, in fact, the relevant documents had to be submitted in person at the Questura (the central police station) in front of an official. It involved a commitment to make a tax contribution. It also presented an ethical dilemma: was it justifiable for a Christian to break the law in this way?

A new factor had emerged, unheralded, in the formation of a multicultural Christian community. These migrants were not foreigners or criminals, and they were more than mission workers – they were sisters and brothers, leaders and examples of faith, to whom loyalty and love were due. In an example of ethical improvisation, at least 20 church members went through the process or claiming to have domestic workers, child-minders and, in one case, a chauffeur! Tina – a stalwart member who had grown up in the church, had held every office, and was loved and respected by all the members, new and old – was keen to be involved. She was disturbed that it involved 'bearing false testimony', but recognised that it offered a chance of life and enabled people to escape the clutches of unscrupulous employers. Two biblical concerns were colliding: justice and truth-telling. Eventually she went to the Questura with two sets of forms, one for herself and one for her mother-in-law, for whom she had power of attorney. As the young uniformed police official stamped the documentation, Tina resolved the conflict within her by saying to him, 'I don't feel bad for bearing false witness here in front of you, as I am doing it for a good end'. She reported that the officer, young enough to be her grandson, straightened up, looked seriously at her for a moment and then said, 'Signora, we each must live according to our conscience'. He then filed the papers.

The church in Genoa, and the Italian Baptist Union, were becoming multi-coloured in terms of the congregation, but the challenge was to become multicultural in their leadership. This was not the way the situation was framed at the time, but questions were posed in the course of community life as to how well integrated the church really was. Spirituality, leadership and theology were key indicators. There was, at first, an unspoken view, both in the church and in the wider union, that migrants from varying parts of the Global South would bring much-needed vibrancy and enthusiasm, but that the leadership and certainly the theology would be provided by the host church and union. An easy – and maybe over-simplistic – distinction was that the music was welcome, but not the theology, which was viewed as a recycled American import.

At one national assembly, when two African pastors prayed for the healing of a much-loved Baptist national figure, there was public censor. This was born of a desire to maintain a hard-won and well-articulated liberal theology and identity; it was not meant to be harsh on those who had offered heart-felt prayers for a prominent member in their new family of faith. There was a genuine desire to be hospitable and to show real progress in forming communities that expressed the gospel vision of all being one in Christ. Leadership within local churches was being opened, and within the church in Genoa there were several deacons from differing nationalities. This is a first in the churches in their more than 160-year history. Migrants moved into leadership, led services, preached and developed mission initiatives. Theology, though, continued to be a sticking point. Droogers and Van der Laan have noted in this type of context 'a condescending attitude:

"conservative" migrant churches should first be upgraded theologically before they are acceptable in the "progressive" ecumenical movement'.[15]

Developing theological formulations is a notoriously lengthy process, but can emerge as the fruit of persistence in the offer and experience of hospitality, where listening deeply to one another has gone on for many years. Israel Olofinjana wisely notes that,

> cross-cultural theological conversation requires a kind of hospitality that allows the foreigners to feel sufficiently at home to make theological contributions ... In congregations where hospitality and familiar spirituality are experienced, immigrants often stay and dedicate themselves to the congregation's mission, making theological cross-pollination possible.[16]

Through the grace of hospitality, where each person is recognised for having gifts to share, we come to see and know each other as God has made us to truly be: mission workers, leaders, sisters and brothers, as well as teachers and theologians.

Conclusion

Where do such stories leave us? Nowhere very certain, and perhaps they prompt further questions. They are retold, out of gratitude, to draw attention to God's activity in the world through movements of migration and – more in keeping with the gospel – to sisters and brothers in Christ whose identity as disciples trumps their economic and legal status. This is the way God works. It may well be wise for those with influence within the church and within mission agencies to give more consideration to migration as mission, and migrants as God's enlivening gift to the church. The practice of hospitality, as it is performed by migrant and indigenous believers, may be more decisive than any mission strategy.

References

Ross, Cathy, *Creating Space: Hospitality as a Metaphor for Mission*, ANVIL Volume 25 No 3, 2008.

Coakley, Sarah, *God, Sexuality, and the Self: An Essay "On the Trinity"*, Cambridge: Cambridge University Press, 2014.

Coakley, Sarah, *Powers and Submissions: Spirituality, Philosophy, and Gender*, Oxford: Blackwells, 2008.

---

[15] Andre Droogers and Cornelius van der Laan, *Fruitful in this Land: Pluralism, Dialogue and Healing in Migrant Pentecostalism* (Zoetermeer: Boekencentrum/Geneva: WCC, 2005).

[16] Israel Oluwole Olofinjana (ed), *African Voices: Towards African British Theologies* (Carlisle: Langham Global Library, 2017).

Droogers, Andre and Cornelius van der Laan. *Fruitful in this Land: Pluralism, Dialogue and Healing in Migrant Pentecostalism.* Zoetermeer: Boekencentrum/Geneva: WCC, 2005.
Ingleby, Jonathan, Beyond Empire: Postcolonialism and Mission in a Global Context, Milton Keynes, AuthorHouse, 2010.
Jennings, Willie James, *Belief, A Theological Commentary on the Bible: Acts,* Louisville, Kentucky: Westminster John Know Press. 2017.
Olofinjana, Israel Oluwole (ed), *African Voices: Towards African British Theologies,* Carlisle, Cumbria, Langham Global Library, 2017.
Robert, Dana, World Christianity as a women's movement *IBMR* vol 30 no4 Oct 2006.
Russell, Letty, *Church in the Round: Feminist Interpretation of the Church,* Louisville Kentucky: Westminster Knox Press, 1993.
Wall, Andrew, "Mission and Migration," Journal of African Christian Thought 5, no. 2 December 2002.

Internet Sources

Ross, Cathy "Without Faces": Women's Perspectives on Contextual Missiology http://www.methodistheritage.org.uk/missionary-history-ross-without-faces-2011.pdf p. 5, (accessed 07.07.2014).
'The 'me too.' movement https://metoomvmt.org/ (Accessed 10.11.2018).
TIME'S UP https://www.timesupnow.com/ (Accessed 10.11.2018).

Section Three
Missiological Insights

(10) Diaspora Phenomena and the Lausanne Movement: A Case Study of Korean Diaspora Mission in Eurasia

S. Hun Kim

Introduction

In recent years, there have been various discussions among field practitioners and mission theologians seeking to define the missional significance of the diaspora phenomenon worldwide. The most significant of these were the academic conference that celebrated the centennial of the Edinburgh Mission (1910),[1] the Third Lausanne World Evangelization Conference in Cape town (2010), and, more recently, the International Association for Mission Studies (IAMS)[2] assembly in Toronto (2012). In the meantime, Korean diaspora around the world have also held forums to discuss various issues. Korean Diaspora Forum (KDF)[3] was one of the significant forums to have emerged out of those conversations.

This paper will explore three facets of the diaspora phenomenon:

1) A brief overview of major mission theologies of the diaspora phenomenon, which has emerged as an important feature of modern missions;

---

[1] A discussion on the theme was included in the 5th division of the forms of missionary engagement from the conference in 2010.

[2] Toronto Assembly 2012 on 15-20 August. The theme was 'Migration, Human Dislocation and the Good News-Margins as the Centre in Christian Mission'.

[3] The Korean Diaspora Forum was birthed in Baltimore, USA in 2004. Initially it drew the participation of Korean diaspora churches worldwide. Since then, it has been convening annually. The first meeting was held in New York in 2005. The following year it was held in Beijing, and then in Tokyo in 2007, Kuala Lumpur in 2008, Shanghai in 2009, Seol-Ak Mountain, Korea in 2010, LA in 2011, and Johannesburg, South Africa in 2012. Meanwhile, since 2004, KDF has also established several regional forums: the Asian Diaspora Forum in Asia, the Eurovision forum in Europe, and the Latin America Korean Mission network (Lakomnet) in South America.

KDF came into existence with the purpose of addressing three main issues that the Korean migrant churches face – ministry, education, and mission. These three issues can be formulated into the following questions: Firstly, how can these churches be healthy in ministry? Secondly, how can they raise up the next generation to become godly people? And, lastly, how can they contribute to world mission? The Forum was established in order to address these issues among Korean diaspora church communities. As one of the outcomes of the Forum, a book was edited by S. Hun Kim and Won Suk Ma, *The Korean Diaspora and Christian Mission* (Oxford: Regnum, 2011). A pre-published version was distributed during the Third Lausanne Congress: Cape Town 2010.

2) Major diaspora movements that have been conducted worldwide in response to the changing mission environment (focusing especially on Global Diaspora Network, an issue Network of Lausanne Movement);
3) Lastly, considering the Korean diaspora missionary movements in Central Asia with a particular focus on the mission strategy of Russian-Korean, Chinese-Korean, and North Korean diaspora. These are case studies of Korean diaspora mission movements that have not been until now included in the scope of research on modern Korean diaspora mission movements.

World Diaspora Phenomenon

Today, diaspora is becoming a global phenomenon more than ever before in human history, and is part and parcel of the broader dynamism of globalization. Jehu C. Hanciles, who was once a research professor at Fuller Theological Seminary, states that 'important religions have strengthened their place in the past due to immigration and scattering, and Christianity is the most representative of them'.[4] In short, the expansion of Christianity can be said to be a history of the diaspora.

Since the 'diaspora' phenomenon emerged as a global mega-trend, both the evangelical and ecumenical parts of the church are attempting to define it from a theological and missiological point of view. One of the champions of this effort is the Global Diaspora Network (GDN) of the Lausanne movement. The Global Diaspora Network published a compendium of Diaspora Missiology in 2016 as the fruit of a five-years study that involved many practitioners, missiologists and theologians. Apart from Global Diaspora Network, there were also various research papers and presentations related to worldwide 'diaspora' during the past decade. However, it will take more time to establish a robust theological framework for the diaspora mission, mostly because of its diversity and the complexities it raises, which go beyond our contemporary mission traditions.

Four Major Theological Perspectives on the Diaspora Phenomena

Daniel Groody[5] *and Migration Theology*

Groody focuses on migration issues in South America. According to him, there are three levels of migration theology. Firstly, there is the *pastoral* level, which refers to efforts to meet the needs of immigrants. Secondly, there is the *spiritual* level: what are the spiritual contributions of migrants and what can we learn from

---

[4] Jehu Hanciles, 'Migration and Mission: The Religious Significance of the North-South Divide', in Andrew Walls and Cathy Ross (eds), *Mission in the 21st Century: Exploring the Five Marks of Global Mission* (London: Darton, Longman and Todd, 2008), 118.
[5] D. Groody and G. Campese (eds), *A Promised Land, A Perilous Journey: Theological Perspectives on Migration* (Notre Dame: University of Notre Dame Press, 2008). G. Campese is Professor of Theology in Scalabrini International Migration Institute.

them to enhance our own spirituality? Thirdly, there is the *theological* level, which combines the previous two aspects to give a fuller picture of theological interpretation. Groody has four theological viewpoints; 1) *Imago Dei* must be restored equally to immigrants because all humans bear the image of God; 2) the word of reconciliation through *Verbum Dei* – entailing unity and forgiveness – must be made through immigration; 3) the redemptive ministry of Jesus Christ, *Missio Dei*, must be achieved without discrimination towards anyone; 4) visions of God's Kingdom, *Visio Dei*, must be realised without discrimination on the border.

In summary, he argues that immigration is no longer a social, economic, or political issue that governments are discussing, but a theological framework for human life and dignity.

Peter C. Phan's Views on Migration in the Patristic Period[6]
This is how the Vietnamese theologian, Peter C. Phan, articulated the characteristics of immigration that can be observed within the age of the Fathers in the early churches. First, early church Christians experienced massive immigration. Second, this movement began in conjunction with the missionary activities of the church. Third, the movements arose because of religious and political persecution, and at the same time, it was facilitated through trade networks, and, most importantly, was motivated by the call to preach the gospel. Fourth, this movement occurred simultaneously with both Christian (internal) and non-Christian (external) movements. Fifth, as in other movements, the movement came from within the centre of the metropolis. Sixth, like the Jews, Christians formed a dynamic community through long-term settlement in the city. Seventh, unlike the Jews, they were treated as outsiders without any vested rights. Eighth, they quickly adapted to local cultures, like other immigrants. Ninth, they were, at the same time, distinct from the surrounding societies in various ways, especially in terms of religious practice. Tenth, the Christian diaspora is a pattern of movement in the population that has been repeated in history.

Theological Framework of Enoch Wan's 'Diaspora' Missiology and Joy Tira[7]
Enoch Wan defines 'Diaspora Missiology' as the systematic and academic study of the phenomenological approach towards diaspora, and as the effort to understand the mission of God through theological interrogation. For the diaspora phenomenon in the Old and New Testaments, Wan found patterns of scattering and gathering, and presented a series of examples in the Bible. The

---

[6] Peter C. Phan, 'Migration in the Patristic Era: History and Theology', in *A Promised Land, A Perilous Journey*, 46-47.
[7] Enoch Wan and Joy Tira (eds), *Diaspora Missiology, Missions Practice in the 21st Century*, Diaspora Series No. 1 (Pasadena: WCIU Press, 2009), 27-54.

difference between traditional and diaspora missiology is summarised in the following figure.

		Polarised/dichotomised	
1	FOCUS	-'great commission' ←→ 'great commandment' -saving soul ←→ social Gospel -church planting ←→ Christian charity -paternalism ←→ indigenisation	-Holistic Christianity with strong integration of evangelism with Christian charity -contextualisation
2	CONCEP-TUALIZATION	-territorial: here ←→ there -'local' ←→ 'global' -lineal: 'sending' ←→ 'receiving' -'assimilation' ←→ 'amalgamation' -'specialisation'	-'de-territorialisation'[8] -'glocal' -'mutuality' & 'reciprocity' -'hybridity' -'inter-disciplinary'
3	PERSPECTIVE	-geographically divided: foreign mission ←→local, urban←→rural -geo-political boundary: state/nation←→ state/nation -disciplinary compartmentalisation: e.g. theology of missions / strategy of missions	-non-spatial, -'borderless', no boundary to worry, transnational & global -new approach: integrated & interdisciplinary
4	PARADIGM	-OT: missions = gentile-proselyte --- coming -NT: missions = the Great Commission --- going -Modern missions: E-1, E-2, E-3 or M-1, M-2. M-3, etc.	-New reality in the 21st Century –viewing & following God's way of providentially moving people spatially & spiritually. -moving targets & move with the targets

Figure 1:2 Comparison of traditional missiology and diaspora missiology[9]

The methodology of Diaspora Missiology covers a range of disciplines, and the major areas include cultural anthropology, demography, economics, geography, history, law, politics, and sociology. In addition to these areas of study, research topics such as migrants, immigrants, ethnic conflict, diaspora phenomenon research, globalisation, urbanisation, pluralism and multiculturalism are necessary. As the diaspora phenomenon becomes more and more widely spread, the application of missiology of diaspora becomes more prominent in our mission practice as a way of discerning how missionary engagement should be conducted in the future.

---

[8] 'De-territorialisation' is the 'loss of social and cultural boundaries' (Wan).
[9] Ibid., 48.

To support the framework of Wan's missionary study on the diaspora phenomenon (above), Tira, in his own paper,[10] pointed out that God's sovereignty is at the centre of the whole diaspora phenomena, and he identified the following themes as playing a significant role within theological reflection upon diaspora:

1) *God of the Trinity.* God as Creator and human saviour intervenes in the movement of human history (Acts 17: 26-27). He also gives human beings stewardship – responsibility for all created things – and he takes care of them through the freedom of residence. As a result of human depravity and expulsion by sin – the wandering of Cain, and the events of the Tower of Babel – 'culture has developed and flowers of civilization have emerged... [and] racial and ethnic gaps in modern society have become prominent'. However, the consequences of the act of God ultimately result in the completion of God's plan (Rom. 11).

The incarnation of Jesus Christ is of great importance as a theological model of 'Purpose driven Immigration (Diaspora)'. Through his earthly life, he showed his disciples what life should be for the kingdom of God, and moreover not only understood the sufferings of the scattered, but gave them hope. The earthly commandment of Matthew 28 convinced the disciples that God's kingdom would be extended beyond space and time.

The Holy Spirit, who is the conductor of mission and who participated in the history of creation, is involved in the formation of Israel and the creation of the church, and ultimately plays a leading role in the divine plan for the redemption of mankind. The Holy Spirit is present to the disciples, scattering them around the world to preach the gospel of the kingdom in fulfilment of the earthly mandate (Matt. 28:20).

2) *The church's identity and mission in Jesus Christ.* The 'mobility instinct' implied in Acts 1:8 goes beyond all boundaries in conjunction with the missional purpose; and the universal church transcends the boundaries of local churches in all ages and spaces. In Christ's prayer for the disciples in John 17:11-21, we see that the scattering of the church is the intent of Jesus.

3) *The union of the scattered ones at the end* (eschatology). The kingdom of God is present, and all Christians are heavenly citizens; but in this land, they live as witnesses as 'pilgrims with purpose'. And at the end of time, all the people who were scattered around the world will be gathered together before the throne of the Lamb (Rev 7:9-10).

4) *Cosmic conflict and spiritual warfare.* When the disciples were scattered for the preaching of the gospel, Jesus gave them the ability to overcome the power of darkness (Luke 9:1-2). The apostle Paul says that all Christians participate in universal conflict and spiritual warfare (Eph. 6:12) Amongst immigrants, the abuse of women and children through human trafficking and the sex industry is a prime example of spiritual warfare. Christians in the diaspora

---

[10] Enoch Wan and Joy Tira (eds), *Diaspora Missiology, Missions Practice in the 21st Century.*

are exposed to spiritual warfare, which is part and parcel of the expansion of the kingdom of God. We must firmly believe that the initiative within this war against evil is with God; and at the same time, we must acquire all the training necessary to attain spiritual growth and engage in the conflict.

5) *Scripture as a mission manual.* The Bible is the final, authoritative manual for world mission. It contains the theology of progressive redemption, the history of the early church, the progress of the gospel, and the apostolic ministry. This means that theological and missiological thinking about the diaspora phenomenon should be based on the Bible and its principles.

Jehu Hanciles's View on Africa's 'Diaspora' History and Missionary Significance[11]

In an article on the relationship between immigration and the expansion of religion,[12] Hanciles notes that immigration in its current form will have a profound impact on religious activities in the twenty-first century. Samuel Escobar, in turn, points out that 'the migration model of today is an important flow of the Christian mission in the future, but has received little attention from the institutional missions'.[13]

Hanciles examined closely the expansion of Christian mission during the era of Western imperialism and colonialism, and analysed the flow of mission work that corresponded with the great wave of migration amongst large populations of European and non-Western labour forces in that period. Imperialism and colonialism eventually led to the creation of a new phenomenon known as 'global migration'. In particular, colonialism established a transnational structure or interstate system, which brought about the era of global immigration; and the disintegration of imperialism in Western Europe caused a massive number of workers from non-Western countries to move to Europe. It was in the era of global immigration (what we call 'post-colonialism') from the 1960s that migration was accelerated from non-Western areas to the West, and from the South to the North. Various phenomena ensued, as follows.

1) They took their religion with them. Religion is a link to the places from which immigrants originated, and provides an important means by which they can retain their identities. Even if they are not religious from the beginning, they tend to pursue religious devotion as a way of dealing with isolation and the loss of life.

2) Immigration also affects the countries that they have left. In the case of Africa, the loss of human resources has caused a 'brain drain', for one third of skilled workers from African countries have moved to Europe. As a result of this, and of the imbalance of global economies, international immigration

---

11 Jehu Hanciles, 'Migration and Mission: The Religious Significance of the North-South Divide'.
12 Ibid., 118.
13 Samuel Escobar, *A Time for Mission* (Leicester: Inter Varsity Press, 2003), 17.

contributes to the immigration nation. From another perspective, immigrants are perceived as a potentially huge source of income for their home countries.

3) Within the current pattern of international immigration, people do not settle in one foreign country. Instead, they come to view both their country of origin and the country to which they have immigrated as places to live; and they act as bridges between the two countries. This pattern is referred to as 'transnational migration'.

4) Modern immigration (diaspora) is 'a network-driven phenomenon. At first, they move from the established contact point to the centre of the immigration'.[14] Thus, unlike the Western linear structure, 'non-western immigration forms are cellular organized and move along already established relationships in the society, lead to leadership and understand communication and human relationships in the context of the community that have been set up'.[15]

5) The movement from the South to the North created a link between the former colonies and the ruling countries, and many Christians of the former colonies migrated along this new passage. For example, Africans who came have been coming since the 1960s due to economic immigration or as refugees together form 3000 faith communities in England alone. The corresponding number across Europe is estimated at three million.

6) The growth of non-Western Christianity promotes immigration. In particular, the fast-growing African Charismatic or New Pentecostal churches are the most mobile groups for social mobility and capital. Moreover, these churches have an international network, which tends to further promote immigration.

7) The South-to-North movement follows a New Testament model, which is pervaded by the themes of church-centred life, incarnate witness, individual creativity, and which places an emphasis upon spiritual power, house churches, and a self-supporting lifestyle.

Summary of Key Elements of Diaspora / Immigrant Mission Theology

1) *It is the sovereignty of God.* Within the events of the Exodus and the Babylonian Exile, it is clear that God himself establishes His sovereignty and His intention for the redemption of human beings by scattering people. Groody described it succinctly as *Imago Dei* ('restoration of image'), *Missio Dei* ('redemption ministry'), and *Visio Dei* ('vision of God's kingdom'). When we lose the identity associated with being scattered, He puts the bridle of slavery on us, and at the same time teaches us to restore the lives of witnesses. Eventually, this leads us from despair to hope. In this sense, God still exercises sovereignty through his 'radical dislocation'.

---

[14] Waldinger, 'Strangers at the Gates', 3.
[15] Jehu Hanciles, *Beyond Christendom: Globalization, African Migration, and the Transformation of the West* (Maryknoll, New York, Orbis Books, 2008), 200-201.

2) *It is the incarnation of Christ*. Jesus Christ exemplifies the diaspora identity most vividly. Through the Lord's Supper, God first showed us the typical pattern of purpose-driven migration. From the perspective of the world, immigration is viewed as a social, economic, and political issue; but in the context of the Eucharist, it is a theological issue which signifies the unconditional union of all humans towards reconciliation with God.

3) *Christian identity*. Christians are essentially immigrants (*paroikoi*). They are 'the third race', meaning that they live in harmony with the world, but are not of the world, for they have 'kingdom' minds. They have faith in the future eschaton, and a desire for spiritual things and for the coming union of believers at the end of the world.

Immigration theology is cross-cultural and counter-cultural character. 'Counter-culture', as defined by Leslie Newbigin's Gospel and Our Culture Network movement, means not a denial of secular culture, but rather a criticism of human culture; it gives the initiative to the gospel as that which creates a new culture.

4) *The identity of the church*. As some scholars have argued, the essential features of the church are the mobility instinct (Acts 1:8) and 'migrantness'. The theologian Phan argued that only immigrant churches with these features were able to obey Christ's earthly orders and truly care for immigrants in the world with faith, hope, and love. A true church should be understood as a diasporic faith community standing in a prophetic tradition, not a religion (temple concept) based on tradition.

The Direction of the Lausanne Movement and the Korean Diaspora Mission
Recent data indicate that the Chinese Coordinating Committee for World Evangelism (CCOWE) was the first global expression of Diaspora Mission within the Lausanne Movement, which came to Hong Kong in 1976 after its founding in 1974. After the Second Manila Lausanne Convention in 1989, the South Asian Concern (SAC) was founded in the UK, and the North American Consultation of South Asian Christians (NACSAC) was founded in 1993. The Filipino International Network (FIN) was founded in Canada, also in 1993.

The Lausanne Diaspora movement was officially organised for the first time in 1998 through the pioneering work of Tom Houston (chairman of the Manila conference), TV Thomas (current chairman of Global Diaspora Network) and others. The International Diaspora Leadership Conference was held in Edmonton, Canada. The Lausanne occasional paper 55 – entitled, 'The New People Next Door' – came out of the Lausanne Forum in Pattaya, 2004. It was a significant document which highlighted the breakthrough in evangelical thinking about missions. At the same Lausanne Forum, copies of *Scattered: The Filipino Global Presence*, a book edited by Luis Pantojo Jr, Sadiri Joy Tira and Enoch

Wan, were distributed to all forum participants. This book brought fresh insight to the diaspora phenomena as it relates to the global church.

In 2007, the Lausanne Movement appointed Dr Sadiri Joy Tira as its Senior Associate for Diasporas. In 2008, Tira assembled the Lausanne Diaspora Leadership Team at a Conference in Budapest, Hungary. Its purpose was to formulate an evangelical diaspora theology and strategy, which were to be presented at the Lausanne Cape Town conference in 2010. At that time, I was commissioned to publish a booklet on the Korean Diaspora. The publication of this booklet was in conjunction with the Korean Diaspora Forum (KDF) and the Korean Diaspora Mission Network (Kodimnet). Entitled *Korean Diaspora and Christian Mission*, a thousand copies of this book were published in October 2010, and it was officially distributed to the delegation. The revised edition has been published by the Regnum publishing house in Oxford and by the Korean Diaspora Research Institute (KRID) in April 2011 as a series of mission studies associated with the Oxford Centre for Mission Studies (OCMS).

At Manila in 2009, various diaspora ministers, theologians, missionaries, field workers, mission strategists, and others tried to set up the Theological Foundation of Diaspora as part of an ongoing conversation about evangelical diaspora theology and strategy. Following this, the Seoul Declaration on Diaspora Missiology was established in Seoul towards the end of 2009. In April 2010, a conference on European diaspora issues was held at Oxford, and the results were presented in *Transformation*, a journal of the Oxford Centre for Mission Studies.

At the 3rd Lausanne Evangelical Congress, held in Cape Town, South Africa in October 2010, the topic of 'Diaspora' was one of five key foci. During the meeting, many panels explored specific issues in the mission field; and 'diaspora' was interpreted in this context as an overarching phenomenon manifested within twenty-first-century missions, and as a significant factor in solving the challenges of field missions. It was also recognised that the diaspora was already positioned by this point as a new paradigm, and as the direction that the new missions should take. The so-called 'Divine Conspiracy' through the diaspora is God's mission strategy, specifically designed for the long and gradual unfolding of Christian history.

After the Cape Town Congress, the Lausanne Diaspora Leadership Team (LDLT) was dissolved, and the Global Diaspora Network (GDN) was formed. Enoch Wan, Sadiri Joy Tira, Hun Kim, Ted Yamamori and other diaspora ministry practitioners held a post-Cape Town meeting in Paris from 20-21 February 2011 to organise an Executive Committee. They created a roadmap to prepare for the Global Diaspora Forum in Manila, which was held in 2015.

The Global Diaspora Network consists of two organizations: the International Board of Reference and the International Advisory Board. The network established an office at the Philippine Security Exchange Commission in Manila, Philippines as a way of symbolising that the global church is leading the movement. The goal of the Global Diaspora Network is to form partnerships with regional organisations and groups related to diaspora missions. It seeks to discover and nurture the next generation of leaders, and to conduct academic research related to diaspora, thus acting as a trailblazer in the field of diaspora missions. The Lausanne Global Diaspora Forum, held in Manila in March 2015, aimed to produce a Compendium of Diaspora Missiology by bringing together 360 field workers and scholars with a deep understanding of the diaspora by region, ethnicity and country. Draft chapters in the compendium were vetted by those present, and so, each chapter was critiqued by an international cast of scholars and ministry practitioners.

The Global Diaspora Network (GDN) strives to find ways to cooperate with other groups engaged in the diaspora cause, such as the Korean Research Institute for Diaspora (KRID) and the Korean Diaspora Networks (KDF, KODIMNET, KODIA-KWMA Diaspora Division). During the Korean-American Diaspora Forum Conference in Los Angeles in 2011, a partnership was formed between the Global Diaspora Network and the Korean Diaspora Network (KDN), the intention of which was to promote the diaspora cause.

The current task of Global Diaspora Network (GDN), along with the Lausanne Movement, is to introduce the theology, missiology, and practices of the diaspora perspective, and to disseminate them appropriately to seminaries, to mission training groups, and to formal and non-formal training programmes. For this purpose, regional diaspora networks are being organised for each continent.

A Case Study of Korean Diaspora Mission in Eurasia:
Considerations of Diaspora Mission Strategy for Central Asia

It is necessary now to revisit the missionary importance of Korean Russians[16] for the Central Asian mission strategy. Korean Russians are viewed as a new potential mission field, which God providentially scattered across Central Asia more than a century ago. They have been playing an important role of guides for Korean missionaries, especially since the collapse of the Soviet Union in 1991, when Protestant missions in general – and missions in Korea in particular – were suddenly flooded.

For Korean missions to flourish in Central Asia, it has been necessary to generate a new perspective by incorporating Korean Russians into their strategy. At present, there are not many studies published in Korea reflecting strategic research related to mission work involving Korean Russians in Central Asia. Since the mission perspective aims to produce 'holistic missions' which consider both social salvation (demonstration of the gospel) and evangelism (proclamation of the gospel), it is inevitable that a symbiotic paradigm will be developed which approaches the diaspora from a cross-disciplinary perspective.

---

[16] This is how ethnic Koreans living in the post-Soviet states refer to themselves. Korean communities can be traced back to the Koreans who were living in the Russian Far East during the late nineteenth century.

As I visited Ukraine in March 2012 and chatted with Korean missionaries in Kiev, two points caught my attention from a diasporic standpoint. The first is that there are very few ministries to the 20,000 Koreans living in Odessa and Crimea. Currently, there are about 120 Korean missionaries in Ukraine, who are ministering to locals and to Russians. But it is necessary that we develop a strategy that includes the possibility of drawing those who are deeply familiar with these local contexts into this missionary work. Around the world, Ukraine has exported its workforce (World Bank 2010) – 6.5 million people, or 14 per cent of the population of Ukraine – to Mexico, India, Russia and China. 4.4 million have gone to Russia, 2.4 million to Kazakhstan, 150,000 to Uzbekistan, and 100,000 to Kyrgyzstan.

The missiological significance of this phenomenon requires us to be intentional about changing our mission perspective. For example, if the Koreans living in Ukraine are to be evangelised, there would need to be a vision to evangelise 7 million Ukrainians as well, along with the Koreans living in the former Soviet Union. Furthermore, an appropriate strategic application of diaspora missiology is needed in order to develop the ministry associated with the diaspora people who have become scattered around the world from Central Asia. (For example, there needs to be a mission to the 2.5 million Ukrainian people living in North America.) This kind of ministry to Ukranians can be efficient and reduce the need for Korean missionaries directly in Ukraine.

It seems that the efforts to utilise the Korean-Chinese diaspora reserved for Central Asia, China, and North Korea missions are more urgent than ever. The history of the Korean-Chinese diaspora developed in various ways. The two major periods in this history are divided into two geographical regions. The first covers the area from the Korean peninsula to the north-east of China. The second ranges from the north-east of China to the Korean Peninsula and, from there, to the rest of the world. The first migration in the late nineteenth century was to what is now the province of Jilin. The second migration consisted of independents and some farmers, who came to the Jilin province in the 1910s. The third migration was carried out in the 1920s and 1940s by the Gyeongsang Peasants in the Heilongjiang Province and the Liaoning Province, in accordance with the forced migration policy of Japan. The fourth migration occurred in the 1950s and after the 1960s, when Korean immigrants moved to North Korea to try to avoid the cultural revolution and the famine. The fifth migration has been occurring since the 1980s. This is a Chinese immigration to Korea, corresponding to the Chinese reform and opening, and to the Korea-China diplomatic ties. The sixth migration, from 1990 to present time, involves movement to other Western countries such as Japan, USA, and Australia. Since the 1990s, the seventh migration has involved Chinese immigrants moving to the Chinese coastal area and the inland metropolitan area.

As this history demonstrates, the Korean-Chinese diaspora has, since the 1980s, developed dynamically in line with the Chinese opening policy. Everywhere, one can see Korean-Chinese churches that have been established, and that work closely with Korean missionaries. In recent years, these groups have moved to Europe and have established churches in the centre of the Korean community in London; and in Germany, a recently-ordained Korean-Chinese minister is now working with a German congregation.

With 1.83 million Chinese in China and 500,000 in Korea, it is more important now than ever that steps are taken to implement the evangelisation of, and the mission strategy[17] designed for, the Korean-Chinese diasporas around the world. Rev Hae Hong, who is the pastor of a Korean-Chinese church, writes in his book, *Diaspora Korean-Chinese*, that

> If the Christian culture is strongly settled to 500,000 Korean-Chinese people in Korea, then the power will reach 2 million Korean people and mission in China … It is expected that it will cause a huge wave in China. For the future of China, we should also positively look at the role of the Korean-Chinese in the middle.[18]

In addition, Seung-ji Kwak, a team leader of Yeunhap News agency in Korea, recognised that their role in rebuilding North Korea after the reunification was absolutely vital. He noted that 'Korean-Chinese are the key unification forces most closely related to the reunification of the Korean peninsula. It is a preliminary task for them to actively participate in the reunification discourse.' Moreover, unlike Koreans, the Korean-Chinese people are slightly at tension with North Korea and North Koreans. In addition, the Korean-Chinese have little administrative constraints in accessing North Korea, they also have less language (including dialects) and cultural barriers. In fact, Korean-Chinese people are frequently visiting Pyongyang or Rajinsunbong area, and they often make contact with North Koreans officials through business activities. Given these points, it is anticipated that as relations with North Korea change – whether towards greater openness or reunification – the Korean-Chinese will be able to play an active and efficient role in all areas of society, including sharing the gospel.[19]

---

17 The majority of the Korean-Chinese diasporas are small in size and low in acceptance of the gospel due to the influence of atheism and materialism in China. This is characteristic of the livelihood of immigrant or a resident. The few diaspora churches among them are not voluntary or self-forming in operation, they depend heavily on Korean-born ministers, of which there is a small number. Therefore, it is now appropriate to prioritize evangelization for them and to concentrate on a small number of devotees in a more time-consuming process. On the other hand, the Korean-Chinese people have more pioneering spirit and stronger mobility than Koreans. Therefore, even a small number of people have the potential to play a very good mission role when they are mobilized. (January 12, 2013, written interview with overseas Korean-Chinese workers).

18 Hae Hong, *Diaspora Korean-Chinese* (Seoul: Kumlan Publishing Co., 2012) (Korean version).

19 Excerpts from the written interview of overseas Korean-Chinese on 12 January 2013.

Although the link between Korean-Chinese and Korean-Russians in Central Asia should be developed with a long-term perspective, it is expected that the next generation of the region will be able to cooperate by means of educational opportunities within Korea and at Yanbian University in China. Some believe that the role of the Korean-Chinese church will be very important in rebuilding the church after the unification of North Korea. According to the leaders of the Chinese churches in Yanbian and Beijing, they are currently free to travel to North Korea several times a year for short-term missions and to establish a framework for North Korean missions. When North Korea is opened, Korean-Chinese churches hope to pay special attention to helping North Korean churches. The reason for this is that there are concerns about reproducing the kind of confusion within Protestant missionary activity which occurred after the collapse of the Soviet Union. After the opening of the Soviet Union, the infiltration of heresy was so severe that the truth of the gospel was distorted.

Figure 1.3 Members of Selected Cults in the Former Soviet Union

Countries	Jehovah's Witnesses	Mormon	Other	Total
Armenia	450	240		690
Azerbaijan				0
Belarus	5,270			5,270
Estonia	5,140	420		5,560
Georgia	580			580
Kazakhstan	4,570			4,570
Kyrgyzia	500			500
Latvia	1,150			1,150
Lithuania	1,700			1,700
Moldova				0
Russia	61,100	8,500*	70,000	139,600
Tajikistan	240			240
Turkmenist an	240			240
Ukraine	117,000	13,000		130,000
Uzbekistan	1,420			1,420
Totals	199,360	22,160	70,000	291,520

Brierley gives a figure of 30,000 Mormons in Russia, but this appears to be inaccurate. Mormons themselves put the 1998 figure at 8,500 (Associated Press, 'Despite Pessimism, Mormons Achieve Legal Status', 15 May 1998).[20]

---

[20] Source: Peter Brierley, *World Churches Handbook* (London: Christian Research, 1997). Figures are derived from the 1995 update of the database used by Patrick Johnstone in *Operation World* (Grand Rapids, MI: Zondervan, 1993).

On the other hand, the identity problem within the Korean-Chinese diaspora is becoming an important issue from a sociological point of view. An anonymous minister made the following observation:

> It is important to affirm and nurture the identity and historical consciousness of the Korean-Chinese people like Korean-Russian, which is crucial to the holistic mission and the mobilization of the mission. The concept of roots and historicity is too weak, so that the individual's direction of life is weakened They are also lacking in knowledge of Korean history and world history, and surprisingly ignorant in Chinese history. They do not put any value on the Christian worldview of God's intervention in history, therefore value money and success. This becomes extremely temporal, instant, low-level view of life. In addition to the harmful effects of communism, Chinese maneuverings of the nation's absorption of the people has made a brilliant contribution to the racialization of ethnic minorities in China, including the Korean people. I think it is therefore crucial in any evangelization of the Korean-Chinese diaspora to consider mission education that connects to their roots of identity and history.[21]

Any global mission network which seeks to foster the missionary mobilisation of the Korean diaspora must create links between Korean-Russian and Korean-Chinese people in Central Asia, including North Korean refugees. Currently, there are more than 7 million Korean diasporas scattered across 170 countries around the world, and about 5,000 Korean churches are seen as the bridgeheads of missions. Up to the present, Korean churches (both large and small), mission councils and diaspora nets have been organised – particularly in North America, South America, Europe, Asia, South Africa and Australia – and steps are being taken by these groups to pursue regional unity and cooperation. The two organisations that I have been working closely with exemplify this development: the Korean Diaspora Missions Network (KODIMNET) and the Korean Diaspora Forum (KDF). In addition, the Korean Diaspora Network (KDN), which was recently proposed and formed by the Korean Diaspora Forum, advocates for the diaspora cause worldwide. Koreans in Central Asia and China should also be encouraged to engage in the mission movement as part of a Korean diaspora workforce.

Conclusion

Now that world mission has shifted 'from everywhere to everyone', the common perception that one's own area is a mission field has grown stronger than ever. In this age, no one can deny that the historical movement of humans is like an infinite tsunami. This phenomenon calls for a significant change in the existing

---

21 The contents are excerpted from the pastor of overseas Korean-Chinese in London on 15 January 2013.

Christian mission. The diaspora mission must seek new breakthroughs as part of God's ultimate 'Divine Conspiracy' for the salvation of all nations. This new breakthrough will not be possible if we merely improve upon existing programmes and practices. In essence, we have to think deeply about what mission actually *is*. What is crucial is that we recognise God's sovereignty in deliberately dispersing man (Acts 17: 26-27); that we reflect on the meaning of Christ's incarnation; that we develop the awareness of the identity of Christians as *paroikoi* ('immigrants'; see 1 Pet. 1:1); and, finally, that we restore mission as the essence of the church. In order to restore this essence, we must practice truly biblical, evangelical ecumenism in our everyday lives, and thus follow the guidance of the Holy Spirit.

Ministry in Central Asia is no longer regionally-isolated. Numerous tribes of this land are moving to every corner of the earth today (e.g. to Ukraine), and the Korean-Russian people, whom God has hidden, are expected to play an important role in future evangelism projects. The Korean church – which, in the past, established the bridgehead of mission through the Korean Diaspora Church, and has been working with Korean missionaries in Central Asia – will be a leading partner among the various global churches that are on the front lines of gospel outreach.

References

Brierley, P., *World Churches Handbook*, London: Christian Research, 1997.
Escobar, S., *A time for Mission*, Leicester, Inter-vacity press, 2003.
Groody, D. & amp; Campese, G. (eds.), *A Promised Land, A Perilous Journey-Theological Perspectives on Migration*, Notre Dame Indiana, University of Notre Dam, 2008.
Hanciles, J., *Migration and Mission: The Religious Significance of the North-South Divide*, in Andrew Walls & Cathy Ross (eds.), *Mission in the 21st Century*, Darton, Longman and Todd, 2008.
Kim, Sung-Hun & Ma, Wonsuk, (eds.) *Korean Diaspora and Christian Mission*, Oxford, Regnum 2011.
Phan, Peter C., *Migration in the Patristic Era, History and Theology*, in *A Promised Land, A perilous Journey*, Notre Dame Indiana, University of Notre Dam, 2008.
Roswith Gerloff, *"The African Christian Diaspora in Europe, Pentecostalism, and the Challenge to Mission and Ecumenical Relations"* (Paper presented at the Society for Pentecostal Studies, Third-first Annual Meeting, Lakeland, Fla., March 14-16 2002.
Wan, Enoch & Tira, Joy (eds.), *Diaspora Missiology, Missions Practice in the 21st Century*, Diaspora Series No. 1, Pasadena, California, WCIU Press, 2009.
Kim, Sung-Hun, *'Theological discussion on the phenomenon of diaspora'*, Journal of Frontier Missions (KJFM), Vol.
Hong, H., *Diaspora Korean-Chinese*, Seoul, Qumran Publishing House, 2012.

(11) Cross-Cultural Mission from a British Gujarati Context
Usha Reifsnider

Introduction

This chapter attempts to demonstrate some aspects of the historical interaction of Gujarati Hindu migrants with Britain and with indigenous British Christians, and to demonstrate how this interaction has impacted conversions from Hinduism to Christianity. The personal accounts that have been shared in this chapter have been selected from over 20 interviews and personal notes taken from ethnographic and auto-ethnographic research undertaken by the author between 2015 and 2018.

The examples aim to offer a glimpse into the personal lives and social backgrounds of South Asians, which may not always be evident to the evangelical church. It shows that adaptation is not just undertaken by migrants entering a new geographical location (nation, city or place of worship) and cultural space. There is also an adaptation and something of a geographical displacement and cultural rearrangement that is experienced by the indigenous British Christians[1] interacting with migrants. This in turn influences how the message of the gospel is received, interpreted, lived and shared. It illustrates the ways in which migratory generational differences sway how the message of the Bible is heard and understood and how conversion takes place, as well as illustrating the impact that these differences have upon the individual, the family, the community and the church.

As attitudes towards the race, culture and belief system of the 'other' change, the approach to how the gospel is given, accepted, lived and reproduced needs constantly to engage with human relational factors, rather than pursuing an outdated traditional model of mission which is rooted in the colonial era.

---

[1] Indians believe that all British people are Christian. This refers to all indigenous white people, whether they practice their faith, are nominal Christians, are agnostic or are atheist.

Historical Interactions between British Christianity
and British Gujarati Hinduism[2]

The Gujarati arrived in Britain shortly after the nation gained independence in 1947. Two hundred years of occupation by the British Empire meant an uncertain future in their newly independent home country. Two world wars left Britain's manufacturing industries, nationalised public transport systems and national health services with large gaps in terms of the working-class labour force. It was convenient for the British to be able to turn to a former colony to fill a labour shortage. The majority of Indians in Britain are Hindu, and the largest group of these are from Gujarat.

Prior to arriving in England, lower-middle-class Gujarati experienced aspects of British Christianity through colonialism. In positive terms, their perception of Christianity included recognition of missionaries who cared for the poor and destitute by providing food, medicine and education. In negative terms, Christianity was perceived as a foreign religion. Like the spread of Islam in India (before the arrival of Christianity), the spread of a foreign religion in this case was perceived has having exploited the resources and the people.

Hinduism is a non-proselytising lifestyle which incorporates many different belief systems and allows for individuals and communities to express their faith in ever-changing ways. Until the colonisation of India by the British, Hinduism was not demarcated as a religion. Thus, the myriad religious expressions of the people of India were categorised as aspects of 'Hinduism'. Western thinkers sought to use classifications of this sort to contain a belief system vastly different to their own.[3]

Daily interaction in India would not have included opportunities for most Hindus to meet Christians. Migrants' exposure to, and interaction, with Christianity would only have begun with their arrival in Britain. Historically, Hinduism among migrants adjusted over time as local practices were absorbed into the broader belief system. The earliest Gujarati migrants were medieval traders. Their influence was evident throughout the ports along trade routes in the Indian Ocean. This movement of Hinduism was the precursor for the influences of Hindu practice around the world. Unlike Islam – which, like Christianity, emphasises text, confession and proselytism – there was not an impulse within British Hinduism, initially, to carve out a physical space for religious and cultural practices in Britain.

---

[2] 80 per cent of the population of India is Hindu. In the state of Gujarat, 90 per cent of the people are Hindus. Among the British Hindu population, more than 70 per cent are Gujarati.

[3] According to Will Sweetman, colonialism and Western ideas of religion shaped the definition of Hinduism. Will Sweetman, *Mapping Hinduism: 'Hinduism' and the Study of Indian Religions, 1600-1776* (Halle Franckesche Stiftungen: Neue Hallesche Berichte, 1991).

The young South Asian men arriving in Britain did little in the way of establishing communal Hindu rituals. The main way in which they fulfilled their religious duty (or *dharma)* was by leaving home to provide financially for the extended family back in India. Additionally, the effort to expand the horizons of future generations through education and lucrative business was seen as an admirable religious duty and social ambition. In India, the ritual practices which constitute one's daily religious duty often fall within the domain of women and the elderly, especially during the working years of life.

Originally, the young men who migrated to Britain were planning to work for a season and then return to India, as had been the habit of their medieval ancestors (the traders) and the indentured labourers of the more recent colonial past. Changes in the British migration laws which threatened to restrict labour migration led wives and children to move to Britain. As young children entered the British school system, they were exposed to Christianity through teachers and schoolmates as well as through the education curriculum itself. In addition to attending classes in religious instruction and daily assemblies which included Christian prayers, teachings and the singing of Christian hymns, students were taught from a curriculum that was influenced by a Christian worldview.

The practice of Hinduism does not rely on text-based teaching, but upon performing daily rituals alongside elders in the home. Without the older generations in the home teaching the younger by example, there was a gap within the religious legacy that was meant to be reproduced within the British Hindu home. In addition, young women coming from India adjusted their religious habits to suit their new lifestyles in Britain. Hindu practices pervade every aspect of day-to-day life in India. Just as it would be impossible to avoid Hinduism in India, it would be equally difficult to replicate it in its entirety in Britain.

A more structured British Hinduism began in the 1970s. This was influenced by a number of factors. Firstly, African independence movements led to Indians indentured to the British being expelled from East Africa. Multiple generations of East African Gujarati Hindus thus became twice-diaspora. As such, they were able to shift and adapt their religious practices across this progression from India, through East Africa to Britain. Secondly, British society became more pluralistic and came to recognise the identities reflected in other religions. This pluralistic dynamic created the need for a separate identity that was distinct from the identities associated with other faiths. Indians were familiar with the proselytising nature of Islam and the continuing violence in India amongst Hindus, Sikhs and Muslims. Thirdly, a growth in the financial means of British Hindus and their desire to maintain their cultural values for younger generations through networking activities led to the establishment of Hindu cultural centres and temples.

Hindu parents encouraged success in education, sometimes as a personal and (often as a) familial religious duty. The traditional Christian education system continues to be held in high esteem throughout the Majority World, where, amongst other advantages, it is seen as promoting social mobility. Success in education therefore benefits Hindus as a mode of enculturation within indigenous British society. Furthermore, Hindus welcome the inclusion of other belief systems into their own. This is one of the reasons for which Hindu children attended Sunday school at the local church with their indigenous British friends – a practice that was also common for the large numbers of Hindus who came to Britain from East Africa from the late-1960s onwards. These twice-diaspora people had the advantage of a bilingual education (English and Gujarati or Swahili and English) that was heavily influenced by Western Christianity in East Africa. They managed to adjust Hindu practices to their multigenerational lifestyles.

The young migrants to Britain of primary school age maintained stronger linguistic – and, therefore, cultural – connections with their parents' generation. They acted as translators of language and culture, and became the generation that had to balance and negotiate the interaction between Britishness and Indianness.[4] The generations born in Britain related to India as a historical land with little-to-no connection to their present life in Britain. Some of them did not learn to speak their mother tongue well, perhaps due to self-orientalism – further alienating them from their parents' generation.[5] As parents tried to encourage their children to connect with their Hindu roots, they did not always have the ability or the time to teach the Hindu religion in the same way that Christianity was taught in school.

The crisis of religious identity often took place in the teenage and university years. For example, Kamala and Urmila[6] shared unconnected yet similar experiences of attending primary schools in separate towns in the West Midlands and being invited to Sunday school by local friends. The ideals of racial and gender equality, and the seemingly clear guidance to approaching God in this life and beyond, appealed to the sense of belonging at a time when the awareness of being foreign could not be escaped either inside the home or outside in the British community. The large Hindu communities had not yet developed in the early 1970s, and the images of Indians in the media were not generally positive. All of these things added to the feelings of cultural dissonance for the 1.5- and second-generation British Hindus.[7]

---

[4] By using the terms 'Britishness' and 'Indianness', I wish to convey the sense of gradual (as well as back-and-forth) movements, rather than conveying the notion of a definitive British or Indian cultural identity.

[5] Self-orientalism refers to our self-perception coming from a colonial perspective – the idea that we view ourselves, and indeed limit ourselves, based to some degree on how the Western world saw us.

[6] Kamala, Urmila, and the other converts whose experiences have been used in this paper have shared their stories in public forums, through publications, and also through interviews with me as part of my research.

[7] I use 'first generation' to refer to those arriving in Britain as adults. '1.5 generation' refers to those who are born in India, but come to Britain when they are under the age of 13. 'Second generation' refers to those born in Britain.

Hindu cultural centres and temples were just beginning to be established in the London and Leicester areas. The perceived freedom of indigenous British (and therefore Christian) friends, and the sense of individual choice, especially in the areas of education, career choice and marriage, were very appealing to young British Hindus. By comparison, the traditional Hindu cultural and religious practices seemed primitive and oppressive. There was an inability to articulate or replicate a version of Hinduism in Britain that was aligned with the Western cultural context. As they left for further education, the now highly Western-influenced British Hindu young people experienced clashes within their own identities.

Opportunities and Obstacles to Conversion

While some British Hindus did convert to evangelical Christianity, their experiences were not without problems, especially in the early years. Many of these problems were underplayed and perhaps difficult to articulate to the indigenous British Christians in leadership. Most clergy were either unaware of the extent of the difficulties experienced, or they offered inappropriate solutions to the converts and their families.

In the 1970s, Kamala and Urmila[8] shared very similar conversion experiences. They each attended local Sunday schools with their parents' permission. In time, they understood that to be a Christian meant to make a confession of faith that entailed a denial of Hinduism and its culture entirely. When they refused to participate in Hindu religious or cultural events, friction emerged in the home. The evangelical church encouraged them to self-identify as Christian to their Hindu families. However, there was little understanding as to why this was necessary, and little explanation provided.

Conversion to Christianity was seen as the ultimate betrayal of family, community, culture and country. Conversion in India was most common amongst the lowest caste, which lived in abject poverty. The missionaries of that era were perceived as having used food, education and medicine as a means of expanding Christianity in India. By spreading Christianity within this demographic, converts were seen as 'rice Christians' who used a foreign religion for socioeconomic gain. Indians without social and economic needs were often beyond the influence of this Western religion.

British Hindu families believed that conversions to Christianity in Britain would force them to decline socially, both in India and in England. Working-class families who depended on the community support of those from higher-caste backgrounds assumed this would affect every aspect of life. This included concerns that conversion would jeopardise the possibility of forming family alliances through the marriage of siblings and relatives. Secondly, when the 'converts' declared they were no longer Hindu, the family believed them to be

---

8 Names have been changed to respect the privacy of the individuals.

stating they were no longer their children, or a part of the family, or even Indian. Culturally, individualism and independence from the family are understood to be shameful, and are punished with enforced exile. This was often the initial effect of the news of conversion upon the Hindu family.

At the same time, within the British evangelical church, the opportunity for foreign mission had come home. Converting the 'heathen' was no longer far away. The British Hindu converts to Christianity were encouraged to share testimonies in the local church, and often used these testimonies as outreach to Hindu friends. This was seen by the British Hindus as an attempt to destroy their families and communities. Implicitly, the church expected converts to turn their backs on all things Indian, including their families, and to encourage others to do the same. These practices perpetuated a colonial aspect of Christianity.

While cultural extraction is not the goal of evangelical Christianity, the lack of understanding within the local church meant that Hindu-background converts to Christianity rejected their Hindu families and communities in both Britain and India. This in turn reinforced the idea that Christianity was purely ethnocentric. Many took on English names, a practice that was commonly forced upon the converts in India by the early missionaries from the William Carey era. The name-choosing and name-giving ceremony is deeply significant within Hindu homes. Before modern means of communication emerged, families waited weeks for letters from India in which senior family members and Hindu priests gave specific direction in the selection of auspicious names. The destiny of future generations, the quality of family relationships, and the goal of perpetuating and promoting cultural and religious continuity were all implicated within the naming ritual. The rejection of the carefully-given name in favour of a popular English name, the alteration in dress, and the change of diet all contributed to the retreat of the convert further and further away from their community. The families of the converts suffered considerably, and in many cases, family relationships were never the same again.

These early converts had zeal to share their newly-found faith. The believers of British Hindu background identified with some of the stories of persecution and suffering among converts in other nations. The evangelical church, often inadvertently, encouraged their new converts to push back against their Hindu roots and culture, and to 'suffer for the cause of Christ'. They would do so by standing against their families in decisions about marriage and other cultural practices that the church deemed un-Christian. These new converts possessed a worldview that was now heavily influenced by Western Christianity and – to some degree – by Western secularism. Often, however, they felt a pull towards sustaining an expression of spirituality in their daily lives that was similar to the practices within Hindu homes. As Western evangelical Christianity became the prevalent lens through which they understood their personal and communal religious identities, their traditional, pre-conversion values diminished, as did the family connectivity that was fostered by familiar rituals in the home.

Since Hindu practice does not rely upon the knowledge of sacred texts or theological rituals, the Christian faith appeared particularly inviting in its emphasis upon the accessibility of the Bible and the connection of the individual to the biblical historical timeline. There was an inability to articulate or replicate a version of Hinduism in Britain that fit within Western modes of practice. Young Hindu converts would often thrust themselves into what they believed was a living example of New Testament faith within evangelical Christianity. Their cultural Hindu values of family and communal loyalty, while evident in the Bible, were not necessarily replicated in the indigenous British Christian community. Thus, conversion led to an estrangement from their British Hindu and South Asian culture, and certain foreignness amongst the indigenous white evangelical church culture as they were in the minority and not fully accepted.

Successful Progress

Things changed considerably in the decades that followed these earlier conversions of British Gujarati into the indigenous white evangelical Christian church. By the late 1980s, many second-generation migrants were coming of age and had become a part of the British community. While anti-racism laws and equal pay laws were introduced in the 1970s,[9] the younger generations of British Gujarati were far more familiar with Britain and had achieved success in the areas of education, while their parents had found gaps in the fields of small business – that is their parents started businesses such as grocery stores which were need at the time.

Indigenous British and British Hindus interacted with each other – especially in the large cities and towns – through the use of public transport, public health, and education. The younger generations within both groups adapted more quickly to life in Britain than the older. British celebrations of Christmas led to friendly, festive interactions with migrants, and often included sharing food and giving gifts. These bridges provided cultural crossover points.

Sharing food is a distinct religious duty for Hindus and Sikhs. For Hindus, giving and receiving food from those around them is seen as means of levelling the social and spiritual ground. Hospitality and service – viewed as aspects of the religious duty of Hindus and Sikhs – helped to bridge cultural gaps. It is a rare thing to find an indigenous British neighbour who has never been offered a plate of food from a British South Asian of any religious persuasion. These simple acts led to neighbourhood friendships, and influenced strong relationships that built mutual trust and respect.

British Hinduism was becoming established within areas that were heavily populated. This increase in visibility led the church to make an effort to learn

---

[9] Race Relation Act 1976, http://www.legislation.gov.uk/ukpga/1976/74/pdfs/ukpga_19760074_en.pdf (Accessed 21st September 2018).

about Asian faiths. While this was an admirable goal, the Western approach to study was trapped within the idea that each religion was monolithic in expression. Many went to great pains to study the theology of Eastern religions as a means of both sharing their knowledge with British Hindus and equipping the church. This time-consuming task was ultimately ineffective in achieving its goal, which was to prove the supremacy of Christianity by making comparisons between Christianity and Hinduism and generating debate.

Many problems emerged from this effort. Firstly, the knowledge of these people impressed indigenous British Christians, but it also caused those within the church who did not have theological training to shy away from sharing the gospel with British Hindus out of fear of giving offence. Secondly, the attempt to use this information to train British Gujarati converts resulted in a paradox: the British Gujarati converts were expected to learn from indigenous British churchmen who themselves had very little understanding of the culture and language in question, and to use methods prescribed by these people to interact with their own families. Thirdly, as stated earlier, the practice of Hinduism is not based upon a single text or upon one fixed theology. This meant that in order to be introduced to Christianity, British Gujaratis, who had no interest in Hindu theology, were expected to engage in theological discussions that were completely irrelevant to their own faith practises.

While the visible growth of the British Hindu communities might be seen as a negative from the perspective of evangelical Christianity, it had an important impact on the religious landscape. Despite the increase of Western secularism, the presence of Hindu temples brought an increase and renewed interest into personal and communal religious backgrounds. As British Hindus engaged with subjective spiritual questions, many were drawn to aspects of Christianity, especially to its emphasis upon kindness during times of crisis. The indigenous white Christian communities now had a particular view of the British Hindu lifestyle and were able to engage with it more effectively.

While entry-point cross-cultural experiences amongst the British Hindus were very similar in the early years, there was a wider variety within their lifestyles in the years that followed due to vast individual differences in terms of integration, social mobility, education and career choices. Mixed-race marriages became more common. The English language and aspects of British culture, now heavily influenced by pluralism, appeared to become prevalent.

Manoj was a successful property investor. In 2008, his life was dramatically affected by two major crises. The first was the global financial crisis, which resulted in massive losses in his business investments. The second was the life-threatening illness of his only son. Parents of his daughter's friend who were practising Christians visited the hospital to pray for Manoj's son. The specialists at the hospital gave no signs of hope that the two-year old would regain consciousness. The continued and committed prayer and support of the Christian family was deeply moving. Profoundly touched by the subsequent healing of their young son, Manoj and his wife decided to visit the church. Several visits later they decided to become followers of Jesus.

Interestingly, Manoj noted that he had met indigenous British Christians many times through his business contacts. He was even invited to lunch meetings with Christian businessmen, but no one had ever engaged him in conversation about faith. For Christ followers of British Hindu background in the evangelical church, this is something of an oddity. It suggests to the convert that while evangelism is promoted, celebrated and encouraged from the pulpit, the indigenous British evangelical Christian does not take practical steps toward evangelism outside the physical confines of the church building. Within the evangelical church, evangelism is considered essential, and the congregation is expected to be involved in the process of proselytization. It would seem that in practice, this is not the case. This may be due to the reserved British culture or to the distinct way in which Hindus express their religious beliefs amongst others; or perhaps the task of evangelism is seen as the responsibility of professional missionaries, pastors or evangelists.

The idea of pluralism has made inroads into the indigenous British culture. Arguably, this could attributed to the influence of Hindus in Britain. Notably, it has made the exploration of Christianity more acceptable for those of other faiths. The British Hindus became an accepted part of the British cultural landscape. In many cases, their presence was more acceptable than that of Muslims due to their reputation for not engaging in proselytization, and for the degree to which they have managed to integrate socially.

In time, the Western cultural ideal of individualism – reflected in the emphasis upon independent life choices – became far more conventional amongst the British Hindus. Some limitations to this acculturation were still apparent. These included favouring jobs that provided a good salary, choosing a (non-Muslim) South Asian spouse, and accepting indigenous British spouse. Colourism[10] continued to play an important role. Amongst twice-diaspora British Gujarati, colourism could be directly related to the privileged status that was afforded to them by the British during the period of indentured servitude in Africa. The issue predates colonial occupation, and is associated with the ancient caste system,

---

[10] Colourism is a form of racism based on skin tone. It is widely and openly practised amongst Asians in the West and in Asia, for instance, in the selection of a spouse or an employee. See Joanne Rondilla and Paul Spickard, *Is Lighter Better?: Skin Tone Discrimination Amongst Asian Americans* (Maryland: Rowman and Littlefield Publishers, 2007) and Radhika Parameswaran on 'colourism' in India. https://www.cmc.edu/keck-center/asia-experts-forum/radhika-parameswaran-on-colorism-in-india (Accessed 21st September 2018).
In the West, statistics show that darker skin tones are closely related to social issues including lower-paying jobs, fewer educational advantages, and conviction of crimes against white people. See J. Viglion, 'The Impact of Skin Tone on Prison Time for Black Female Offenders', in *The Social Science Journal*, Vol. 48 No. 1 (January 2011), 250- 258.

inherited occupation and other issues influencing social status. Marriage to African or African Caribbean people is less common amongst the twice-diaspora British Gujarati, although it has become more acceptable since the turn of the century.

Dharma, as a definitive expression of religious duty, was implied rather than expected, and the practice of taking responsibility for the extended family gave way to the independence of the nuclear family – especially among those who were wealthy enough not to need financial help from relatives or the wider community. British Hindu religious practices, like the practices of indigenous British Christians, were now more likely to be relegated to specific holy days and family events, such as births, deaths and marriages. For British Hindus, these were valuable times for catching up with their extended families and networking with kinsmen.

These more neutral cultural interactions led to the re-exploration of contextual approaches to evangelism.11 Those missionaries and local church leaders who were able to relate to British Hindus beyond the colonial historical identity were more successful in this respect. A broad variety of contexts was apparent; hence, a course similar to Alpha12 was created to explain, and foster an understanding of, the cultural differences that influence divergent belief systems and practices. 'Discovering Jesus Through Asian Eyes'13 was used to help those within the church who had a desire to share the gospel in a culturally-appropriate way. While this was not intended as a complete and definitive tool, it opened the door to more respectful and contextually-appropriate efforts. Prayer guides and other training materials provided insight into the British Hindu culture as something relevant and commendable, rather than as something primitive and foreign.

Journeying to Christ

Pritesh and Poonam grew up in the tradition of Jainism, which, like Buddhism, has roots in Hinduism and shares many similar beliefs and cultural practises. Pritesh is a second-generation migrant. As a youngster, he participated in youth activities at the local church. He had no personal interest in Jainism, but followed the traditions and rituals of his parents and grandparents. As a young adult, he became involved with a youth-focused Jain organisation as a way of learning something about his religion. He married a twice-diaspora, 1.5 generation young woman. Their marriage was not entirely arranged, but they were introduced to each other through the Jain organisation. Around the time of his marriage, he

---

11 The missionary Roberto De Nobili (1577-1656) was the earliest scholar of Indian religious thought. His writings have only recently been published, but contain information about contextual approaches to mission.
12 The Alpha Course was created by the Holy Trinity Church in Brompton, an Anglican church in London.
13 https://www.discovering-jesus.com (Accessed 21st September 2018).

met an American missionary who was familiar with contextual approaches to Christianity and invited Pritesh to a group in which men were learning to be better husbands. Through this group, Poonam was invited, a little while later, to a 'Mum's and Tot's' group meeting at the contextually-appropriate church gathering.

This gathering was known as a *Yeshu Satsang* (Jesus Worship). It aimed to connect with the local residents of that particular part of north London. The area is highly populated by middle-class, multigenerational British Hindus. The advanced level of education among this demographic meant that the English language was used well in this context, but Gujarati was a strong second language. Multiple Hindu temples and businesses run by British South Asians evince the strong, vibrant cultural presence of the British Hindus.

By addressing the salient aspects of British Hindu culture, the *Yeshu Satsang* provides a place of gathering for fellowship and relationship, without any pressure to convert. The journey to consider the relevance of Jesus is explored through relationship, rather than through church attendance or the expectation of conversion. People like Pritesh and Poonam feel able to invite their family members to the gatherings, as they include familiar symbols that point to the cultural aspect of worship rather than the religious. A *divo*[14] is lit at the beginning of the service, and the wearing of shoes in the worship space is optional. While the public address is given in English, the Bible is read and displayed in both Gujarati and English. The gatherings often include vegetarian meals, and there is always time to talk over hot tea and biscuits or Indian sweets.

The overall impression is one of acceptance, regardless of the outcome of attendance. In this atmosphere, Pritesh, Poonam and others feel very comfortable inviting their practising British Jain and British Hindu friends. This is an example of how British Gujarati Christ followers engaged in evangelism giving a positive picture of Christianity. It is seen as self-improvement in this context as both Jainism and Hinduism allows for exploring other ways to improve oneself. While this may take time, the journey to Christianity is never forced; and family members feel at ease to welcome this spiritual exploration, since following Christ in this context is initially perceived as a means of self-improvement. Pritesh recalls that his family attended his baptism service, noting that the goal of Jain religious practice was to become a better person. The family saw clear evidence of this in the lives of Pritesh and Poonam as they lived lives committed to honouring their families as they worship Jesus. Hence, their willingness to accept Pritesh's and Poonam's choice to follow Christ makes for strong extended intrafamilial relationships. This has resulted in their family members and friends attending events at the *Yeshu Satsang*, making prayer requests, and welcoming people from the *Yeshu Satsang* to family events.

---

14 *Divo* is a small homemade lamp. Traditionally, the wick is made from a hand-twisted cotton ball, and the fuel is ghee. At the *Yeshu Satsang*, a small tea light candle is often used.

Kamala and Urmila, whose stories were shared earlier, had similarly positive experiences when they were able to reconnect with their families after decades of separation. Urmila's parents, having retired and returned to live in Gujarat, both became Christ followers (independently of each other) after the family relationship was restored. Urmila was able to share her faith in Jesus in a way that her parents could understand. They saw what they determined were positive changes in their daughter's life. This was evidenced in Urmila's ability to choose to follow Jesus whilst remaining culturally-faithful to her family. Her recognition of the value of Gujarati culture for herself and for her family, despite her mixed-race marriage, healed many wounded relationships in both Britain and Gujarat.

Similarly, Kamala's mother lives close to a *Yehsu Satsang* and occasionally attends. She joined Kamala and others on a mission trip to India, where she met other Gujarati-speaking Christ followers. Since then, she has begun to understand her own language and culture – an knowledge which is sustained as she joins in prayer in Jesus' name for peace and healing. Moreover, the mother is in relationship with her daughter and with other Gujarati and Western Christ followers while on her own journey to Jesus. This has had an impact on the wider family as they meet at family gatherings.

From Here to Worldwide Mission

While this section of the paper ought to offer something by way of conclusion, it is hoped that it will actually be more of an introduction to look into the realm of possibilities of diaspora mission among those who have come to Christ from British Gujarati Hindu backgrounds. In terms of mission – both to and through the British Gujarati Hindu background Christ followers – there is a growing range of opportunities which combine the efforts of converts, indigenous British evangelical churches and Western mission agencies. What is still lacking is the capacity for mission activity among the British Gujarati Hindu converts, and indeed, among other diaspora converts who are not entirely culturally Western.

The lack of missional engagement among British Gujarati Hindu background Christians can be attributed to several factors. It has been assumed that the pattern of decline in church attendance in the Western world is true of the entire world, and this assumption has caused the church to try and halt attrition at the expense of mission. In fact, current statistics show that the largest population of Christians are now in Africa.[15]

The Western world's interpretation of theology may have come to a place of natural decline. It is till useful; however, the Majority World Christians from Africa, Latin America and Asia need to contribute their voices and actions to the

---

[15] Global Christianity: A Look at the Status in 2018. http://www.gordonconwell.edu/ockenga/research/documents/CSGC_Newsletter_Summer_2018.pdf (Accessed 1st October 2018).

global mission forums. Furthermore, the emphasis on Western theology, based upon seminary training, as the necessary qualification to do mission is deeply embedded within the post-colonial perspective. This perspective, in turn, is unintentionally filtered through to new generations of Christ followers from other faiths. Many of them believe their ideas to be irrelevant. Indigenous Western church leaders expect their own particular training programmes to be promoted and used by those of other cultures who know and understand their own identifiable people groups better. Sadly, they are rarely afforded the opportunity to use their abilities and skills to exercise influence within the church, or to take adequate leadership or creative strategic roles.

Many Western mission leaders are spending millions of dollars to create and perfect strategies for penetrating the world of mission to the diaspora. They often ignore the successful – albeit perhaps unorthodox – outreach and evangelism efforts of first-generation converts. Instead, they favour Western-influenced Christians in the Majority World who are themselves trapped in a colonial, self-oriental methodology within their own nation, and who have little-to-no understanding of their countrymen in the Western world. For example, they inadvertently expect diaspora converts to completely accept and adhere to Indian-British, colonially-rooted Christianity. In addition to this are the out-dated practices based on a bygone missionary era which is still present in Indian Christian culture within India, but totally foreign in British South Asian culture.

Often, indigenous British Christian churches and ministry leaders desire their schemes to be approved and implemented by mature converts from Hindu, Muslim or Sikh backgrounds. Including them in the leadership or creation of such strategies is far too rare. Allowing first-generation converts[16] to train, lead and mentor indigenous British Christians, as well as others from similar backgrounds, would go a long way to improving these missional strategies. Such efforts would also create wider networks that would lead to a greater understanding of who Jesus might be to the Hindu and to people of other faiths within the worldwide diaspora. There is a scarcity of traditional and contextual church planters working alongside first-generation converts from Majority World backgrounds in the worldwide mission force. This could be resolved by critically reviewing the traditional mission perspective on what are considered the necessary qualifications for church planting and missionary work, and by welcoming new perspectives – including those of first-generation converts – on how people should be trained for missions.

The problems are multifaceted, but far from insurmountable. The solutions must allow a complete shift in perceptions. Outside of the religious milieu – in the areas of the arts, business and media – there has been a steady improvement in cross-cultural awareness, which has in turn promoted the multicultural and multi-ethnic features of life in the twenty-first century. The evangelical church

---

16 By 'first-generation converts', I am referring to those who identified with a non-Western religion prior to self-identifying as a Christ follower or convert.

has access to the same human resources as these other sectors, and a far worthier cause; yet there is a world of difference between what is perceived to be multicultural and 'multi-coloured'.multi-coloured in the sense of diversity being present, for example a church congregation may have people of different nationality and ethnicity represented in the church but that does not mean that the leadership and structure of that church reflects that. In essence, that church is multi-coloured but not multicultural in terms of its leadership and structure.

Outsiders to this context of diaspora mission (including the experienced Western missionaries in India) – no matter how well-meaning, integrated, experienced and educated they are deemed to be – should be considered supplementary, and should themselves seek to encourage the convert to speak out rather than wait for permission. The first-hand experiences of diaspora converts – as authentic British Gujarati Hindu background insiders – could be breathtakingly innovative, and should be nurtured. Many of them are trapped by self-orientalism, and feel that there is far more authority within Western theology and expertise. It is time for a deconstruction of traditional mission thinking; it is time to make room for and encourage alternative voices to make the cause of Christ known through and from the diaspora.

References

Banks, Taunya Lovell, 'Colorism Among South Asians: Title VII and Skin Tone Discrimination' in *Global Perspectives on Colorism* Washington University Global Studies Law Review Vol.14, Issue 4 (Symposium Edition), 2015.
Bhabha, Homi, *The Location of Culture*, New York: Routledge, 1994
Bharati Dayanand, *Living Water Indian Bowl* Pasadena, CA: William Carey Library, 2004.
Clark, Peach & Vertovec (eds.), *South Asians Overseas* Cambridge: Cambridge University Press, 1990.
Cohen, Robin, *Global Diasporas: An Introduction* Oxon: Routledge, 2008.
Dufoix, Stéphane, *Diasporas,* Berkeley, CA: University of California Press, 2008.
Poros, Maritsa, *Modern Migrations: Gujarati Indian Networks* Stanford, CA: Stanford University Press, 2011.
Rondilla, Joanne and Spickard, Paul, *Is Lighter Better?: Skin Tone Discrimination Amongst Asian Americans,* Maryland, USA, Rowman and littlefield Publishers, 2007.
Vertovec, Steven, *The Hindu Diaspora: Comparative Forms* Oxon: Routledge, 2000.
Viglione, Jill, 'The Impact of Skin Tone on Prison Time for Black Female Offenders' in *The Social Science Journal* January 2011, Vol. 48 No. 1, pp. 250- 258.
Said, Edward, *Orientalism* New York: Pantheon Books, 1979.
Sheikh, Samira, *Forging a region: Sultans, Traders and Pilgrims in Gujarat 1200-1500* New Delhi: Oxford University Press, 2010.
Shukla, Sandhya, *India Abroad* Princeton, NJ: Princeton University Press, 2003.
Sweetman, William, *Mapping Hinduism: 'Hinduism' and the Study of Indian Religions, 1600-1776,* Halle Franckesche Stiftungen: Neue Hallesche Berichte, 1991.
Wan, Enoch, *Diaspora Missiology* Portland, OR: Western Seminary, 2011.

Williams, Raymond Brady, *An Introduction to Swaminarayan Hinduism* Cambridge: Cambridge University Press, 2001.

Internet Sources

Discovering Jesus through the Asian eyes: https://www.discovering-jesus.com [accessed 21/09/2018]
Global Christianity: A Look at the Status in 2018:
http://www.gordonconwell.edu/ockenga/research/documents/CSGC_Newsletter_Su mmer_2018.pdf [accessed 01/10/2018]
Jha, Saumitra, *Trade, Institutions and Religious Tolerance: Evidence from India,* Working Paper, 2007 https://www.gsb.stanford.edu/faculty-research/working-papers/trade-institutions-religious-tolerance-evidence-india [accessed 21/09/2018]
Race Relation Act 1976:
http://www.legislation.gov.uk/ukpga/1976/74/pdfs/ukpga_19760074_en.pdf [accessed 21/09/2018]
Radhika Parameswaran on 'colorism' in India: https://www.cmc.edu/keck-center/asia-experts-forum/radhika-parameswaran-on-colorism-in-india [accessed 01/10/2018]

(12) African Diaspora Christianity: Towards an African British Theology and Mission
Israel Oluwole Olofinjana

Introduction

This chapter investigates the mission initiatives of African Christians in the European diaspora, using Britain as a case study. The paper argues that African Christians and churches have had a long presence in Europe and are far from being a homogenous unit. The diversity that exists within the African Christian diaspora is demonstrated throughout the chapter, with various examples illustrating their different typologies, ecclesiological standpoints, and approaches to mission. I subsequently argue that the different types of African churches have varying mission strategies in their attempts to evangelise Europe. Some are reaching mainly African diaspora communities, while others are reaching beyond the African diaspora; and analysis of the latter group yields a mixed picture. With a view to developing an African Theology and Mission in the British context, two critical questions are asked. Firstly, how can Africans who still believe in the world of spirits, angels and demons engage in mission with Europeans who have been brought up with an Enlightenment mode of thinking which reduces religion to fairy tales and views it has having lost its relevant? Added to this is are the European perceptions of African economic migrants and refugees as people who are in need of Western welfare. And secondly, to what extent is African identity an important factor in terms of the efforts of Africans to do mission work in Europe? Should they assimilate, integrate or segregate? I am writing as an African missionary and pastor in Britain, employing an insider's perspective which makes use of contemporary church history and a missiological approach.

History and Mission of African Churches in Europe: Types and Profiles

The history of African churches in Europe reveals that these churches have been engaging in mission for more than a century. Take, for example, the first African Pentecostal church in Europe, which was founded in London in 1906.[1] This was

---

1 'The First African Pentecostal Church in Europe (1906–Present)', May 2012. Available at http://israelolofinjana.wordpress.com/2012/05/06/the-first-african-pentecostal-church-in-europe-1906-present/ (Accessed 20th March 2019).

Sumner Road Chapel, founded by Rev Thomas Kwame Brem-Wilson in Peckham. Rev Brem-Wilson, a businessman and schoolmaster, was born into a wealthy family in Dixcove, Ghana in around 1855. He migrated to Britain in 1901 and later founded Sumner Road Chapel in Peckham, which is known today as Sureway International Christian Ministries and is now located at Herne Hill, south-east London. As an African Pentecostal church, Rev Brem-Wilson's church was also involved with the origins of the Pentecostal movement in Britain. This was largely because of his networking with individuals such as Alexander Boddy (the Anglican priest who is recognised as the father of British Pentecostalism), Cecil Polhill (one of the pioneers of the Pentecostal missionary movement in Britain), D. P. Williams and W. J. Williams (founders of the Apostolic church in Britain).2 While Brem-Wilson's church was quite pioneering, it was not the first African church in Europe; that honour goes to a church founded by John Jea (1773-18__?) in the early nineteenth century. After a fruitful itinerant ministry in North America and Europe, John settled down in Portsmouth with his wife, and started a church in their house between 1805 and 1815.3 John Jea was from Old Calabar in Nigeria and at the age of two he was sold into slavery and trafficked to New York. He was uneducated, but through divine revelation, he later taught himself to read the Bible. He gained his freedom and became an itinerant evangelist, travelling across different parts of the United States, Europe and South America and preaching the gospel before settling down in Britain.4

In 1931 Daniels Ekarté founded African Churches Mission (hereafter, ACM) in Toxteth, Liverpool. Ekarté's official biographer suggested that he was probably born in Calabar, Nigeria in the 1890s.5 As a boy, Ekarté was influenced by the Scottish missionary, Mary Slessor (1848-1915), who worked amongst the Calabar people in Nigeria. Ekarté became a seaman and migrated to Liverpool around 1915. Liverpool's prosperity in the mid nineteenth century depended largely on the slave economy. The black population increased during and after the First World War in places such as Liverpool, Bristol and London. The war in Liverpool led to an increase in unemployment and poorer living conditions. Coupled with this was the widespread racial discrimination of the time. For example, intermarriages between black men and white women were a major source of tension in Liverpool, and the children of such marriages were termed 'half-caste' children (known today as mixed-race) and were rejected by many

2 Babatunde Adedibu, *Coat of Many Colours* (London: Wisdom Summit, 2012), 26.
3 See John Jea, *The Life, History and Unparalleled Sufferings of John Jea, The African Preacher* (Cornwall: Dodo Press, 2009).
4 Ibid.
5 Marika Sherwood, *Pastor Daniels Ekarte and the Africa Churches Mission* (London: the Savannah Press, 1994) 24.

people in society. These children were actually labelled 'mongrels'.[6] This was the socioeconomic milieu into which ACM was born.[7]

After the Second World War, many half-caste children were born from unions between African American soldiers and English women. These children were rejected by society, and so, Ekarté decided to transform the ACM into an orphanage home, which would both serve these children and acted as a rehabilitation centre for their mothers. His vision was realised, but in 1949, this community project was forcibly shut down, and the children were transferred to the city's home for children. Ekarté was barred from any further contact with the children. In 1964, the local authorities demolished the building that housed the Mission. The blow of seeing the Mission shut down was too much for Ekarté, and he died not long after, in 1964.

These three stories illustrate the early missionary efforts of African Christian migrants to share the gospel in Europe by planting independent churches without denominational attachments and affiliations. It is worth noting at this stage that there are three types of African churches in Britain: African Initiated Churches (AICs), African Newer Pentecostal Churches, and African congregations within historic churches.[8] My typology here follows that of Afe Adogame.[9] In the Swedish context, Nils Malström has identified four types of diaspora churches:

1) *'Mega Churches' from the 'Global South'*: he noted that these churches got started in Africa in the 1970s. These are global Pentecostal and Charismatic churches, although they attract mainly diaspora people in Sweden.

2) *Independent Pentecostal immigrant churches which started in Sweden*: This second category consists of churches that were started in Sweden by immigrants and which have continued to develop there.

3) *Pentecostal 'Mega churches in-the-making' created in Sweden with congregations in several countries*: This third group contains churches which have been so successful in Sweden that they have managed to build a base there, from which to expand to other countries in Europe and the Global South.

---

6 Sherwood, *Pastor Daniels*, 13.
7 Afe Adogame, 'African Christian Communities in Diaspora', in Ogbu Kalu (eds) *African Christianity: An African Story* (Trenton: Africa World Press, 2007), 431-451.
8 Historic churches in this context refer to the following groups: Roman Catholic, Church of England, Baptist, Methodist, Lutheran and United Reformed Church.
9 Afe Adogame, *The African Christian Diaspora: New Currents and Emerging Trends in World Christianity* (London: Bloomsbury Academic, 2013), 62-73.

4) *Pentecostal immigrant churches with connections to Swedish churches*: this fourth group includes immigrant churches which have started within or as part of an already-established Swedish church.[10]

In the German context, Claudia Währisch-Oblau's typology also includes four categories:

1. Independent Local New Mission Churches: No affiliation.
2. New Mission Megachurches: Affiliation to a strong leader.
3. New Mission Church Groups: Affiliation through language, nationality or creed.
4. Denominational New Mission Churches: Affiliation to a mother church.[11]

While there is overlap between Nils' and Claudia's typologies, it is worth noting that Claudia's third category is distinct. We shall also see that my own typology in the British context also overlaps with both Nils' and Claudia's.

African Initiated Churches in Britain (1960-80)

The second wave of church planting was carried out by African Initiated Churches (AICs hereafter).[12] The independence of African countries, starting with Ghana in 1957, led to African diplomats, students and tourists coming to Britain and other European countries. Like the Caribbean migrants before them, they were rejected by the British churches and by society at large. This rejection, as well as their own impulse for mission, led to the formation of AICs in London. Adogame and other commentators on African Christianity have identified two types of AICs in the diaspora. The first are branch churches that were planted in Britain and other European cities and have church headquarters in Africa; the second are churches founded in Britain which either emerged from a split with

---

10 Nils Malmström, Pentekostala Migrantkyrkor, in Jan-Åke Alvarsson (ed) *Pentekostalism i Sverige på 2000 talet* (Uppsala: Institutet för Pentekostala Studier, 2013).
11 Claudia Währisch-Oblau, '"We shall be Fruitful in this Land": Pentecostal and Charismatic New Mission Churches in Europe', in André Droogers, Cornelius van der Laan & Wout van Laar (eds), *Fruitful in this Land – Pluralism, Dialogue and Healing in Migrant Pentecostalism* (Zoetermeer: Boekencentrum, 2006).
12 AICs are African Independent Churches. As the name implies, they were churches founded by Africans for Africans and were theologically, financially and organisationally independent from mission churches. African Independent Churches, as they were initially termed, were later called African Indigenous Churches, and more recently, African Instituted Churches, or African Initiated Churches. See Victor Hayward, *African Independent Church Movements* (London: SCM Press Ltd, 1963), Harold Turner, *History of an Independent Church: The Church of the Lord Aladura* 2 Vol (Oxford: Oxford University Press, 1967) and Allan Anderson, *African Reformation: African Initiated Christianity in the 20th Century* (Trenton: African World Press, Inc, 2001), 10-11.

an already-existing denomination or started up independently.₁₃ Examples of the former include the Church of the Lord *Aladura*, planted in London in 1964; Cherubim and Seraphim Church, founded in 1965; The Celestial Church of Christ, founded in 1967; Christ Apostolic Church (CAC) Mount Bethel, founded in 1974; and Musama Disco Christo Church (MDCC), founded by Rev Dr Jeri Jehu-Appiah in 1980. Examples of the latter include Divine Prayer Society, founded by Archbishop Owusu Akuffo in the early 1960s in London; Aladura International Church, founded in London by Rev Father Olu Abiola in 1970; and Born Again Christ Healing Church, founded in London by Bishop Fidelia Onyuku-Opukiri in 1979.₁₄ Some of the typologies developed by Nils and Claudia reflect this distinction between AICs that emerged from denominational affiliations in Africa and those that started in Britain independently.

Since the 1970s, there has been a growing presence of AICs in other European countries, such as Germany, the Netherlands, Switzerland, Belgium, France, Portugal, Spain, Ukraine, Austria, Switzerland, Luxemburg and Denmark. The first of the AICs established in a European country outside the UK was probably the Celestial Church of Christ, founded in Munich, Germany in 1974. The Kimbanguist Church, whose members are from the Central African countries of the Democratic Republic of Congo (formerly Zaire), Congo-Brazzaville and Angola, was started among a group of African students in Belgium in 1978.₁₅ Since then, other Kimbanguist Churches have been established in France, the Netherlands, Switzerland, Germany, Spain and Portugal. Also noteworthy is the True Teachings of Christ's Temple, founded in Amsterdam in (around) the 1980s by Rev Daniel Himmans-Arday (the first African church in that country).₁₆ Due to their strong emphasis on African cultural identity, AICs tend to attract mainly African diaspora to their churches. These churches appeal to Africans who want to reaffirm their sense of African identity in a postmodern society such as Britain. This is why some Africans have a dual church membership. From my own observation and field research, some African Christians attend historic churches, but remain members of AICs.

₁₃ Adogame, *The African Christian Diaspora*, 67-68.
₁₄ Israel Olofinjana, *Partnership in Mission: A Black Majority Church Perspective on Mission and Church Unity* (London: Instant Apostle, 2015), 26-27.
₁₅ Kimbanguism owes its name to Simon Kimbangu (1887-1951) a Belgian-Congolese prophet who founded the Church of Jesus Christ on Earth. Kimbanguism, as it is popularly known, is one of the largest AICs in central Africa.
₁₆ Gerrie Tar Haar, *Halfway through Paradise: African Christians in Europe* (Cardiff, Cardiff Academic Press, 1998), 32.

African Newer Pentecostal Churches in Britain (1980–Present)

In the 1980s and 1990s, a new type of African church emerged across European cities, termed African New Pentecostal Churches (hereafter, ANPC).[17] Nils' and Claudia's typologies clearly apply to these churches as well, for among them are those that started as denominational church plants in Europe which sought to gather existing members who have relocated to Europe. For example, the Church of Pentecost started in Ghana around 1937 through the efforts of one of the Apostolic Church missionaries, James McKeown (1900-89). It began in London in collaboration with Elim Pentecostal Churches around 1988 to 1989. Today, it has more than 150 branch churches in major cities in the UK such as London, Birmingham, Manchester, Liverpool, Nottingham, Cardiff, Leicester, Sheffield, Leeds and Glasgow. ANPCs with strong affiliations to their mother churches in Africa tend only to reach out to African migrants. The mission of these churches within European cities is often affected by denominational constraints and by the transnational identity of their members.

However, there are some African denominational church plants that have sought to do things differently. This is the case for Faith Ministries in Zimbabwe, which came to Britain in 2004 through the pioneering strategy of Pastor Anderson Moyo. Mayo decided to set up the church with fewer denominational constraints in the UK. Faith Ministries in the UK was set up independently in order to allow its leaders some flexibility in their understanding of and approach to mission in the UK. Faith Ministries is also part of the network of churches known as Salt and Light Ministries, which is one of the Charismatic churches in the UK.

There are also ANPCs that started independently in Britain. An example is Temple of Praise Church, founded by Dr Tani and Modupe Omideyi in Liverpool in 1980.[18] Temple of Praise Church is a unique example of a church led by Africans that has nevertheless worked intentionally to reach beyond the African diaspora. The church can be described as a multicultural church in that the congregation and leadership of the church reflect the diversity in Britain. It is a different kind of ANPC.

Since the 1990s, ANPCs have also been founded in other European countries. For example, the largest church in Eastern Europe (20,000 people) is the Embassy of God Church, founded by Sunday Adelaja (of Nigeria) in Ukraine in 1994. In Hamburg, Germany, there is the Christian Church Outreach Mission International (CCOMI), founded by Dr Abraham Bediako in 1991. Another example is International Evangelical Church (IEC), founded in 1992 by

---

[17] The ANPC are independent Pentecostal churches in Africa, of which the majority were born out of the Charismatic revival of the 1960s and 1970s in West Africa. The term is also used to describe other Pentecostal churches that are not classic Pentecostal churches.

[18] Dr Modupe Omideyi, *Transformed to be Transform: A Journey to Bring Change to a Community* (Liverpool: Love and Joy Ministries Ltd, 2017), 19-24.

Ghanaian-born Robert Agyei-Mensah. Additionally, African Ecumenical Church which was founded in Berlin in 1991, with many French-speaking Africans in attendance. Another African church in Germany is the African Christian Council (ACCH), which acts as an umbrella for over 60 African churches in Hamburg. The significance of this council of churches is that they come under a German church, Arbeitsgemeinschaft Christlicher Kirchen.[19] Worth noting in Copenhagen, Denmark, finally, is the International Harvest Christian Centre, founded in 1994 by Ghanaian, James Conney.[20]

African Christians and Congregations within Historic Churches

The majority of studies on the mission of African diaspora appear to focus on independent Pentecostal and Charismatic churches from Africa. What is obscured is the fact that there is a strong and growing presence of Africans within historic churches. For example, black Anglicans in Britain virtually doubled between 1992 and 1998, from 27,000 to 58,200 attendees.[21] Additionally, in the year 2000, the largest concentration of black church-goers was found in the Roman Catholic Church, with in 61,000 – a remarkable contrast to the total Pentecostal population of 70,000.[22] African Christian migrants within historic churches stand a better chance of reaching beyond African diaspora people in their mission engagement because they serve within a multicultural church context. This is the case for some of the African Baptist pastors in London. My own story serves as an example in this respect. Since coming to the UK in 2004, I have served with Baptists Together, leading two multicultural churches and a white majority church in London. The same is also happening across European cities. Pastor Peter Rong from Sudan, for instance, leads an international refugee church in Bucharest, Romania, called Spiritual Revival Baptist Church. Peter Rong went to Romania in 1992 to study economics and later studied at a Baptist theological institute to prepare him for Baptist ordination and ministry. Since then, his ministry within the Baptist context has been to refugees of various nationalities who have come to Romania.

Nevertheless, there are also African congregations within historic churches which mainly reach out to African diaspora communities. An example is Trinity Baptist Church, one of the largest Baptist churches in Britain, which is led by

---

19 Adogame, *The African Christian Diaspora*, 62.
20 Haar, *Halfway Through*, 100-102.
21 Joe Aldred, 'The Black Church in Britain and Their Relations with the Ecumenical Movement, with Particular Reference to Black Pentecostalism', in Christoph Dahling-Sander, Kai M. Funkschmidt and Vera Mielke (eds), *Beiheft zur Okumenischen Rundschau: Pfingstkirchen und Okumene in Bewegung* (Frankfurt am Main: Verlag Otto Lembeck, 2001), 184.
22 Peter Brierley, *The Tide Is Running Out: What the English Church Attendance Survey Reveals* (London: Christian Research, 2000).

Pastor Kingsley Appiagyei.23 Despite its success in terms of church planting and promoting church growth in Europe, the church still mainly attracts African diaspora people, largely Ghanaians.

Mission Initiatives of African Diaspora Christians in the UK

African diaspora Christians in Britain have different mission strategies that they employ in their evangelisation of Europe. A key mission strategy employed by many African churches is to plant churches. These church-planting initiatives vary in nature, and include monocultural church plants as well as multi-ethnic church plants. As already noted, some of these church plants only reach African diaspora communities. For instance, this was the case for the Ethiopian and Eritrean evangelical churches which started in the 1980s.24 This was also the case for many of the African churches planted in the 1980s, which are best described as church extensions, since they were founded for the purpose of providing care to church members in Africa who had relocated to Europe. Likewise mentioned above are the Africans who lead multicultural, multi-ethnic churches – whether in the context of an independently-founded church or a historic church – that reach beyond the African diaspora. This is the case for Peter Rong in Bucharest and Tani Omideyi in Liverpool.

There are different transnational activities and strategies used by AICs and ANPCs in their missionary expansion outside Africa. One of these strategies is to hold international conferences. For instance, Kingsway International Christian Centre (KICC) organises an annual international conference called the International Gathering of Champions (IGOC). This conference hosts renowned speakers from the United States, Africa and Europe, as well as utilising multimedia such as satellite television and cable networks. In addition, KICC now has its own TV station, called KICC TV, which attracts viewers in Africa, Europe, the United States and Asia. By using multimedia for global coverage, these conferences reach an international audience.

Evangelism and prayer form another aspect of the mission strategy used by African Christians. The reason for this is that African Christians cannot separate evangelism from prayer; thus, they combine them. One strategic initiative that combines evangelism and prayer and has had tremendous success in reaching beyond African diaspora communities is called The Turning. The Turning was started in 2016 in the town of Reading by an African Baptist pastor, Yinka Oyekan.25 Its purpose was to turn the hearts of people back to their Father God through prayer and street evangelism. This evangelism initiative was very

---

23 Israel Olofinjana, *Reverse in Ministry and Mission: Africans in the Dark Continent of Europe*, (Milton Keynes: Author House, 2010), 46.
24 Hirpo Kumbi, *Mission and Movement: A Study of Ethiopian and Eritrean Evangelical Churches in the UK* (Watford: Instant Apostle, 2018), 82-83.
25 The Turning History http://theturning.eu/history/ (Accessed 25th March 2019).

successful in Reading; many people became Christians. In partnership with other churches, the same initiative was also carried out in Oxford, Liverpool, Southampton, Wales, Scotland and France, where the same result was achieved. Yinka's passion is to see the nation saved for Jesus.[26]

Towards an African British Theology and Mission

There are two important questions related to the mission of African Christians in the European diaspora. Firstly, how can Africans who still believe in the world of spirits, angels and demons engage in mission among Europeans who have been brought up with Enlightenment thinking that reduces religion to fairy tales and thus finds it no longer relevant? Added to this is the perception of Africans as economic migrants who are here on benefits and are exploiting the system. And secondly, to what extent is African identity an important factor in terms of the attempts of Africans to conduct mission work in Europe? Should they assimilate and give up their African culture so that they can reach white Europeans, or should they segregate and retain their Africanness?

In seeking answers to these questions, I have started developing a theology of mission around African identity, which I refer to as African British Theology. As an African theology, African British Theology is a contextual, postcolonial theology which takes into consideration the existential realities of Africans living in a multicultural British society. It relates in this sense to Black British Theology, which takes seriously the black experiences of Africans and Caribbean peoples as crucial aspects of theological reflection. This means that African British Theology is a subset of Black British Theology. African British Theology is also a practical theology which seeks to improve upon the missional practices of African pastors and churches in Britain.

African British Theology is a contextual theology which seeks to interpret the essential aspects of Christian theology in a way that affirms African identity and the African worldview, thus helping African Christians to engage meaningfully and in a relevant way with postmodern, secular Britain.[27] Two of these aspects of African British Theology – the affirmation of African identity and the engagement of African Christians with the postmodern and secular ethos of the West and Britain – are, at times, in tension, but they nevertheless compliment each other. The affirmation and nurturing of African identity is important because we have to be confident as Africans bringing our own, unique cultural contributions to a contested, multicultural society.

When Paul claimed that to the Jews he became a Jew and to the Greeks he became a Greek so that he can win some to the gospel (1 Cor. 9:20-23), this did not mean that Paul had lost his identity. Instead, it entailed the maturing of his

---

26 The Turning is currently planning to come to London.
27 Israel Olofinjana (ed), _African Voices: Towards British Theologies_ (Carlisle: Langham Partnership, 2017), 11.

dual identity in Christ. In Verse 19 of the same text, Paul stated, 'I am free and belong to no man'. In other words, Paul's identity as a Jew born in the diaspora was secured in Christ. Paul was confident in his dual identity as a Jew from Tarsus who had both Jewish and Roman citizenship because he understood that this dual identity in Christ empowered him to show flexibility – to make adjustments and to adapt – in order to contextualise the gospel for his audience. This confidence comes through in Paul's speech to the crowd after his arrest, when he had been confused by the soldiers with an Egyptian terrorist: 'I am a Jew from Tarsus in Cilicia, a citizen of no ordinary city' (Acts 21:37-39). Here, Paul is affirming his Jewish roots as well as his Roman citizenship.

African Christians ministering in Britain must exhibit this kind of confidence in their cultural identity. There have been situations in which this has not been the case. Take, for example, certain African and Caribbean congregations within the Baptist denomination in Britain. There have been occasions in which some of these congregations have preferred to have a white pastor rather than a black pastor. While such congregations always point to the cross-cultural mission of the church as an excuse for this preference, one often wonders whether there is a subconscious, residual colonialism at work here: do they see white as being superior and, by default, better than black?

The second task of African British Theology follows on from the first. It is to help African Christians and churches engage with postmodern secular Britain. One of the defining characteristics of postmodern secular societies such as Britain is multiculturalism. It is one of the realities of our mission context. This is one of the reasons for which, at a sociological level, one can question whether reverse mission is actually happening in cases in which, for instance, a Nigerian pastor leads a Nigerian church in London? Added to this are the existential realities of second- and third-generation African and Caribbean people. While their parents might be content and secure to be in a monocultural church, the children question it because it does not match their experience at school, in their social networks and within their general surroundings. How can they relate and integrate with people of different ethnicities, cultures, nationalities and social backgrounds from Monday to Saturday, and then settle for just one culture or nationality on Sunday?

Another important point to consider is that African Christians face a double challenge in evangelising Europe. The first is the fact that the European worldview no longer accepts God or institutional religion. The second relates to the way in which African Christians are viewed by Europeans. In order to meet the first challenge, we have to build a good reputation that is equal to the second challenge. Take, for example, an African church in south-east London which disturbs its neighbours with its loud music, or by taking up lots of residential parking on the street. This sort of difficulty fuels the already-existing perception that African Christians are not here for us but for themselves; for if the narrative already suggests that Africans are here only as economic migrants living on benefits, these sentiments are only going to be fuelled when church members disturb the neighbours through what is considered noise pollution (despite this 'noise' being understood as praise and worship to God by the church). Such perceptions certainly are not going to help the reputation or mission of African churches. African churches therefore need a two-way approach in their mission strategy and engagement. The first aspect of this approach is to build bridges into their communities, presenting themselves as good citizens who have come in peace to bring shalom. This bridge can be built by demonstrating authentic care for the communities in which their churches are located. One example of this would be to join local groups of neighbours which handle issues of safety and welfare within the community. This would then permit them to confront the second challenge of aggressive secularism which says that God does not exist, or, at least, is not relevant.

African churches must understand that their mission context demands them to rethink rather than perpetuate and replicate church extension practices – that is, those practices which stand in opposition to the model of church planting which engages with the local community. Consider, for example, the Redeemed Christian Church of God (RCCG), which is perhaps the most well-known of African Newer Pentecostal Churches in Britain. The church's leadership and congregations are very monoethnic, drawing mainly Nigerian immigrants in Britain. This model reflects the mission strategy that was employed by many African Newer Pentecostal Churches in the 1980 and 1990s, when pastors were sent to recruit church members among people already living in Britain, as opposed to planting churches that reflect the demographics and ministry context of Britain. This strategy thus led to the rise of monoethnic churches – a process which, deploying the 'homogenous unit' principle of church growth, culminated with the emergence of mega churches.[28] Ukah, a Nigerian sociologist of religion, critically investigated the mission of RCCG in the UK, using data he collected from Nigeria as well as the UK. He came to the conclusion that RCCG was not only homogenously Nigerian, but also very tribalistic. It attracted mainly Yorubas, with the effect that non-Yoruba Nigerians felt like outsiders.[29] If this analysis is correct, then it challenges the phenomenon of Nigerians leading Nigerian churches, and raises the question as to whether this can accurately be termed 'reverse mission'. It should be noted that there are strategies currently being formulated by the national leadership of RCCG in the UK to change this pattern.

However, it is important to mention that 'reverse mission' does not only mean reaching out to white British indigenes as if it is a white hunt! Reverse mission does not just happen when an African pastor leads a white British church; it also

---

[28] D.A. McGavran, *Understanding Church Growth*, 3rd ed (Grand Rapids: Eerdmans, 1990).
[29] Ukah Azonkeh, 'Reverse Mission or Asylum Christianity? A Nigerian Church in Europe', in T. Falola and A. Agwuele (eds), *Africans and the Politics of Popular Culture* (Rochester: University of Rochester Press, 2009), 113-119.

happens when an African pastor leads a church full of African British, Caribbean British and Asian British people. Underpinning these versions of reverse mission there is a challenge the assumption that to be white is to be British; this simply is not the case. The authenticity of reverse mission cannot merely be determined by whiteness, for this position would assume a narrow and faulty sociological definition of mission. Crossing cultures is an essential part of the gospel, for Jesus encouraged his followers to make disciples of all nations. African churches must therefore seek to engage in mission not only to white British people, but also to the people of various nationalities who make Britain a truly multicultural, multi-ethnic society.

As highlighted above, there are African churches whose missional initiatives reach beyond just Africans in the diaspora. For example, one of the African Newer Pentecostal Churches that reaches the wider British society with its evangelism and social action is New Wine Church, founded in 1993 by the late Tayo Adeyemi in Woolwich. Each year, the church gives Christmas hampers to the community. People of different ethnicities and cultures in the immediate community and from afar benefit from this initiative as people travel from different parts of London to receive these gifts. Another example is Freedom's Ark Church in London, whose Peace Alliance initiative engages with issues of youth violence and gun and knife crime, which are currently plaguing the capital and other parts of the nation.

While I want to commend these efforts to provide social services to the community, reverse mission cannot stay at the level of evangelism, church planting and social and community engagement; it has to address deeper structural issues, with a view to bringing lasting socioeconomic and political change to society. This will mean shifting from just providing social services – which the African Newer Pentecostal Churches do very well – to seeking changes to structures and institutions. Referring to the mission of Black Majority Churches, Apostle Alfred Williams of Christ Faith Tabernacle in London said, 'Prayer without participation is not effective'.[30] Ade Omooba, co-chair of National Church Leaders Forum at the same gathering, said, 'We have too many prominent ministers without influence'. He also said, 'We need to tackle the issue of racism as it brings imperfection to our society'.

Both of these African Newer Pentecostal Church leaders recognise the need to participate in the political process and effect change in society. There are several issues in our society that demand political action from the church, and, in particular, from African Newer Pentecostal Churches. Examples of systems and structural issues that need to be addressed include institutional racism, unemployment, poverty, educational under-achievement among African and

---

[30] He said this at an event with the theme, 'Black Church Leaders Review of Cities and Communities', organised by the National Church Leaders Forum (NCLF) on Saturday 25 November 2017 at Christ Faith Tabernacle in Woolwich, London. In attendance were black church leaders, activists and practitioners.

Caribbean children, inequalities in the healthcare system, immigration policies, and the prison system. As stated above, one of the tasks of African British Theology is to engage with the postmodern mission context of Britain. African Christians must therefore engage with these systemic and structural issues, for they affect three categories of people (among others): migrants, deprived ethnic communities, and the white working classes. Within this task, African British Theology can be enriched not only by African Political theology, but also by the liberative praxis of Black British Theology. The goal of reverse mission cannot just be to evangelise and plant churches; it must also be to engage in prophetic actions that change structures and influence policies. While the African church in Britain has not yet attained this goal, there are signs – reflected in the words of Alfred Williams and Ade Omooba that – that point in the right direction and give us hope.

Concluding Reflection

African Christians have been engaging in mission in Europe for more than a century; their contribution to Diaspora Missiology is not a new phenomenon. This chapter has argued that there are different types of African churches in Europe, with different profiles. Thus, any scholarly analysis which caricatures them as a homogenous unit is not sufficiently robust, and has not taken cognisance of their histories or their present actions. I have also demonstrated that there are different mission initiatives used by African Christians and churches in their attempt to evangelise Europe. Some do this through the use of media and by developing transnational networks, while others evangelise and plant churches. Some of these initiatives only reach Africans, while others reach a multicultural audience. Lastly, I have explored the idea of an African Theology in Britain which takes seriously African identity and its importance for diaspora mission. This theology seeks to empower African identity so that Africans can engage meaningfully in a post-secular, multicultural British society. The conclusion here is that the task is far from over.

Reference List

Adedibu, Babatunde, *Coat of Many Colours: The Origin, Growth, Distinctiveness and Contributions of Black Majority Churches to British Christianity*, London: Wisdom Summit, 2012.

Adogame, A., *The African Christian Diaspora: New Currents and Emerging Trends in World Christianity*, London, Bloomsbury Academic, 2013.

Adogame, A, "African Christian Communities in the Diaspora". In Ogbu Kalu (ed), 2007, *African Christianity: An African Story*, Trenton, NJ, African World Press, Inc, pp. 431-450, 2007.

Aldred, Joe, "The Black Church in Britain and Their Relations with the Ecumenical Movement, with Particular Reference to Black Pentecostalis", in Christoph Dahling-Sander, Kai M. Funkschmidt and Vera Mielke, eds., *Beiheft zur Okumenischen*

Rundschau: Pfingstkirchen und Okumene in Bewegung, Frankfurt am Main: Verlag Otto Lembeck, 2001.

Brierley, Peter, *The Tide Is Running Out: What the English Church Attendance Survey Reveals*, London: Christian Research, 2000.

Jea, John, *The Life, History and Unparalleled Sufferings of John Jea, The African Preacher*, Cornwall: Dodo Press, 2009.

Kumbi, Hirpo, *Mission and Movement: A Study of Ethiopian and Eritrean Evangelical Churches in the UK*, Watford, Instant Apostle, 2018.

Malmström, Nils, Pentekostala Migrantkyrkor, in Alvarsson, Jan-Åke, (Ed) Pentekostalism i Sverige på 2000 talet, Institutet för Pentekostala Studier, Uppsala 2013.

McGavran, D.A., *Understanding Church Growth*, 3rd ed, Grand Rapids, Michigan, William B Eerdmans Publishing Company, 1990.

Olofinjana, I.O., (ed), *African Voices: Towards British Theologies*, Cumbria, Langham Partnership, 2017.

Olofinjana, I.O., *Partnership in Mission: A Black Majority Church Perspective on Mission and Church Unity*, London, Instant Apostle, 2015

Olofinjana, I.O, *Reverse in Ministry and Mission: Africans in the Dark Continent of Europe*,(Milton Keynes: Author House, 2010.

Omideyi, Modupe, *Transformed to be Transform: A Journey to bring change to a Community*, Liverpool, Love and Joy Ministries Ltd, 2017.

Sherwood, Marika, *Pastor Daniels Ekarte and the Africa Churches Mission*, London, the Savannah Press, 1994.

Tar Haar, Gerrie, *Halfway through Paradise: African Christians in Europe*, Cardiff, Cardiff Academic Press, 1998.

Währisch-Oblau, Claudia,*"We shall be Fruitful in this Land": Pentecostal and Charismatic New Mission Churches in Europe. in Droogers, André & van der Laan, Cornelius & van Laar, Wout (eds), Fruitful in this Land – Pluralism, Dialogue and Healing in Migrant Pentecostalism*, Boekencentrum, Zoetermeer, The Netherlands, 2006.

Internet Sources

The Turning History http://theturning.eu/history/ (Accessed 25th March 2019).

The First African Pentecostal Church in Europe (1906–Present), May 2012. Available at http://israelolofinjana.wordpress.com/2012/05/06/the-first-african-pentecostal-church-in-europe-1906-present/ (Accessed 20th March 2019).

Contributors

Tope Bello grew up in south London and came to know the Lord in her late teenage years. Her upbringing encouraged her to become involved in youth and prison work, before attending Oak Hill College to study Theology. She is now a member of a Christian organisation called Black Berea, which hopes to engage the Black British culture and community with the Gospel of Jesus Christ.

Dr Stephen D Dye, PhD, Biola University is the founding pastor of CrossWay International Baptist Church in Berlin, Germany and missionary field leader of the Association of Baptists for World Evangelism (ABWE) in Germany.

Dr Rosalee Velloso Ewell is Principal of Redcliffe College, UK. She is on the editorial boards of *Evangelical Review of Theology* (World Evangelical Alliance theological journal) and *International Review of Mission* (World Council of Churches journal).

Flavio Gurattos was born and brought up in Brazil. He comes from a business background but closed his company to become a full time cross-cultural missionary. For over twenty-five years he pioneered and coordinated a movement of partnerships between Brazilian, British and European churches and charities. More recently he was part of the Public Policy and Advocacy Team of the Evangelical Alliance UK as the coordinator of Speak Up and is now working as a policy advisor for the British Government. He has a Masters in International Relations from the University of Westminster. Flavio is married to Karen, father of three children and grandfather of two boys.

Hun Kim is Diaspora Consultant for Wycliffe Global Alliance and Korean Research Institute for Diaspora. He is the visionary behind Equip 7 Learning Community, which is a pioneering diaspora training organisation in Germany.

Nils Malmström has a BDiv. from Lund University. He has been doing research about African Pentecostalism in both Nigeria and Sweden since 2004. For several years, he has been working to increase knowledge and understanding of the new ecclesiastical landscape due to the emergence of Pentecostal Migrant churches in Sweden.

Dr Dulcie Dixon McKenzie is the Director of the Centre for Black Theology and Tutor in Black Theology and Ministries at Queens Foundation for Theological Ecumenical Education, Birmingham. She is also an executive member of the Society for the Study of Theology (SST) and a member of the Common Awards Management Board at Queens.

Rev Claire Ord is a Baptist minister and a Baptist Missionary Society (BMS) mission worker. She has an MA in Applied Theology and is a hospital chaplain. She is a mother of three children.

Rev Mark Ord is a Baptist minister and director of training of Baptist Missionary Society (BMS) in Birmingham. He also lectures with Moorlands College and is currently working on a PhD in Theology at Vrije Universiteit, Amsterdam through Queens Foundation in Birmingham.

Rev Israel Oluwole Olofinjana is the founding director of Centre for Missionaries from the Majority World. He is an Honorary Research Fellow at Queens Foundation for Ecumenical Theological Education, Birmingham. He is the pastor of Woolwich Central Baptist Church in south-east London.

Usha Patel Reifsnider is a first British Gujarati Christ follower, transcultural mission consultant and PhD researcher. She is also one of the directors of Centre for Missionaries from the Majority World. Usha is on the Executive Team of Lausanne Europe.

Jim Stewart is currently pursuing a PhD at the Oxford Centre for Mission Studies and works for Open Doors as Church Relations Manager, Wales. Before that, he worked for twelve years with Evangelical Alliance in Wales as Public Policy Officer. He has worked extensively among refugees and asylum seekers and has developed strong links with Majority-World Christian communities in Wales. His wife is a former refugee from Eritrea and the couple have a young boy, Caleb.

BV - #0008 - 210420 - C0 - 229/152/11 - PB - 9781913363314